The
Reference Shelf®

Income Inequality

The Reference Shelf
Volume 94 • Number 4
H.W. Wilson
a Division of EBSCO Information Services, Inc.

Published by
GREY HOUSE PUBLISHING
Amenia, New York
2022

The Reference Shelf

Cover photo: istock

Publisher's Cataloging-in-Publication Data
(Prepared by Parlew Associates, LLC)

Names: Grey House Publishing, Inc., compiler.
Title: Income inequality / [compiled by Grey House Publishing].
Other Titles: Reference shelf ; v. 94, no. 4.
Description: Amenia, NY : Grey House Publishing, 2022. | Includes bibliographic references and index. | Includes b&w photos and illustrations.
Identifiers: ISBN 9781637002940 (v. 94, no. 4) | ISBN 9781637002902 (volume set)
Subjects: LCSH: Income distribution -- United States. | Economic policy. | Equality -- Economic aspects -- United States. | Taxation -- United States. | United States — Economic conditions. | BISAC: BUSINESS & ECONOMICS / Economics / General. | BUSINESS & ECONOMICS / Economics / Macroeconomics. | POLITICAL SCIENCE / Public Policy / Economic Policy.
Classification: LCC HC110.I5 R44 2022 | DDC 339.2 R--dc23

Contents

5

Preface

Fairness and Equity

Income inequality is a complex and multifaceted topic, but the central, underlying issue is relatively simple. All workers, no matter their jobs and no matter their "level" within the American workforce, contribute to the productivity of the companies that sell goods and services to customers, and so fuel the economy. Anyone who works shares some portion of the revenues collectively generated by American businesses, but the central question is, are the revenues generated by these businesses being *fairly* distributed among the workers?

According to data from 2020, around 11 percent of Americans live in poverty and between 3 and 4 million Americans live in poverty despite working at least forty hours per week or more in a full-time job.[1] The fact that Americans can work full time and still fail to earn sustainable wages is an example of what economic analysts call "income inequality," which can be defined as the unequal distribution of economic resources. Public welfare and antipoverty activists have long argued that any job should pay workers a living wage, but critics argue that increasing salaries to provide sustainable wages would place a strain on businesses and weaken the economy.

Across political lines, more than 60 percent of Americans believe that income inequality is a problem in America, but this includes only 41 percent of conservative voters. By contrast, nearly 80 percent of progressive voters identified income inequality as a major problem and believed that economic reforms were needed.[2] Although majorities of Americans agree that income inequality is a problem, most Americans are more concerned with other issues. Only around 2 to 4 percent of Americans list income inequality as their top concern in polls.[3]

Wealth in America

In the United States, the wealthiest 20 percent of Americans control a staggering 52 percent of all income earned, which means that the remaining 80 percent of Americans collectively share just 48 percent of all wealth and assets. The concentration of wealth increases the further one moves up the income chain, and the top 5 percent of American earners control over 20 percent of the nation's wealth. Studies have also shown that wealth inequality in America has increased markedly over time. In 1968, the top 20 percent earned 43 percent of the nation's wealth, as compared to 52 percent in 2020, which means that the concentration of wealth has increased by nearly 10 percent over the past half century.[4]

The "Gini coefficient" is a measure of how income is distributed among members of a population, and therefore provides an important measure of equality with regard to the distribution of revenues. The Gini rating ranges from 0, which means total equality, to 1, which would mean that 100 percent of a nation's income is unequally distributed. No society has yet reached 100 percent inequality. Looking at the Gini index indicates that the nation with the highest level of income inequality is South Africa, which has a Gini index of 63.0 percent, indicating that over 60 percent of the nation's revenues are concentrated among the wealthy class. Nations with low levels of income inequality include Iceland, which had a Gini index rate of 26 percent, and Belgium, which had an estimated 27 percent inequality. The vast majority of countries at the higher end of the Gini spectrum are developing countries, nations suffering from political turmoil in which there are insufficient safeguards in place to protect the welfare of the populace from exploitation by corrupt leaders and corporations. However, even in developed countries with strong economies, it is possible for wealth inequality to become a major problem, and the United States provides the most familiar example. The United States has a Gini coefficient of 41 to 43 percent, which is the highest of all the economically dominant nations in the world.[5] By contrast, the United Kingdom has a Gini score nearly 10 percent lower than in the United States. Economic analysts have found that one of the key differences between the United States and the United Kingdom is the level of corporate regulation. In the United States, legislators have tended to prioritize corporate profit over individual income, and this has led to limited advancement among the populace.

Wages and Taxes

Two of the most prevalent debates in the field of income and wealth inequality concern whether or not the nation should adopt a higher minimum wage and whether or not the corporate tax structure and taxes on the wealthiest Americans should be altered to redistribute the nation's wealth.

If wealthy Americans command an unfair amount of the nation's wealth, one way to combat this would be to increase their taxes or to decrease the tax burden for workers. A majority of Americans agree that taxes on wealthy Americans should be higher, but there is significant resistance among those that identify as conservative. Even across political lines, nearly half of voters identifying as conservative still favor increasing taxes on the wealthy.[6] Income inequality became a major issue in the 2020 presidential campaign, and polls indicate that interest in taxing wealthy Americans increased among voters. A Morning Consult poll from September of 2021 found that 68 percent supported raising taxes on the wealthy, with 62 percent supporting increasing tax rates on American corporations.[7]

The so-called wealth tax proposals overlap with proposals to cut corporate tax breaks, or to increase taxes on corporations. Advocates for income and wealth redistribution have long argued that the American tax system provides too many benefits to large corporations, which deprives the federal government and states of revenues that could be used to provide assistance for workers, for education, and for other goals. According to the Institute on Taxation and Economic Policy (ITEP), 55 of the largest corporations in the United States, such as Nike and FedEx, paid no tax revenues in 2020, despite earning increased profits from the previous year. The 55 companies identified by ITEP would have paid $8.5 billion in taxes, and received a further $3.5 billion in tax rebates, which meant a total loss of more than $12 billion in tax revenues to the nation. American corporations avoid taxes by storing profits overseas and in other countries, where US tax laws do not apply. In addition, corporations lobby conservative legislators to support tax bills lowering corporate tax rates or providing tax rebates. Advocates of wealth redistribution argue that the federal government should end tax loopholes that allow large corporations to avoid reporting or paying taxes on income, as well as increase corporate taxes overall.[8]

One of the ways that Americans have sought to rebalance the nation's wealth distribution over time is to increase mandated minimum wages, at both the state and federal level. The minimum wage is the lowest acceptable hourly wage for people working in certain fields or occupations, and can be thought of as a legal safeguard against corporate and employer exploitation. Minimum wages were introduced in the states at the beginning of the twentieth century, with the federal minimum wage first appearing in 1938 as part of a series of reforms aimed at lifting up the working and middle class in the wake of the Great Depression. Increasing the minimum wage has been positively correlated with the reduction of poverty levels and with increased spending power among the working class and middle class. But neither states nor the federal government have kept pace with inflation and increased cost of living when establishing minimum wage laws. The controversial "fight for $15" campaign, which seeks to establish a $15 minimum wage in the United States, is one of the most aggressive and widespread minimum wage campaigns in recent history, but economic experts have argued that minimum wage rates would need to be closer to $23 to $24 per hour in order for minimum wages to reflect America's economic productivity and inflation rates.[9]

Causes and Solutions

Researchers have identified many economic and sociological factors contributing to income inequality in America. For one, the decline of labor unions and labor union participation has eliminated what was once one of the most powerful ways for workers to achieve higher wages and improved conditions in the workplace. A combination of misconduct and propaganda has continued to encourage American skepticism in the labor union industry, despite the role that unions have played in helping the working and middle class to come closer to economic parity. Modern union debates, such as the campaign to unionize companies like Starbucks and Amazon, have helped to bring the issue of workers' rights and organization back into the debate over income and equity.

Automation and the possibility of future automation through artificial intelligence has also played a major role in creating the modern patterns of income inequality. The loss of workforce jobs to automation began in the 1800s but intensified in the mid- to late twentieth century, as mechanized assembly plants and robotics replaced hundreds of positions once staffed by skilled and semiskilled workers. With scientists making progress in the construction of "thinking" machines capable of automating advanced tasks, Americans have become increasingly concerned that more and more jobs will be threatened by automation. Studies indicate that millions of jobs could be automated over the next decade, spanning a wide range of fields from management to high-level programming and design. This does not mean, of course, that millions of Americans will certainly lose their jobs between the 2020s and 2030s, but merely that technology will make it possible for employers to replace employees with mechanized systems.[10] Nevertheless, historians and economists have noted that automation and mechanization have played an important role in the levels of income inequality seen in America in the 2020s and will likely continue to play an important role in the future of the nation's economic debates.

When it comes to solving economic inequality in America, economists and sociologists have long warned that there are no simple solutions to this complex problem. Academics and economic activists have proposed numerous potential governmental and policy changes that might help to redistribute the nation's wealth. For instance, it has been suggested that protecting and improving affordable access to healthcare helps to combat economic inequality by reducing healthcare debt for individuals and families. Likewise, activists have suggested that reducing student debt or helping students to better fund their educational goals without accruing high levels of debt may be key to creating a more equitable American population in future generations.

Works Used

"Gini Index." *World Bank*. World Bank Group. 2022. https://data.worldbank.org/indicator/SI.POV.GINI?name_desc=false.

Horowitz, Juliana Menasce, Ruth Igielnik, and Kochhar Rakesh. "Views of Economic Inequality." *Pew Research Center*. 9 Jan. 2020. https://www.pewresearch.org/social-trends/2020/01/09/views-of-economic-inequality/.

Marquart, Sarah. "Reports Reveal Millions of Jobs Are Threatened by Automation: Does This Spell Doom?" *Futurism*. 25 Feb. 2016. https://futurism.com/85-jobs-threatened-automation-spell-doom.

Miller, Andrea. "How Companies Like Amazon, Nike and FedEx Avoid Paying Federal Taxes." *CNBC*. 14 Apr. 2022. https://www.cnbc.com/2022/04/14/how-companies-like-amazon-nike-and-fedex-avoid-paying-federal-taxes-.html.

"National Poverty in American Awareness Month: January 2022." *Census*. Census Bureau. Jan. 2022. https://www.census.gov/newsroom/stories/poverty-awareness-month.html.

Newport, Frank. "U.S. Public Opinion and Increased Taxes on the Rich." *Gallup*. 4 June 2021. https://news.gallup.com/opinion/polling-matters/350555/public-opinion-increased-taxes-rich.aspx.

Schaeffer, Katherine. "6 facts About Economic Inequality in the U.S." *Pew Research Center*. 7 Feb. 2020. https://www.pewresearch.org/fact-tank/2020/02/07/6-facts-about-economic-inequality-in-the-u-s/.

Shapiro, Thomas M. *Toxic Inequality: How America's Wealth Gap Destroys Mobility, Deepens the Racial Divide, & Threatens our Future*. Basic Books, 2017.

Williams, Claire "The Tax Man Cometh for the Wealthy and Corporations in House Democrats' Plan: And Voters Are OK with It." *Morning Consult*. 22 Sept. 2021. https://morningconsult.com/2021/09/22/house-democrats-tax-plan-raising-taxes-wealthy-corporations-poll/.

Notes

1. "National Poverty in American Awareness Month: January 2022," *Census*.
2. Horowitz, Igielnik, and Kochhar, "Views of Economic Inequality."
3. Newport, "U.S. Public Opinion and Increased Taxes on the Rich."
4. Schaeffer, "6 Facts About Economic Inequality in the U.S."
5. "Gini Index," *World Bank*.
6. Newport, "U.S. Public Opinion and Increased Taxes on the Rich."
7. Williams, "The Tax Man Cometh for the Wealthy and Corporations in House Democrats' Plan: And Voters Are OK with It."
8. Miller, "How Companies Like Amazon, Nike and FedEx Avoid Paying Federal Taxes."
9. Shapiro, *Toxic Inequality: How America's Wealth Gap Destroys Mobility, Deepens the Racial Divide, & Threatens Our Future*.
10. Marquart, "Reports Reveal Millions of Jobs Are Threatened by Automation: Does This Spell Doom?"

1

The Wealth Gap

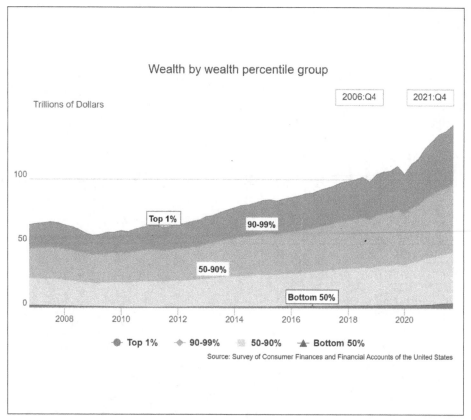

Wealth by wealth percentile group

Trillions of Dollars

2006:Q4 2021:Q4

Top 1% 90-99% 50-90% Bottom 50%

Top 1% 90-99% 50-90% Bottom 50%

Source: Survey of Consumer Finances and Financial Accounts of the United States

By Survey of Consumer Finances and Financial Accounts of the United States.

The above graph from the Federal Reserve indicates how extreme the disparity in the distribution of household wealth in the United States has become.

The Uneven Distribution of Wealth in the United States

According to 2018 Census Bureau data, the wealthiest 5 percent of Americans controlled a staggering 20 percent of the nation's wealth, and the top 20 percent of earners collectively controlled more than half of all the money flowing through the nation. This means that 8 out of 10 workers, more than 80 percent of the American workforce, collectively share less than half of the nation's wealth.[1]

The gulf in both assets and income between the wealthy class and the middle or working class in America places the United States on par with many of the world's developing economies, like that of Peru in South America, the Ivory Coast of Africa, Bulgaria in Europe, and the troubled island nation of Haiti, all of which have similar levels of economic inequality. The United States has the highest level of income inequality among the G7 countries—the seven advanced economies that dominate the global economy and include Canada, France, Germany, Italy, Japan, and the UK.[2]

Colonial Equality

While the American independence movement of the 1700s is celebrated as a key moment in the history of global democracy, the framers of the American independence movement weren't really trying to create an egalitarian, fully democratic system. The leaders of the revolution were business owners and prominent figures in colonial communities and many of the them were members of the colonial aristocracy of the era—wealthy people from wealthy families, some of whom were descended from wealthy families in England. The many letters and other documents left behind by the men known as the Founding Fathers indicates that most of them would probably be called "elitist" by modern standards. They believed that wealthy, prominent families should lead society and that it is acceptable for wealthy individuals to build their wealth by exploiting those at lower levels of the income spectrum. There is no clearer evidence of this than the fact that many of the founding fathers owned slaves, the ultimate form of human exploitation in furtherance of economic gain. George Washington at one point owned more than 300 slaves, who spent their entire lives laboring to build and maintain the Washington family's wealth.[3]

The American Revolution began as a rebellion led by America's elite class against what they saw as unfair taxation on the part of the British crown. In many ways, the revolution was similar to a "worker's rights movement," in which workers band together to protest unfair treatment by their employers or whatever company they work for. In the case of the American colonies, the British crown was essentially the parent company, and the colonies can be seen as "franchises" of British culture and the British economy. The "patriots" as they came to be called, weren't initially trying to win independence from England, but wanted the equivalent of new workers' contracts, with England agreeing to allow the colonists to have more autonomy and to control a larger share of the wealth generated by their plantations and exports.

As the patriots promoted their movement, they told colonial workers in their communities that independence would increase welfare across the board, and that all Americans would share in the increased revenues produced by independent American businesses no longer under the yoke of the tyrannical British regime. When the independence movement succeeded, however, most American laborers did not see an increase in personal wealth or purchasing power. Instead, the land-owning elite of the nation saw the highest level of rewards, and essentially replaced the aristocracy of England with a constitutional aristocracy of landowning colonial men.[4]

From the Gilded Age to the Corporate Age

Though the elite and wealthy class promoted the independence movement, and reaped the lion's share of the benefits, income inequality wasn't nearly as pronounced in the 1700s as it would become in later centuries. Historians have found that the wealthiest 1 percent of Americans around 1776 controlled about 8.5 percent of the total income, whereas this same group would control more than 20 percent by the twenty-first century. In fact, income and wealth distribution in the Colonial Era was more egalitarian than anywhere in Western Europe. This changed over the course of the nineteenth century, largely thanks to the rise and spread of the nation's first ultrawealthy corporations.[5]

The era of the "robber barons," or "industrialists"—a small number of extremely wealthy men who dominated politics and the American economy for nearly a century—features prominently in studies of the American economy and economic equality. Men like John Jacob Astor, Andrew Carnegie, Jay Gould, and John Warne Gates dominated the United States for many years, at times controlling 90 to 100 percent of key industries, like oil and gas, the railroads, and lumber. Many modern articles have compared these wealthy industrialists to the "tech billionaires" of the twenty-first century, like Elon Musk, Mark Zuckerberg, and Jeff Bezos, and like these men the industrialists of the 1800s had an outsized impact on American culture. Politicians allied with the industrialists shaped the laws to limit corporate taxation and to limit the rights of workers to unionize and organize against perceived unfair treatment. In some cases, the industrialists had such enormous political influence that local police forces essentially became private security for their companies, employing violence and threats to prevent workers from organizing to force the companies to accede to their demands.

Mark Twain, one of the great icons of American literature and culture, coined the term "Gilded Age" to refer to the period of the late 1800s and early 1900s when industrialization was driving massive changes and technological advancement across the United States. The term "gilded" refers to the process of coating an otherwise unremarkable item with a thin veneer of gold, which could make an item appear luxurious and expensive even though beneath the thin skin of gold, the item itself might be intrinsically worthless. The industrialists and their political supporters frequently claimed, in this era, that the changes they were fostering in society was creating a new "golden age" for Americans, but Twain argued that it was really a "gilded age," where flashy new technologies and urbanization hid the fact that the nation's growth had been gained at the expense of working-class families and slaves.[6]

The status quo of America's wealth inequality changed over the course of the first half of the twentieth century. This tumultuous period saw the erosion of personal wealth among the elite class and saw the rise of a political movement championing "collectivism" and the idea that a greater share of the nation's collective wealth should be shared by the lower classes. After World War II, income for laborers rose sharply, for the first time nearly catching up with inflation, and this is what produced the once dominant "American middle class," a cohort of American workers who were wealthy enough to afford lower-end luxuries, though not wealthy enough to be classed among the wealthy. This period marked the closest that the United States ever came to economic equity, though only for white men and their families. Women and people of color would not begin to realize any level of parity for many further decades.

Things began to change again in the 1960s, as the result of many different factors. Technological development led to increased outsourcing, which is when companies hire outside of their state, region, or country to find cheaper, typically marginalized workers. Outsourcing increases corporate profits at the expense of local workers and this practice was very controversial in the 1970s and 1980s, but it had become commonplace and largely accepted by the twenty-first century. At the same time, robotics and advanced mechanical engineering allowed corporations to fully replace workers with machines in many industries, especially those involving manufacturing and fabrication. As a result, many industries saw massive reductions in jobs for unskilled and skilled workers. This increased the demand for jobs, while decreasing the supply of jobs, a pattern that ultimately led to stagnant salaries for workers and increased the gulf of wealth between the upper and lower classes.

At the same time, the conservative political establishment in the United States was becoming more closely allied with the corporate sector, in part resulting from the popularity of the theory that reduced corporate regulation and lower corporate and wealth taxes would lead to higher levels of corporate hiring and spending among the wealthy, thus fueling growth at the lower end of the economy. This "trickle down" theory was popularized in the 1980s, and has continued to be a popular strategy among conservative politicians, but has proven ineffective at redistributing wealth. Increasing profits for corporations typically results in increased executive salaries and compensation for investors and ownership, but less often results in advancement at lower levels of the economy.

One example can be found in the tax laws passed by the Republican-controlled Congress in 2017. This new tax system reduced tax burdens on large corporations by as much as 30 percent, representing billions in additional revenues for many companies. However, Bureau of Labor Statistics data indicates that only 6 percent of the companies that received tax breaks hired additional workers. Though supporters argued that the 2017 tax program would create "millions of jobs" by 2019, with the tax cuts in place for two years, progress in creating new job opportunities was negligible. The Institute on Taxation and Economic Policy (ITEP) reported that about a quarter of the benefits of the new tax plan went to the wealthiest 1 percent of Americans in 2018, and that 65 percent of tax savings benefitted the wealthiest 20 percent of Americans. While this tax plan failed to advance working class Americans, it also reduced revenues available for environmental and social service programs, by eliminating billions in corporate tax revenues.[7]

Layers of Inequality

A survey of American history shows clearly that wealth inequality has always been a hallmark of the American system and Americans have yet to adopt a strategy that can effectively redistribute the profits of the nation's productivity to balance advancement between different levels of the economy. Researchers and experts in the field have produced numerous studies showing how wealth inequality impacts Americans in many different ways, from the education system, to the job market, to retirement and end-of-life care.

The debate over economic inequality has evolved, however, because of digital media. In the not-too-distant past, it was difficult for any nonspecialist to gain an understanding of the American economy and its evolution, but the proliferation of research and free access to digital data has allowed the American public to become far more informed on the way that resources are both produced and usurped within the American economy. This process has gradually increased awareness of income and wealth inequality in the United States, but it remains to be seen if the democratization of data can create the level of consensus and popular support that might be needed to return America to the post–WWII levels of working-class and middle-class growth.

Scholars and activists interested in wealth and income inequality in the twenty-first century often break the issue down to the example of how wealth inequality manifests in different parts of society. Some studies have focused on patterns of change over time, looking at how various political strategies impact wealth and equality over the span of decades and centuries, while other studies are more focused on the present or recent history. There are studies, for instance, trying to determine how the COVID-19 pandemic, or the recession of 2008–9, changed the balance of wealth in America. Other studies focus on how wealth inequality manifests in different subsets of America, and this leads to a focus on the "gender gap" and the "racial gap" in American wealth and equity.

Works Used

"Gini Coefficient by Country 2022." *World Population Review*. https://worldpopulationreview.com/country-rankings/gini-coefficient-by-country.

Hanauer, Amy. "Faulty Fact Check on Tax Breaks for the Rich and Corporations." *ITEP*. 5 Feb. 2021. https://itep.org/faulty-fact-check-on-tax-breaks-for-the-rich-and-corporations/.

Lindert, Peter and Jeffrey Williamson. "Unequal Gains: American Growth and Inequality Since 1700." *Vox EU*. CEPR. 16 June 2016. https://voxeu.org/article/american-growth-and-inequality-1700#:~:text=Colonial%20America%20was%20the%20most,than%2020%25%20of%20total%20income.

Mekouar, Dora. "Today's Democracy Isn't Exactly What Wealthy US Founding Fathers Envisioned." *VOA*. 24 Jan. 2021. https://www.voanews.com/a/usa_all-about-america_todays-democracy-isnt-exactly-what-wealthy-us-founding-fathers-envisioned/6201097.html.

Schaeffer, Katherine. "6 Facts About Economic Inequality in the U.S." *Pew Research*. Pew Research Center. 7 Feb. 2020. https://www.pewresearch.org/fact-tank/2020/02/07/6-facts-about-economic-inequality-in-the-u-s/#:~:text=The%20share%20of%20American%20adults,from%2025%25%20to%2029%25.

Semuels, Alana. "The Founding Fathers Weren't Concerned with Inequality." *The Atlantic*. 25 Apr. 2016. https://www.theatlantic.com/business/archive/2016/04/does-income-inequality-really-violate-us-principles/479577/.

White, Richard. *And the Republic for Which it Stands*. Oxford UP, 2017.

Notes

1. Schaeffer, "6 Facts About Economic Inequality in the U.S."
2. "Gini Coefficient by Country 2022," *World Population Review*.
3. Mekouar, "Today's Democracy Isn't Exactly What Wealthy US Founding Fathers Envisioned."
4. Semuels, "The Founding Fathers Weren't Concerned with Inequality."
5. Lindert and Williamson, "Unequal Gains: American Growth and Inequality Since 1700."
6. White, *And the Republic for Which It Stands*.
7. Hanauer, "Faulty Fact Check on Tax Breaks for the Rich and Corporations."

Has Wealth Inequality in America Changed Over Time? Here Are Key Statistics

By Ana Hernández Kent and Lowell Ricketts
Federal Reserve Bank of St. Louis, December 2, 2020

If you Google "wealth inequality in America," you may find our blog post *What Wealth Inequality in America Looks Like: Key Facts & Figures*. In it, we showed the state of wealth and income inequality in the U.S. using 2016 data—at the time, the most recently available—from the Federal Reserve Board's Survey of Consumer Finances.

So, how has wealth inequality in the U.S. changed over time? What does the wealth distribution in America look like now? Well, groups that historically have had low wealth had notable increases in median wealth from 2016 to 2019. For Black families, Hispanic families and families with a high school degree (but no more), these impressive gains ranged from 25% to 60%.

Groups that historically have had higher wealth, like white families and families with at least a bachelor's degree, gained only 4% to 5% more wealth in the same time period. However, since these families had higher wealth to begin with, small percentage gains translated into large gains in dollar terms. Thus, wide wealth gaps remained, and wealth levels among Black, Hispanic and less educated families remained low—making it difficult for these groups to fully participate in the economy and have financial stability.

In this article, we'll use updated (2019) data from the Fed's latest Survey of Consumer Finances, which was released this year, to refresh our previous primer on wealth inequality.

WHAT IS THE SURVEY OF CONSUMER FINANCES?

The Federal Reserve Board's Survey of Consumer Finances (SCF) is considered the gold standard on wealth data in the United States. It is conducted every three years, most recently in 2019, and allows researchers to explore the finances of specific groups—for example, "college-educated Blacks"—with detail that would not be possible in other datasets.

The Federal Reserve Board's Bulletin also summarizes changes between the 2016 and 2019 SCF. Our estimates may differ slightly due to accessing the public versus private datasets and slight variation in demographic definitions.

Just a note: Though the most recent SCF data are from 2019, they do not capture the impact of the pandemic on families' economic well-being and wealth, which has the potential to erode some of the gains seen that year.

Let's begin by looking at family wealth and wealth inequality for different demographic groups:

- **Race and ethnicity:** non-Hispanic, white; non-Hispanic, Black and Hispanic of any race.[1]
- **Education:** GED or less than high school, on-time high school degree, associate degree, bachelor's degree and post-graduate degree.
- **Age.**

At the St. Louis Fed's Center for Household Financial Stability, we've found these demographics are strong indicators of which families are *more* likely or *less* likely to experience economic resilience and upward mobility.

We see demographics as relatively stable across time and strongly associated with family wealth.[2] Think of family wealth as what a family *owns*, minus what they *owe*.

Black Families Made Gains, but the Wealth Gap with White Families Remains Large

The wealth gap between Black and white families remains large, despite Black families' real (i.e., inflation-adjusted) wealth gains in dollar terms.

In 2019, the typical non-Hispanic Black family had about $23,000 of wealth. That's up 32%, from $17,000 of wealth in 2016 (using unrounded numbers). By "typical," we mean a family at the middle or median. (The median is a useful approximation of the typical family's experience because it's not as likely to be affected as the average by the inclusion of data on extremely high- or low-wealth-holding families.)

That's also 12 cents per dollar of the typical non-Hispanic white family, which had about $184,000 of wealth in 2019. Non-Hispanic white family wealth was up 4%, from $177,000 in 2016.

> **The wealth of the bottom half of families—roughly 64 million families—adds up to only 1% of total U.S. household wealth.**

The Median Wealth Gap Between White and Black Families

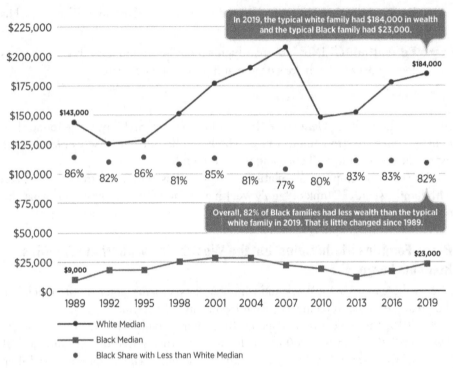

In 2019, the typical white family had $184,000 in wealth and the typical Black family had $23,000.

$184,000

$143,000

86% 82% 86% 81% 85% 81% 77% 80% 83% 83% 82%

Overall, 82% of Black families had less wealth than the typical white family in 2019. That is little changed since 1989.

$23,000

$9,000

1989 1992 1995 1998 2001 2004 2007 2010 2013 2016 2019

White Median
Black Median
Black Share with Less than White Median

■ FEDERAL RESERVE BANK OF ST. LOUIS

NOTES: White and Black median family wealth and share of Black families below white family median. Dollar values are adjusted to 2019 dollars using the consumer price index for all urban consumers (CPI-U) and rounded to the nearest $1,000.
SOURCES: Federal Reserve Board's Survey of Consumer Finances and authors' calculations.

The graphic above displays white and Black median family wealth from 1989 to 2019. Also shown are the share of Black families with less than the typical white family at the median (i.e., the 50th percentile). For example, while half (50%) of white families had less than $184,000 in 2019, the majority (82%) of Black families had less wealth.

This illustrates vastly different, longstanding wealth outcomes between the groups. As a group, Black families owned 3% of total household wealth—an amount unchanged from 2016—despite making up 15% of households. White families, on the other hand, owned 85% of total household wealth—down slightly from 87% in 2016—but made up 66% of households.

Hispanic Families Made Bigger Gains, but Their Wealth Gap with White Families Also Remains Large

The typical Hispanic family of any race had $38,000 of wealth in 2019. That amount is up an impressive 60%, from $24,000 in 2016 (using unrounded numbers). That's also 21 cents per dollar of white median wealth.

Similarly to Black families, Hispanics in 2019 owned 4% of total household wealth—up slightly from 3% in 2016—while making up 13% of households.

The graphic below displays white and Hispanic median family wealth from 1989 to 2019, as well as the share of Hispanic families with less than the white family median. You can observe that the majority of Hispanics, 76%, had less wealth than the median white family (i.e., the 50th percentile) in 2019.

The Median Wealth Gap Between White and Hispanic Families

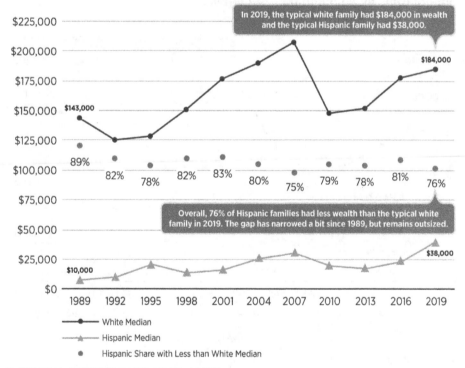

In 2019, the typical white family had $184,000 in wealth and the typical Hispanic family had $38,000.

Overall, 76% of Hispanic families had less wealth than the typical white family in 2019. The gap has narrowed a bit since 1989, but remains outsized.

- White Median
- Hispanic Median
- Hispanic Share with Less than White Median

■ FEDERAL RESERVE BANK OF ST. LOUIS

NOTES: White and Hispanic median family wealth and share of Hispanic families below white median. Dollar values are CPI-U adjusted to 2019 dollars and rounded to the nearest $1,000.
SOURCES: Federal Reserve Board's Survey of Consumer Finances and authors' calculations.

The Wealth Gap Favoring College-Educated Families Is Still Growing

Thirty-nine percent of families had at least a four-year college degree in 2019, up from 36% in 2016. As a collective group, highly educated families continue to have considerably more wealth than less educated families.

Families headed by someone with at least a bachelor's degree had 77% of the wealth pie in 2019 and $310,000 in median wealth. That is up from their holding of 75% of the wealth pie in 2016, with $293,000 in median wealth.

Meanwhile, the typical family *without* a bachelor's degree had $66,000 in wealth in 2019, up from $54,000 in 2016. The wealth gap between these broad groups grew by about $5,000, even though it declined in percentage. That is, while the wealth of less educated families grew more rapidly in percentage terms (narrowing that gap), more educated families had greater median wealth to start with and thus their absolute growth in dollar terms was larger.

Wealth Gaps by Educational Attainment

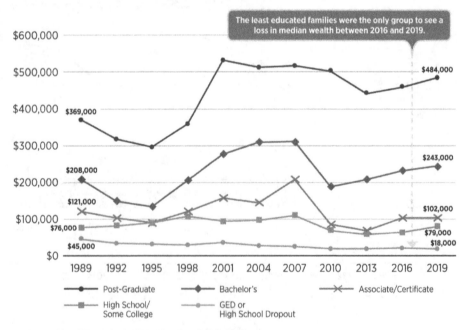

NOTES: Median (50th percentile) family wealth. Dollar values are CPI-U adjusted to 2019 dollars and rounded to the nearest $1,000.
SOURCES: Federal Reserve Board's Survey of Consumer Finances and authors' calculations.

The graphic above displays the educational wealth gap from 1989 to 2019. We show median household wealth values of five educational groups. An in-depth look at the data also reveals a more complex story.

Family respondents with:

- **a GED, or with less than a high school diploma,** had $18,000 in median wealth in 2019. That means this group had about $2,000 (8%) *less* median wealth in 2019 than in 2016 in inflation-adjusted dollars.

- **a high school degree, or some college but no degree,** had $79,000 in median wealth in 2019. Family respondents with, at most, an on-time high school diploma had about $16,000 (25%) *more* wealth in 2019 than in 2016.

- **an associate degree or certificate** had $102,000 in median wealth in 2019. Their wealth was *unchanged* from 2016 to 2019.

- **a terminal bachelor's degree** had $243,000 in median wealth in 2019. So, they had about $12,000 (5%) *more* wealth in 2019 than in 2016.

- **a postgraduate degree** had $484,000 in median wealth in 2019. That means from 2016 to 2019, those with a postgraduate degree had about $25,000 (5%) *more* wealth.

Those with, at most, a high school diploma saw large gains in percentage terms. However, this was still less than those with a postgraduate degree in absolute terms. The least educated were the only group to see a loss in median wealth between 2016 and 2019.

The Wealth Gap Between Older and Younger Families Continues to Widen

The median wealth of younger families (ages 25-35) has remained fairly flat between 1989 and 2019. In contrast, the wealth of older families (ages 65-75) grew rapidly between 1995 and 2007 and has nearly recovered to those levels.

Of course, the people in these groups change over time. In 1989, the younger group was made up of younger baby boomer families. In 2019, those in the younger group were millennial families. They had $24,000 in median wealth, or 9 cents per dollar of the $269,000 in median wealth held by older, mainly boomer families.

While inflation-adjusted younger family wealth barely budged between 1989 and 2019, older families in 2019 had much more median wealth than older families in 1989.

Wealth Gaps by Age

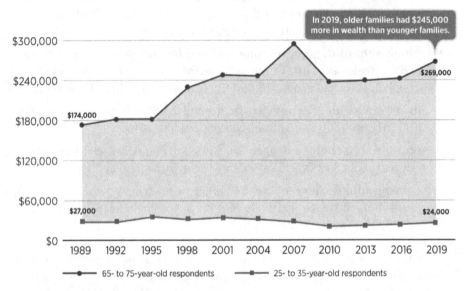

In 2019, older families had $245,000 more in wealth than younger families.

- 65- to 75-year-old respondents
- 25- to 35-year-old respondents

■ FEDERAL RESERVE BANK OF ST. LOUIS

NOTES: Median (50th percentile) family wealth of 25- to 35-year-olds and 65- to 75-year-olds. Dollar values are CPI-U adjusted to 2019 dollars and are rounded to the nearest $1,000.
SOURCES: Federal Reserve Board's Survey of Consumer Finances and authors' calculations.

The graphic above displays the wealth gap for older and younger families from 1989 to 2019. It shows the median household wealth of families headed by 65- to 75-year-olds, as well as the median household wealth of families headed by 25- to 35-year-olds. In 1989, these values were $174,000 and $27,000, respectively. In 2019, these values were $269,000 and $24,000, respectively.

Overall Wealth Inequality Remains High
The demographic breakdowns above illustrate large wealth gaps. Looking at the population as a whole, without demographic lenses, offers a broader, though less nuanced, snapshot on how wealth is distributed. On average, families across the wealth distribution accumulated more wealth between 2016 and 2019.

In 2016, total U.S. household wealth amounted to $92.4 trillion in 2019-adjusted dollars. The 2016 population was about 126 million families. To be in the top 10% of the wealth distribution in 2016, a family needed at least $1.26 million.

In 2019, total wealth had grown to $96.1 trillion. The 2019 population was approximately 129 million families.

- **To be in the top 10%,** a family needed $1.22 million or more (slightly less than in 2016). Together, these roughly 12.9 million wealthy families owned 76% of total household wealth in 2019.

- **To be in the middle 40%,** a family needed at least $122,000 in wealth. Together, these approximately 51.5 million families owned 22% of U.S. wealth in 2019.

- **To be in the bottom 50%** meant a family had less than $122,000 in wealth. That represented about 64.3 million—or half of—families in 2019, owning just 1% of the nation's wealth. Further, of this group, some 13.4 million families (about 1 in 10) had negative net worth—they didn't even have a slice of the pie.

Wealth is what a family owns, minus what they owe. This is how wealth was concentrated (or not) among the U.S. population of 129 million families. The graphic below shows this distribution of total U.S. wealth in 2019.

The Distribution of $96.1 Trillion in Total American Wealth

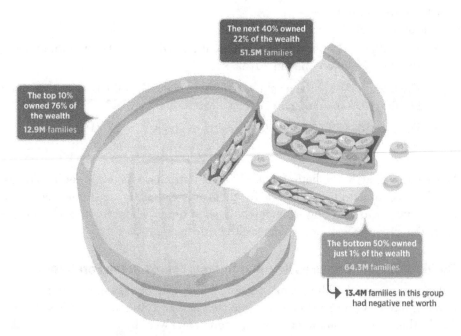

NOTES: Figures do not add up to 100% due to rounding.
SOURCES: Federal Reserve Board's Survey of Consumer Finances and authors' calculations.

Who is in the top 10% of the wealth distribution?
  Which families were more likely to hold the top 10% of wealth in 2019?

- **White families:** 13% of white families, compared to 1% of Black families and 3% of Hispanic families.

- **Higher-educated families:** 16% of families with at most a bachelor's degree, and 27% of families with a postgraduate degree—compared to 4% of those with less than a four-year degree.

Who is in the bottom half of the wealth distribution?

Groups more likely to be in the bottom half of the wealth distribution include:

- **Black and Hispanic families:** 75% of Black families and 67% of Hispanic families, compared to 41% of white families.

- **Less-educated families:** 79% of respondents with a GED or less than a high school diploma, and 58% of those with at most a high school diploma—compared to 31% of those with a bachelor's degree or more.

How has wealth distribution changed?

In summation, the wealth of the bottom half of families—roughly 64 million families—adds up to only 1% of total U.S. household wealth. This contrasts sharply with income, in which the bottom half of families, or those making less than $59,000, collectively have about 15% of total household income.

The lengthy economic expansion before the pandemic led to growth in wealth holdings for all groups, with proportionately faster growth (though smaller absolute growth) at the bottom.

The average family in:

- The bottom 50% of the wealth distribution had $22,000 of wealth, or about $5,000 (27%) more than in 2016.

- The middle 40% of the wealth distribution had $411,000 of wealth, or about $13,000 (3%) more than in 2016.

- The top 10% had $5,716,000 of wealth, or about $75,000 (1%) more than in 2016.

Despite this growth, the bottom half of families still have modest wealth holdings, which makes it extremely difficult for them to weather financial emergencies in tough times or to gain upward mobility in good times. These findings also underscore the importance of examining wealth by demographics.

Building Wealth Requires Keeping Demographics at the Forefront

Solutions aimed at building family wealth should keep demographic differences in mind in order to promote the economic well-being of American families. For example, there are two prominent ways to accumulate wealth:

1. Earn more income, save more income, or both

2. Own or receive assets that can appreciate in value, such as a home or stocks.

Progress has continued when it comes to improving opportunities for groups that historically have had low wealth to earn more. But ownership of the appreciating assets that are important to building wealth remains highly uneven, magnifying the role played by demographic factors.

Notes and References

1. Note that families are grouped by the primary racial and ethnic identity of the survey respondent. Our definition uses both race and a separate question on ethnicity (added in 2004). The Federal Reserve Board only uses responses to the question on race (which includes Hispanic as an option) for greater comparability to earlier surveys; thus, our estimates will differ from those published by the Board. The remainder of respondents fall into a diverse "other race" group (not included here), which includes Asians, American Indians, Alaska Natives, Native Hawaiians, Pacific Islanders, other races and multiple racial identifications.

2. Estimates may differ from earlier articles due to inflation adjustment to 2019 dollars and changes in assignment of demographic characteristics for households. All demographic characteristics for the family were taken from the survey respondent, generally the most financially knowledgeable person.

Print Citations

CMS: Hernández Kent, Ana, and Lowell Ricketts. "Has Wealth Inequality in America Changed Over Time? Here Are Key Statistics." In *The Reference Shelf: Income Inequality*, edited by Micah L. Issitt, 8–17. Amenia, NY: Grey House Publishing, 2022.

MLA: Hernández Kent, Ana, and Lowell Ricketts. "Has Wealth Inequality in America Changed Over Time? Here Are Key Statistics." *The Reference Shelf: Income Inequality*, edited by Micah L. Issitt, Grey House Publishing, 2022, pp. 8–17.

APA: Hernández Kent, A., & Ricketts, L. (2020). Has wealth inequality in America changed over time? Here are the key statistics. In Micah L. Issitt (Ed.), *The reference shelf: Income inequality* (pp. 8–17). Amenia, NY: Grey House Publishing.

Racial Wealth Gap May Be a Key to Other Inequities

By Liz Mineo
The Harvard Gazette, June 3, 2021

The wealth gap between Black and white Americans has been persistent and extreme. It represents, scholars say, the accumulated effects of four centuries of institutional and systemic racism and bears major responsibility for disparities in income, health, education, and opportunity that continue to this day.

Consider that right now the net wealth of a typical Black family in America is around one-tenth that of a white family. A 2018 analysis of U.S. incomes and wealth written by economists Moritz Kuhn, Moritz Schularick, and Ulrike I. Steins and published by the Federal Reserve Bank of Minneapolis concluded, "The historical data also reveal that no progress has been made in reducing income and wealth inequalities between black and white households over the past 70 years."

It's no surprise. After the end of slavery and the failed Reconstruction, Jim Crow laws, which existed till the late 1960s, virtually ensured that Black Americans in the South would not be able to accumulate or to pass on wealth. And through the Great Migration and after, African Americans faced employment, housing, and educational discrimination across the country. After World War II many white veterans were able to take advantage of programs like the GI Bill to buy homes—the largest asset held by most American families—with low-interest loans, but lenders often unfairly turned down Black applicants, shutting those vets out of the benefit. (As of the end of 2020 the homeownership rate for Black families stood at about 44 percent, compared with 75 percent for white families, according to the Census Bureau.) Redlining—typically the systemic denial of loans or insurance in predominantly minority areas—held down property values and hampered African American families' ability to live where they chose.

The 2020 pandemic and its economic fallout had a disproportionate toll on people of color, and many expect that it will widen the gap in various areas, including wealth. At Harvard, experts from different disciplines are studying the problem to find its roots and possible ways to level the playing field to ensure all have an equal chance to achieve the American dream. Here we will take a look at a few, several of which focus on education as a long-term path out.

A History Older Than the Nation

Khalil Muhammad, Ford Foundation Professor of History, Race, and Public Policy at the Harvard Kennedy School, traces the roots of disparity to the Colonial period, when the European settlement and conquest of North America took place.

The process began in the second half of the 17th century, said Muhammad, when European settlers stripped Natives of their lands and used Africans as enslaved labor, preventing them from fully participating in the economy and reaping the fruits of their work.

"The two dominant non-European populations, Indigenous and Africans, were subjected to various coercive forms of labor that would be distinct from the experience of indentured European servants," said Muhammad, who is also the Suzanne Young Murray Professor at the Harvard Radcliffe Institute. "And as such, racism became an economic imperative to harness land and labor for the purpose of wealth creation, and that did not change in any substantial way until really about the 1960s."

In fact the founders discovered that the issues of Black slavery and equality were so divisive that they opted to kick the can down the road, hoping some future generation would prove wiser or better.

With the Voting Rights Act of 1965, a crowning achievement of the Civil Rights Movement, African Americans finally gained full citizenship. Many believed that would end the era of Black inequality, but it did not, said Muhammad, because that thinking failed to account for how deeply systemic the problem had become.

Such misconceptions have tended to make it difficult to gain widespread public support for the implementation of policies to close the disparities between Blacks and whites. That's why it's important to institutionalize anti-racist practices and policies in civil society and government, said Muhammad, as well to better enforce anti-discrimination laws and investment in schools in low-income neighborhoods. But he also believes a "massive commitment to anti-bias education" starting in kindergarten is necessary.

"If we want to undo the cultural infrastructure that is hand in glove with the economic and political racism and domination of people, we have to start very young," said Muhammad. "Anti-bias education is a social vaccine to vaccinate our children against the disease of racism. Imagine what the world would look like in a generation."

A Legacy That Benefits Some and Hurts Others

Over the past decades, many scholars have examined the Black-white gap in household wealth. But it was in 1995 that sociologists Thomas Shapiro and Melvin Oliver put wealth inequality on the map with their groundbreaking book, "Black Wealth, White Wealth." Their research analyzed the role of wealth, or accumulated assets, rather than that of income in the persistent racial divide.

"Income is unequal, but wealth is even more unequal," said Alexandra Killewald, professor of sociology in the Faculty of Art and Sciences, who studies inequality in the contemporary U.S.

"You can think of income as water flowing into your bathtub, whereas wealth is like the water that's sitting in the bathtub," she said. "If you have wealth, it can protect you if you lose your job or your house. Wealth is distinctive because it can be used as a cushion, and it can be directly passed down across generations," providing families more choices and greater opportunity in the present and the future.

Most scholars agree that the legacy of slavery and other subsequent forms of legal discrimination against African Americans have hindered their ability to accumulate wealth. "Today's African American adults and children are living with the legacy of discrimination, inequality, and exclusion, from slavery to redlining and other discriminatory practices," said Killewald. "And in turn, white Americans are benefiting from legacies of advantage."

The typical white American family has roughly 10 times as much wealth as the typical African American family and the typical Latino family. In other words, while the median white household has about $100,000-$200,000 net worth, Blacks and Latinos have $10,000-$20,000 net worth. Depending on the year or how it's measured, those numbers may change, as shown by a report by the Pew Research Center, but the wealth racial gap has continued for decades. "It's a staggeringly large number," said Killewald.

The divide persists across generations, said Killewald, who researched the subject with co-author Fabian Pfeffer of the University of Michigan in an article that included striking visualizations. One of them shows that Black parents tend to have much lower wealth than white parents, and that Black and white children tend to follow the wealth position of their parents, reproducing inequality across generations. The study concludes that "today's black-white gaps in wealth arise from both the historical disadvantage reflected in the unequal starting position of black and white children and contemporary processes, including continued institutionalized discrimination."

How Inequality Affects Education

Many scholars consider education to be the key to narrowing the gap, and economist Richard Murnane is one of them.

During the last 40 years, Murnane examined the interactions between the U.S. economy and its educational system and the ways in which it has affected the educational opportunities of low-income children, who are disproportionately Black or Latinx.

"The extraordinary income inequality in the United States diminishes opportunities for low-income families and for children of color," said Murnane, Juliana W. and William Foss Thompson Research Professor of Education and Society at the Graduate School of Education.

Rising inequality has led to growing gaps in educational resources and learning opportunities between high-income families and their low-income counterparts, as well as residential and educational segregation by income. As a result, inequality poses a danger to the promise that U.S. public education provides children with an equal chance at a better life than their parents.

"One statement that most everybody across the political spectrum agrees with is that if a child grows up poor, but works hard and takes advantage of opportunities, that child's children will have a better life," said Murnane. "That's less true now."

A study on the "fading American dream" co-authored by Raj Chetty, William A. Ackman Professor of Economics, and others concluded that "absolute mobility—the fraction of children who earn more than their parents—has declined sharply in America over the past half century primarily because of the growth in inequality."

Economic mobility rates are lower in the U.S. than in some European countries, and the American dream seems to grow more unreachable as inequality grows. Murnane warns that the government must address the problem as large sectors of the American population sink into despair and frustration.

"A great many people, especially males, have grown up thinking they would take care of their families, and the inability to do that has left them angry, frustrated, and depressed," said Murnane. "That was what they grew up expecting, and that has not been possible for them. That's a deep challenge to how people feel about themselves. And that's a fundamental problem."

> **Net wealth of a typical Black family in America is around one-tenth that of a white family.**

The American Dream: Out of Reach

Economists Claudia Goldin, Henry Lee Professor of Economics, and Lawrence Katz, Elizabeth Allison Professor of Economics, believe that the solution to reducing income inequality, which is strongly tied to the wealth gap, is to close the educational divide.

Goldin and Katz examined wages and income inequality in the U.S. from the end of the 19th century to the early 21st century in their trailblazing book "The Race Between Education and Technology."

What they found was that in periods where there was improved access to education amid technological change, as in the early 1900s when public high schools sprouted across the nation amid the Industrial Age, workers' earnings rose. Inequality began to grow in the 1980s as the economy started to shift toward knowledge-based industries and the supply of highly trained workers fell below demand.

Around that time, the rates of college graduation began to decrease and overall high school graduation numbers leveled off. For Goldin and Katz, expanding access to higher education could actually help reduce inequality.

"You could wipe out a large fraction of inequality by ramping up the education of individuals who are limited in their ability to access and finish a college education," said Goldin.

The problem of wealth inequality is more extreme than income inequality since the former builds on the latter, said Katz, and their effects persists across generations. The legacies of the Jim Crow era and racism against Blacks are expressed today in residential segregation, housing discrimination, and discrimination in the labor market.

For Katz, who has been studying housing discrimination and its effects on upward mobility, public policies can be implemented to reduce residential segregation. A study Katz co-authored with Chetty and Nathaniel Hendren, professor of economics, found that when low-income families move to lower-poverty neighborhoods, with help of housing vouchers and assistance, it is "likely to reduce the persistence of poverty across generations." Chetty and Hendren, along with John Friedman of Brown University, were the co-founding directors of the Equality of Opportunity Project, now expanded and called Opportunity Insights, based at Harvard.

Growing inequality is spoiling the chances to have a better life than the previous generation. Recent numbers show that the top 1 percent has seen their wages grow by 157 percent over the last four decades, while the wages of the bottom 90 percent grew by only 24 percent.

Inequality is one of the factors keeping the American dream out of reach, said Goldin.

"The American dream has sort of shifted from one in which the economic growth of the nation was shared more across the income distribution, where the growth rate of the income of those at the bottom quartile was about the same, if not more, than the growth at the top quartile," said Goldin. "And today it's not that way at all: the bottom quartile isn't going anywhere and the top is going rapidly up."

To keep the American dream alive and return to the era of shared prosperity, the government must act, said Katz. Both Goldin and Katz believe that an expansion of investment in higher education infrastructure and access to a high-quality college education would have a powerful impact in the lives of many Americans. It could be similar to the effects of the high school movement, which lifted millions of American families out of poverty during the first half of the 20th century.

"In the early 20th century, we allowed everyone access to high school," said Katz. "We have never done that for college, even though college is as essential today as high school was 100 years ago."

Additional Benefits of Higher Education

The economic returns of a college degree are important, but the social returns are also valuable, said Anthony Jack, assistant professor of education at the Graduate School of Education.

"Workers who are more educated tend to be in jobs that are more recession- and pandemic- proof," said Jack, who also holds the Shutzer Assistant Professorships at the Radcliffe Institute. "They also tend to live longer, have better health outcomes, and be more civically engaged. Education means more than just extra dollars in the bank. It's also the constellation of things that come along with it."

But the road to college has become increasingly harder, especially for low-income people, even though access to college for disadvantaged students has increased over the past two decades. A report by the Pew Research Center found that the number of enrolled undergraduates from lower-income backgrounds grew from 12 percent in 1996 to 20 percent in 2016. Most of that growth has taken place in public two-year colleges and less-selective institutions.

Selective universities have also opened their gates to poor students, however. In 1998, Princeton became the first Ivy League university to offer full financial aid to low-income students, and others followed suit. At Harvard, 55 percent of undergraduates receive need-based scholarships, and the 20 percent of Harvard parents who have total incomes below $65,000 don't pay anything at all.

Still, access to college "varies greatly by parent income," according to a study by Opportunity Insights. Children with parents in the top 1 percent are 77 times more likely to attend elite colleges and universities than children with parents in the bottom 20 percent.

To Jack, those numbers showcase that access to college is highly unequal and is influenced by income, race, wealth, and ZIP code. "Education may be the great equalizer, but access to an equal education has never been part of the American story," he said. "Higher education is highly stratified. The wealthier the family, the higher the likelihood that students will enter a selective college. The inequality doesn't end there. What happens if you are one of the few low-income students who make it into these elite schools?"

For Jack, that is not a rhetorical question. The middle son of a single mother who worked as a school security guard, Jack rose from a working-class neighborhood in Coconut Grove, Fla., to attend Amherst College, with the help of financial aid. He then came to Harvard, where he graduated with a doctorate in sociology in 2016. Two years later, Jack wrote the book "The Privileged Poor: How Elite Colleges are Failing Disadvantaged Students" about what it's like to be a low-income student in selective universities, partly inspired by his own life.

Elite universities have made progress in recruiting more low-income students to their campuses, but there is much more work to be done to ensure that those students use their four years there as a springboard to a better future the same way their richer counterparts do, said Jack.

"The real question is not only how to increase access to colleges and universities," said Jack. "We must pay attention to what happens once those low-income students move into campus, because that's where inequality gets reproduced in ways that are sometimes invisible but no less insidious."

A Marshall Plan for Higher Education

So if greater access to public higher education would help close the wealth gap, what we need is a kind of Marshall Plan to fix the system, says economist David J. Deming, professor of public policy and director of the Malcolm Wiener Center for Social Policy at Harvard Kennedy School.

That U.S. government initiative helped rebuild infrastructure and economy in Europe after the destruction of World War II. Deming's ambitious proposal would likewise focus resources on overhauling and expanding the size and number of two- and four-year public institutions, with a goal of making access to college virtually universal.

"We ought to set a goal of increasing access to higher education for low-income students and students of color, to basically equalize education opportunity," said Deming. "We need to invest in public higher education because it actually would make a difference in terms of intergenerational mobility."

For one, public higher education is where most of the nation's post-secondary schooling takes place. A report by the National Center for Education Statistics found that of the 19.7 million college students enrolled in the fall of 2019, 14.5 million attended public colleges and universities compared with 5.1 million enrolled in private institutions.

The number of students enrolled in post-secondary education has skyrocketed over the past five decades. The report predicted that by the fall of 2029, more than 20 million students will be enrolled in college. Of them, nearly 15 million will attend public institutions.

Deming's vision would involve far-reaching investment across two-year colleges and four-year universities, many of which have been historically underfunded and understaffed. Instructors are often adjunct faculty who teach large classes and have high course loads, and many institutions lack tutoring and counseling services to help less-prepared students navigate through college.

In terms of investment per student, the scale of inequality in resources is much greater in higher education than it is at the K-12 level. As an example, Deming points out that a rich school district might spend 20 percent more per student than a poor school district, whereas Harvard spends more than $100,000 per year per student, and Bunker Hill Community College spends about $10,000 or $15,000 per year per student.

"Just purely in terms of dollars and cents, the disparity is much, much greater at the higher education level," said Deming.

Investing in higher public education won't solve all the myriad problems that affect inequality, such as the declining minimum wage and discrimination in the labor market, among others. But it would be a big first step, he said.

Print Citations

CMS: Mineo, Liz. "Racial Wealth Gap May Be a Key to Other Inequities." In *The Reference Shelf: Income Inequality,* edited by Micah L. Issitt, 18–24. Amenia, NY: Grey House Publishing, 2022.

MLA: Mineo, Liz. "Racial Wealth Gap May Be a Key to Other Inequities." *The Reference Shelf: Income Inequality,* edited by Micah L. Issitt, Grey House Publishing, 2022, pp. 18–24.

APA: Mineo, L. (2021). Racial wealth gap may be a key to other inequities. In Micah L. Issitt (Ed.), *The reference shelf: Income inequality* (pp. 18–24). Amenia, NY: Grey House Publishing.

6 Facts About Economic Inequality in the U.S.

By Katherine Schaeffer
Pew Research Center, February 7, 2020

Rising economic inequality in the United States has become a central issue in the race for the Democratic presidential nomination, and discussions about policy interventions that might help address it are likely to remain at the forefront in the 2020 general election.

As these debates continue, here are some basic facts about how economic inequality has changed over time and how the U.S. compares globally.

The highest-earning 20% of families made more than half of all U.S. income in 2018

Share of U.S. aggregate household income, by income quintile

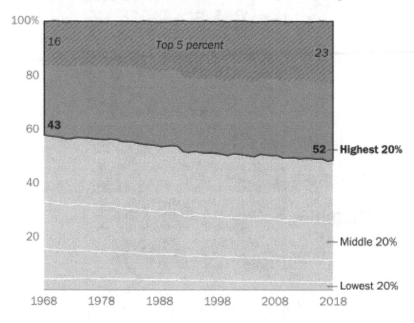

Note: Figures may not add to 100% due to rounding.
Source: U.S. Census Bureau, Income and Poverty in the U.S.: 2018, Table A-4.

PEW RESEARCH CENTER

1. **Over the past 50 years, the highest-earning 20% of U.S. households have steadily brought in a larger share of the country's total income.** In 2018, households in the top fifth of earners (with incomes of $130,001 or more that year) brought in 52% of all U.S. income, more than the lower four-fifths combined, according to Census Bureau data.

In 1968, by comparison, the top-earning 20% of households brought in 43% of the nation's income, while those in the lower four income quintiles accounted for 56%.

U.S. has highest level of income inequality among G7 countries

Gini coefficient of gross income inequality, latest year available

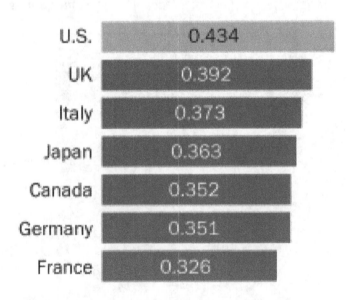

U.S.	0.434
UK	0.392
Italy	0.373
Japan	0.363
Canada	0.352
Germany	0.351
France	0.326

Source: Organization for Economic Cooperation and Development.

PEW RESEARCH CENTER

Among the top 5% of households—those with incomes of at least $248,729 in 2018—their share of all U.S. income rose from 16% in 1968 to 23% in 2018.

2. **Income inequality in the U.S. is the highest of all the G7 nations, according to data from the Organization for Economic Cooperation and Development.** To compare income inequality across countries, the OECD uses the Gini coefficient, a commonly used measure ranging from 0, or perfect equality, to 1, or complete inequality. In 2017, the U.S. had a Gini coefficient of 0.434. In the other G7 nations, the Gini ranged from 0.326 in France to 0.392 in the UK.

Globally, the Gini ranges from lows of about 0.25 in some Eastern European countries to highs of 0.5 to 0.6 in countries in southern Africa, according to World Bank estimates.

In the U.S., black-white income gap has held steady since 1970

Median U.S. household income, in 2018 dollars

White
$84,600
$54,100
$51,600
$30,400
Black

1970 1978 1988 1998 2008 2018

Note: Income is adjusted for household size and scaled to reflect a three-person household. Whites and blacks include those who report being only one race and are non-Hispanic. Source: Pew Research Center analysis of 1970 to 2019 Current Population Survey, Annual Social and Economic Supplements.

PEW RESEARCH CENTER

3. **The black-white income gap in the U.S. has persisted over time.** The difference in median household incomes between white and black Americans has grown from about $23,800 in 1970 to roughly $33,000 in 2018 (as measured in 2018 dollars). Median black household income was 61% of median white household income in 2018, up modestly from 56% in 1970—but down slightly from 63% in 2007, before the Great Recession, according to Current Population Survey data.

4. **Overall, 61% of Americans say there is too much economic inequality in the country today, but views differ by political party and household income level.** Among Republicans and those who lean toward the GOP, 41% say there is too much inequality in the U.S., compared with 78% of Democrats and Democratic leaners, a Pew Research Center survey conducted in September 2019 found.

Democrats are nearly twice as likely as Republicans to say there's too much economic inequality

% saying there is ___ economic inequality in the country these days

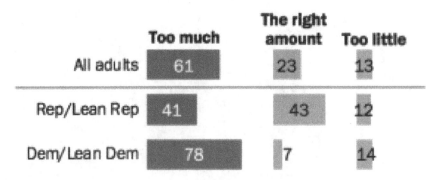

	Too much	The right amount	Too little
All adults	61	23	13
Rep/Lean Rep	41	43	12
Dem/Lean Dem	78	7	14

Note: Share of respondents who didn't offer an answer not shown.
Source: Survey of U.S. adults conducted Sept. 16-29, 2019.
"Most Americans Say There Is Too Much Economic Inequality in the U.S., but Fewer Than Half Call It a Top Priority"

PEW RESEARCH CENTER

Across income groups, U.S. adults are about equally likely to say there is too much economic inequality. But upper- (27%) and middle-income Americans (26%) are more likely than those with lower incomes (17%) to say that there is *about the right amount* of economic inequality.

These views also vary by income within the two-party coalitions. Lower-income Republicans are more likely than upper-income ones to say there's too much inequality in the country today (48% vs. 34%). Among Democrats, the reverse is true: 93% at upper-income levels say there is too much inequality, compared with 65% of lower-income Democrats.

The richest families are the only group to have gained wealth since the Great Recession

% change in median family wealth, by wealth quintile and for the top 5%

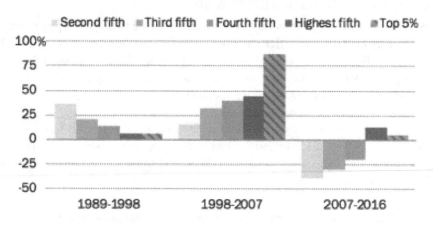

Note: Data for families in the first quintile (bottom 20%) are not shown. Their median wealth was as follows: 1989 – $0; 1998 – $0; 2007 – $36, and 2016 – negative $1,099 (figures in 2018 dollars).
Source: Pew Research Center analysis of the Survey of Consumer Finances.
"Most Americans Say There Is Too Much Economic Inequality in the U.S., but Fewer Than Half Call It a Top Priority"

PEW RESEARCH CENTER

5. **The wealth gap between America's richest and poorer families more than doubled from 1989 to 2016,** according to a recent analysis by the Center. Another way of measuring inequality is to look at household wealth, also known as net worth, or the value of assets owned by a family, such as a home or a savings account, minus outstanding debt, such as a mortgage or student loan.

In 1989, the richest 5% of families had 114 times as much wealth as families in the second quintile (one tier above the lowest), at the median $2.3 million compared with $20,300. By 2016, the top 5% held 248 times as much wealth at the me-

> **The richest families are also the only ones whose wealth increased in the years after the start of the Great Recession.**

dian. (The median wealth of the poorest 20% is either zero or negative in most years we examined.)

The richest families are also the only ones whose wealth increased in the years after the start of the Great Recession. From 2007 to 2016, the median net worth of the top 20% increased 13%, to $1.2 million. For the top 5%, it increased by 4%, to $4.8 million. In contrast, the median net worth of families in lower tiers of wealth decreased by at least 20%. Families in the second-lowest fifth experienced a 39% loss (from $32,100 in 2007 to $19,500 in 2016).

6. **Middle-class incomes have grown at a slower rate than upper-tier incomes over the past five decades,** the same analysis found. From 1970 to 2018, the median middle-class income increased from $58,100 to $86,600, a gain of 49%. By comparison, the median income for upper-tier households grew 64% over that time, from $126,100 to $207,400.

The share of American adults who live in middle-income households has decreased from 61% in 1971 to 51% in 2019. During this time, the share of adults in the upper-income tier increased from 14% to 20%, and the share in the lower-income tier increased from 25% to 29%.

The gaps in income between upper-income and middle- and lower-income households are rising, and the share held by middle-income households is falling

Median household income, in 2018 dollars, and share of U.S. aggregate household income, by income tier

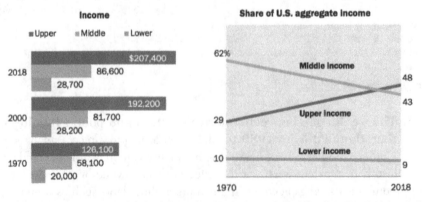

Note: Households are assigned to income tiers based on their size-adjusted income. Incomes are scaled to reflect a three-person household. Revisions to the Current Population Survey affect the comparison of income data from 2014 onwards. See Methodology for details.
Source: Pew Research Center analysis of the Current Population Survey, Annual Social and Economic Supplements (IPUMS).
"Most Americans Say There Is Too Much Economic Inequality in the U.S., but Fewer Than Half Call It a Top Priority"

PEW RESEARCH CENTER

Print Citations

CMS: Schaeffer, Katherine. "6 Facts About Economic Inequality in the U.S." In *The Reference Shelf: Income Inequality,* edited by Micah L. Issitt, 25–31. Amenia, NY: Grey House Publishing, 2022.

MLA: Schaeffer, Katherine. "6 Facts About Economic Inequality in the U.S." *The Reference Shelf: Income Inequality,* edited by Micah L. Issitt, Grey House Publishing, 2022, pp. 25–31.

APA: Schaeffer, K. (2020). 6 facts about economic inequality in the U.S. In Micah L. Issitt (Ed.), *The reference shelf: Income inequality* (pp. 25–31). Amenia, NY: Grey House Publishing.

The Wealth Gap: How the Education World Fails to Fully Measure Students' Economic Disadvantage

By Matt Barnum
Chalkbeat, September 29, 2020

When Ajuah Helton was a college student, her financial aid package came up a few thousand dollars short. What happened next threw her off course.

Her mom took out a high-interest federal loan that she ultimately couldn't repay. The next year, her mom wanted to avoid more loans, but didn't have other funds to tap into. Helton, out of options, left school for a semester to work to make up the difference.

"That's with a mom who was fully employed, college-educated, but did not come from anything that allowed her to say, 'Oh $5,000? Let me just go to my bank account or my stock market and pull out a little bit of cash,'" Helton says.

Helton, who is Black, did graduate. She is now the national director of KIPP Through College, a program designed to help students like herself earn college diplomas. But every day, she sees her own story reflected back at her—the absence of family wealth shaping the trajectories of students, particularly Black students.

"That legacy plays out in any number of ways, starting with what a family has access to pay for education," said Helton. "Often, there is no mortgage to take out of a home. There is no long-term savings."

America's racial wealth gap is massive. The median Black household with children has a net worth of $300, compared to $47,250 for the median white family. Those Black families have 1%, and Hispanic families have 8%, of the average white family's wealth.

The education world often ignores wealth, though, focusing instead on family income, where racial disparities are smaller. It's ingrained in how we study efforts to help students at an economic disadvantage and talk about them, too: How are *low-income* students faring compared to their more affluent peers?

But a small body of new research suggests that wealth matters in a distinct way—and ignoring it means we may be underestimating the extra support that low-wealth students and schools need.

One of those studies, by University of California Berkeley economist Rucker Johnson, finds that wealth directly affects students' chances of completing college.

Johnson hopes it will serve as a call to action, especially because families with little wealth will have a hard time making up for the pandemic's disruption of typical school.

"The fact that we don't typically measure wealth means the default is an income conversation," he said. Wealth, he said, "influences access to educational opportunity pretty much at every stage—I'm talking about pre-K affordability all the way to college."

The Education World Thinks About Family Income: It Rarely Accounts for Family Wealth

Family income does matter. It predicts—and likely contributes to—students' success in school.

That's why the education world explicitly considers income in so many ways, from eligibility for early childhood education programs to federal school funding decisions. The nation's free and reduced-price lunch program is based on family income, too.

The free lunch data, though quite imprecise, is widely used to measure economic disadvantage. "We're groomed to think about just income because of Title I or free and reduced-price lunch," said Mohammed Choudhury, the chief innovation officer for San Antonio schools.

This wouldn't be a problem if wealth and income measured the same thing. But they don't, especially for Black and Hispanic families.

A recent study found that the median Black household with children took in about 50% the income of white families but held just 1% of the wealth. High-income and highly educated Black Americans still have much less wealth than their white peers—a reflection of policies that have excluded Black families from building housing wealth and passing it down to future generations.

"The racial differences in income versus the racial differences in wealth are of a completely different magnitude," said Johnson.

Why Wealth Matters for Families and for Children

Wealth, critically, buffers families from financial hardship.

High-wealth families, regardless of income, are in a better financial position to navigate tumultuous life events, like a divorce or becoming disabled. For low-wealth families, those same events often prompt struggles to pay for food or health care, according to a new study.

Wealth, the study explains, serves as a "private safety net."

Wealth also shapes educational opportunity. It can affect where a family lives, and therefore where children attend elementary, middle, and high school, as well as college. It can influence, too, whether those children experience material hardship and the degree of stress in their household, which can affect their ability to focus on school.

Still, there is not a lot of research on how wealth affects students' performance in school. "I think it's a gap," University of Washington education researcher Dan Goldhaber. "The data is just not available."

The small number of studies that do tackle this question suggest that wealth matters. Students from high-wealth families are much more likely to graduate from high school and complete college, according to a 2018 paper. Even controlling for other factors, including income, children from high-wealth families were 10 percentage points more likely to earn a college degree than those from low-wealth families.

"It's important to understand it as a distinct dimension of inequality," said Fabian Pfeffer, a University of Michigan sociologist and author of the study.

The recent study by Johnson, the Berkeley researcher, goes a step further, suggesting that wealth is not just connected to academic success, but a cause of it.

He found that when a family's housing value spiked by about $50,000 in the years leading up to college, their child's chances of finishing college increased by 3 to 4 percentage points. That may be because students from wealthier families are more likely to attend selective and well-resourced schools that increase their chances of graduating.

"Does parental income matter? Yes," Johnson said. "But parental wealth and parental income in combination matter much more."

Liz Valladares, a recent high school graduate who went to a KIPP middle school, is experiencing those effects firsthand. When COVID-19 hit, her mom's work hours were cut. Without another financial cushion,

> **Wealth directly affects students' chances of completing college.**

she had to tap into a college fund she had started a few years earlier. The added financial strain means Valladares is attending her local community college in Los Angeles rather than the university she'd planned for.

"It was hard for me," said Valladares. "But as a parent it was harder for her to tell her own kid, 'We can't really afford that, you're going to have to change your dream.'"

Valladares says school is going well so far—with the help of money from KIPP to pay for a laptop and books—and she hopes to transfer in a couple of years. But many students lack such support, and research shows students are far more likely to drop out if they attend a two-year rather than a four-year college.

What Should We Do About It?

Whether and how the country should address its wealth gaps is the subject of fraught debate. Some argue that we need to address the issue directly, with a tax on wealth or reparations for descendants of enslaved people.

Of course, school officials don't control economic policy. But they can decide how to respond to students' economic circumstances. If our shared understanding of economic disadvantage is flawed or incomplete, students who stand to benefit from additional help are going without it.

"I'm definitely intrigued," said Zahava Stadler, who works on school funding for Education Trust, an education and civil rights group. "While I wouldn't say that we have enough information to know for sure that it's the right approach, there is an intuitive logic to the idea that family wealth, just like income, is a part of the picture."

Wealth already does play one notable role in education. States usually send extra school funding to communities with limited housing wealth to make up for the fact that they can't collect much in property taxes.

Doing more, Stadler said, will require better data. "We're hampered by what data is easy to get at the student level," she said. "That's a lot of the problem here."

Perfect data might be difficult or intrusive to obtain. But some are figuring out how to measure economic hardship in new ways that extend beyond income.

Choudhury, the San Antonio school official, created a way of measuring economic disadvantage at the neighborhood level. It includes not just median income but family structure, average education levels, and home ownership rates, with that last dimension designed to capture community wealth. The approach has since been taken statewide as part of Texas' school funding formula.

"When we rely on a single measure, we wash poverty in one shade," said Choudhury.

Print Citations

CMS: Barnum, Matt. "The Wealth Gap: How the Education World Fails to Fully Measure Students' Economic Disadvantage." In *The Reference Shelf: Income Inequality,* edited by Micah L. Issitt, 32–35. Amenia, NY: Grey House Publishing, 2022.

MLA: Barnum, Matt. "The Wealth Gap: How the Education World Fails to Fully Measure Students' Economic Disadvantage." *The Reference Shelf: Income Inequality,* edited by Micah L. Issitt, Grey House Publishing, 2022, pp. 32–35.

APA: Barnum. M. (2022). The wealth gap: How the education world fails to fully measure students' economic disadvantage. In Micah L. Issitt (Ed.), *The reference shelf: Income inequality* (pp. 32–35). Amenia, NY: Grey House Publishing.

Modern Society Is as Unequal as 14th Century Europe

By Scotty Hendricks
Big Think, May 14, 2021

Economic inequality is a constant topic. No matter the cycle—boom or bust—somebody is making a lot of money, and the question of fairness is never far behind.

A recently published essay in the Journal of Economic Literature by Professor Guido Alfani adds an intriguing perspective to the discussion by showing the evolution of income inequality in Europe over the last several hundred years. As it turns out, we currently live in a comparatively egalitarian epoch.

Seven Centuries of Economic History

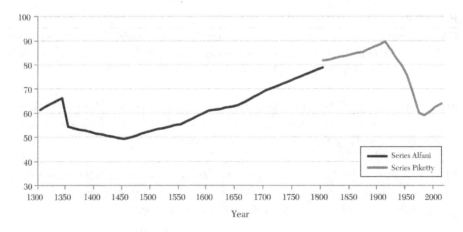

Figure 8 from Guido Alfani, *Journal of Economic Literature*, 2021.

This graph shows the amount of wealth controlled by the top ten percent in certain parts of Europe over the last seven hundred years. Archival documentation similar to—and often of a similar quality as—modern economic data allows researchers to get a glimpse of what economic conditions were like centuries ago. Sources like property tax records and documents listing the rental value of homes can be used to determine how much a person's estate was worth. (While these methods leave out those without property, the data is not particularly distorted.)

The first part of the line, shown in black, represents work by Prof. Alfani and represents the average inequality level of the Sabaudian State in Northern Italy, The Florentine State, The Kingdom of Naples, and the Republic of Venice. The

> **The cause of changes in inequality levels is the difference in the rate of return on capital and the overall growth rate of the economy.**

latter part, in gray, is based on the work of French economist Thomas Piketty and represents an average of inequality in France, the United Kingdom, and Sweden during that time period.

Despite the shift in location, the level of inequality and rate of increase are very similar between the two data sets.

Apocalyptic Events Cause Decreases in Inequality

Note that there are two substantial declines in inequality. Both are tied to truly apocalyptic events. The first is the Black Death, the common name for the bubonic plague pandemic in the 14th century, which killed off anywhere between 30 and 50 percent of Europe. The second, at the dawn of the 20th century, was the result of World War I and the many major events in its aftermath.

The 20th century as a whole was a time of tremendous economic change, and the periods not featuring major wars are notable for having large experiments in distributive economic policies, particularly in the countries Piketty considers.

The slight stall in the rise of inequality during the 17th century is the result of the Thirty Years' War, a terrible religious conflict that ravaged Europe and left eight million people dead, and of major plagues that affected South Europe. However, the recurrent outbreaks of the plague after the Black Death no longer had much effect on inequality. This was due to a number of factors, not the least of which was the adaptation of European institutions to handle pandemics without causing such a shift in wealth.

In 2010, the last year covered by the essay, inequality levels were similar to those of 1340, with 66 percent of the wealth of society being held by the top ten percent. Also, inequality levels were continuing to rise, and the trends have not ended since. As Prof. Alfani explained in an email to *Big Think*:

> During the decade preceding the Covid pandemic, economic inequality has shown a slow tendency towards further inequality growth. The Great Recession that began in 2008 possibly contributed to slow down inequality growth, especially in Europe, but it did not stop it. However, the expectation is that Covid-19 will tend to increase inequality and poverty. This, because it tends to create a relatively greater economic damage to those having unstable occupations, or who need physical strength to work (think of the effects of the so-called "long-Covid," which can prove physically invalidating for a long time). Additionally, and thankfully, Covid is not lethal enough to force major leveling dynamics upon society.

Can Only Disasters Change Inequality?

That is the subject of some debate. While inequality can occur in any economy, even one that doesn't grow all that much, some things appear to make it more likely to rise or fall.

Thomas Piketty suggested that the cause of changes in inequality levels is the difference in the rate of return on capital and the overall growth rate of the economy. Since the return on capital is typically higher than the overall growth rate, this means that those who have capital to invest tend to get richer faster than everybody else.

While this does explain a great deal of the graph after 1800, his model fails to explain why inequality fell after the Black Death. Indeed, since the plague destroyed human capital and left material goods alone, we would expect the ratio of wealth over income to increase and for inequality to rise. His model can provide explanations for the decline in inequality in the decades after the pandemic, however, it is possible that the abundance of capital could have lowered returns over a longer time span.

The catastrophe theory put forth by Walter Scheidel suggests that the only force strong enough to wrest economic power from those who have it is a world-shattering event like the Black Death, the fall of the Roman Empire, or World War I. While each event changed the world in a different way, they all had a tremendous leveling effect on society.

But not even this explains everything in the above graph. Pandemics subsequent to the Black Death had little effect on inequality, and inequality continued to fall for decades after World War II ended. Prof. Alfani suggests that we remember the importance of human agency through institutional change. He attributes much of the post-WWII decline in inequality to "the redistributive policies and the development of the welfare states from the 1950s to the early 1970s."

What Does This Mean for Us Now?

As Professor Alfani put it in his email:

> [H]istory does not necessarily teach us whether we should consider the current trend toward growth in economic inequality as an undesirable outcome or a problem per se (although I personally believe that there is some ground to argue for that). Nor does it teach us that high inequality is destiny. What it does teach us, is that if we do not act, we have no reason whatsoever to expect that inequality will, one day, decline on its own. History also offers abundant evidence that past trends in inequality have been deeply influenced by our collective decisions, as they shaped the institutional framework across time. So, it is really up to us to decide whether we want to live in a more, or a less unequal society.

Print Citations

CMS: Hendricks, Scotty. "Modern Society Is as Unequal as 14th Century Europe." In *The Reference Shelf: Income Inequality,* edited by Micah L. Issitt, 36–39. Amenia, NY: Grey House Publishing, 2022.

MLA: Hendricks, Scotty. "Modern Society Is as Unequal as 14th Century Europe." *The Reference Shelf: Income Inequality,* edited by Micah L. Issitt, Grey House Publishing, 2022, pp. 36–39.

APA: Hendricks, S. (2021). Modern society is as unequal as 14th century Europe. In Micah L. Issitt (Ed.), *The reference shelf: Income inequality* (pp. 36–39). Amenia, NY: Grey House Publishing.

2
The Minimum Wage

A 2016 protest in Minneapolis protest for a $15-an-hour minimum wage.

What Is the Value of an Hour?

The minimum wage refers to a series of laws mandating a minimum rate of pay for any kind of work. In most countries in which minimum wage laws are utilized, minimum wage rates typically fall short of a "living wage," which is the rate of pay at which a person or family can achieve a "normal" standard of living. But the establishment of minimum wage laws is a strategy to combat corporate and employer exploitation of the working class.

Between 2015 and 2022, the minimum wage debate has been heavily focused on the popular movement to establish a $15.00 federal minimum wage, which would guarantee a minimum of $15 per hour for any employee paid directly by the federal government. The establishment of a $15 federal minimum wage would force companies in a number of states to adopt a similar wage in order to remain competitive in the job market. Supporters argue that a $15 minimum wage would raise a significant number of families out of financial insecurity, while critics argue that raising the minimum wage would make it more difficult for small businesses to compete and will limit hiring and expansion for companies. A number of economists have noted that the $15 minimum wage proposal would not raise average compensation levels enough to keep pace with the last fifty years of inflation and cost-of-living increases.

Evolution of an Idea

The world's first minimum wage law was established in 1894 in New Zealand, as part of the Industrial Conciliation and Arbitration Act. The government's decision to establish the law came after a massive series of strikes in New Zealand's cities, and the law also established limits on working hours and required businesses to address workplace safety issues. The passage of New Zealand's minimum wage law was controversial. News coverage within New Zealand in 1894 showed that business and industry leaders warned that forcing them to increase wages would lead to less hiring and would place a strain on businesses.

In an 1894 article from the *New Zealand Herald,* the paper reported, "If the Harbour Board is compelled to pay 10s [10 shillings] per day, they will just employ half the number of men they would do if they had to pay only 5s per day. So far as they are concerned, the other men will have to starve."[1] This kind of argument is strikingly similar to the arguments against the proposed $15 minimum wage in the United States in the twenty-first century. In New Zealand, the wealthy industrialists who controlled the oceanic shipping industry argued that they would be forced to reduce employment and that new jobs would not be available. But the warnings issued by business leaders and pro-business politicians were idle threats. The businesses couldn't actually reduce employment numbers without losing even more revenues and so they were, in the end, forced to pay higher wages. There was no net loss in employment and no evidence of corporate stagnation.

Two years after New Zealand passed the world's first national minimum wage law, the Australian government passed the Factories and Shops Act, which established a system of wage boards, split evenly between employers and employees and managed by an appointed chairman representing the state. Each industry had a wage board, and the members of the board discussed profit margins, taxes, and wages and attempted to establish minimum wages for each job category, rather than a nationwide minimum wage. This Australian system inspired debate in Great Britain, the former colonial power in control of both New Zealand and Australia. There had been a contentious debate over the possibility of establishing minimum wages across Britain from the mid-1800s on, but little progress had been made. In 1909, the British government established a series of wage boards for various industries, and in 1912 it mandated a minimum wage for the national coal industry, which was one of the industries plagued by frequent conflict between workers and management over poor conditions, exploitative working hours requirements, and insufficient pay.[2]

At the time, minimum wage laws were not really the same as minimum wage laws in the twenty-first century, which establish the lowest wage that a worker can be legally paid. In contrast, the early minimum wage laws were an effort to regulate wages so as to prevent companies from establishing exploitative wages. The English news media provided American workers and worker's rights advocates with coverage of the wage debates in Australia, New Zealand, and Great Britain, and this inspired campaigns in a number of states to establish similar laws.

The first minimum wage in the United States was inspired by the previous decade of workers' rights victories in England and Australasia, but it was also the result of the looming mechanization process in American factories. The textile industry was the first to widely embrace the replacement of human workers with manufacturing machines, a process that began in the late 1800s and accelerated in the early years of the twentieth century. Mill workers suffered extremely poor conditions, despite the fact that the majority of workers were female children and adolescents. Factories were crowded and unsanitary, and workers toiled for long hours in rooms filled with toxic chemicals.

Conditions for workers were especially poor in Lawrence, Massachusetts, where a massive milling industry had developed between the late 1800s and the early 1900s, employing hundreds of women. According to William Moran, author of the 2002 *The Belles of New England*, physician Elizabeth Sharpleigh reported in 1911 that a third of the workers in the textile mills in Lawrence died before the age of twenty-five, largely from rapidly spreading diseases like tuberculosis, aggravated by long hours, poor hygiene, and particulate matter within the air at the mills.[3] In 1912, Lawrence became the site for the beginning of a historic workers' strike that eventually spread across the region. Thousands of workers left the mills and factories and marched in the streets, and strikers in other cities and other industries joined in as well. Most of the striking workers were women and one of the slogans they used while marching was "We want bread, and roses, too," which was a way of saying that the workers not only wanted enough compensation to meet their most basic needs (a loaf of bread) but wanted enough to enjoy a modicum of pleasure, like treating oneself to roses or other pleasurable purchases. This slogan led some in the press to call the movement the "Bread and Roses" strike.[4]

The Lawrence textile strike was one of the major factors leading to the adoption of state minimum wages for the industry, which was the first minimum wage law established in the United States. Over the next year, a total of nine states adopted some form of minimum wage law, most of which utilizing the wage commission or wage board strategy first developed in Australia. The establishment of these state minimum wage laws was actually the culmination of many years of dispute between employers and workers across the United States. The states in which minimum wage laws were established, including Massachusetts, Oregon, Utah, Washington, Nebraska, Minnesota, Colorado, California, and Wisconsin, all had large scale-low pay industries, and all had seen numerous widespread strikes and demonstrations over previous decades. In California, for instance, there were numerous strikes and other workers' actions, many of which culminated in violent attacks by police or security, in the railroad and mining industries.

While the minimum wage laws of the early 1900s were a significant victory for workers, and transformed a number of important industries within the country, pro-corporate politicians and lobbyists succeeded to preventing the establishment of new minimum wage standards in most states. Despite the fact that the establishment of minimum wage systems did *not* lead to mass layoffs in the states that adopted such laws, or in the other countries that adopted often more progressive minimum wage systems, the primary argument used to critique minimum wage proposals was that such laws would greatly limit corporate profit, forcing companies to withhold from hiring additional workers or to layoff existing workers. As was the case in New Zealand, in 1894, in most cases such threats were without merit and companies were generally able to accommodate minimum wages. What legislators and critics are typically trying to protect, when arguing against minimum wage laws, are the profits given to corporate ownership and upper management.

The Great Depression, which began in 1929, greatly reduced the influence of the antiminimum-wage movement, as workers in the laboring and middle class joined together to strike against companies offering unfair wages and maintaining poor conditions. This was a turning point in the history of the workers' rights movement and in 1938, as a progressive legislature overruled state minimum wage laws to establish the first federal minimum wage as part of the Fair Labor Standards Act, which also provided the first and most robust protections for labor unions in American history to that point. In October of 1938, the minimum wage was set at $0.25 per hour, though only for employees involved directly in interstate commerce, and so covered by the Congressional power to regulate commerce between the states. States did not have to meet this minimum wage, but the law provided workers in many industries with leverage to use in arguing for increased wages within their states.

The first federal minimum wage established a new frontier for this debate, in the form of legislation increasing or expanding the minimum wage and other workers' rights standards. In the years since the 1938 law, workers' groups have successfully lobbied for numerous minimum wage increases, and many states have outpaced the federal government in terms of protecting certain minimum standards in wages and hours for workers. But critics argue that minimum wage legislation has not been aggressive enough, while critics of the minimum wage continue to argue that forcing increased wages will force businesses to close or cease hiring and argue that unregulated competition between companies provides better wages for workers than can be achieved by mandating wage standards.

Does the Minimum Wage Work?

Since the passage of the nation's first minimum wage law in 1938, minimum wage laws have been updated many times. The first came just a year after the initial minimum wage of $0.25 was established in 1938, and raised the wage to $0.30 in October of 1939. The next came several years later, in 1940, and raised the wage to $0.40, then to $0.70 in 1950, five years after the previous wage increase. The minimum wage finally hit $1.00 per hour in 1956, then climbed to $1.15 in 1961, then $1.25 in 1963. The most recent update of the federal minimum wage prior to the $15 minimum wage debate came in 2009, when a new federal law set the minimum wage at $7.25 for all applicable workers.[5]

While the minimum wage has increased at semiregular intervals since the late 1930s, the federal wage rate has always been insufficient at least in certain states. Many states have adopted minimum wage laws mandating rates significantly higher than the federal limit, and in these states federal legislation has reduced importance. The difficulty with establishing nationwide wage rates is that conditions, costs, and the labor market differ significantly from state to states such that it can be difficult to create a wage rate that will work for workers in all states. This is one of the criticisms frequently raised to counter calls for new federal wage rates. Critics of the minimum wage frequently argue that limiting corporate regulation, and allowing states and companies to compete with workers, will result in higher wages for workers and will be more effective than mandating wage increases.[6]

The problem with allowing free-market competition to determine wage rates is that workers are not free to move between employment opportunities. Many Americans lack the resources to relocate between states or might face other difficulties in relocation, such as family, educational, or interpersonal commitments. Within a state, competition for workers may force companies to increase wages, but this only works when there are more jobs available than workers in need of employment. When companies must compete for workers, wages increase. When workers are readily available, companies can pay the minimum wage necessary to retain their workforce.

Critics of minimum wage increases also argue that small businesses will be negatively impacted, some potentially forced to close, when states or the federal government adopt minimum wage laws. Historical research indicates that larger companies rarely experience any sustained negative impact from even moderate wage increases, but mandated wage increases can prove a significant strain on struggling smaller businesses. States and the federal government have tried to combat this deleterious impact by providing tax breaks and other incentives to small businesses, in an effort to enable small business owners to defray the cost of providing wages that meet the current federal minimum. Federal minimum was laws also typically apply only to businesses above a certain minimum threshold of employees or that bring in a certain minimum of profit annually.

One of the problems with minimum wage laws is that the pace of minimum wage increases has not kept pace with the cost of living, inflation, or corporate profit rates, and some critics argue that minimum wage laws are not particularly useful unless they provide significant, rather than moderate, wage increases. Economic research organizations like the Center for Economic Policy Research (CEPR) have shown that productivity in the American economy has been steadily increasing since the 1960s, but that wages have not kept pace with inflation or the rising cost of living. In 2021, the CEPR released a report detailing the history of wages, inflation, and productivity between the 1960s and 2020, indicating that the average minimum wage in the United States should be closer to $23.00 per hour, if wages had kept pace with the increase in corporate profits and productivity since 1968.[7]

Studies of poverty in America have also proven, conclusively, that the $7.25 minimum wage is insufficient to cover the cost of living for US workers in any state, no matter the local conditions. Numerous studies, produced between 2010 and 2022, proved that the $7.25 wage was insufficient, though twenty-one US states continued to utilize the federal minimum wage as the state standard. Further, studies indicate that the establishment of a $15 minimum wage—the primary focus of the minimum wage campaign in the twenty-first century—would only constitute a sustainable wage in around half of US states. In the remaining states, workers earning $15 per hour would still live dangerously close to poverty and would largely be unable to accrue savings or investments to advance to the next level.[8]

Even in states that have established minimum wages significantly higher than the federal rate, or the $15 proposed wage, data from the Massachusetts Institute of Technology's "cost-of-living" data set indicates that none of the fifty US states provides a minimum wage that meets the standards of a "living wage," defined as a wage that not only allows the average individual and family to survive, but allows them to sustain a normal standard of living. Individuals earning a "living wage" can afford some basic amenities beyond the resources needed to survive, but still may lack sufficient income to build savings or equity.[9]

A living wage is considered, by many activists in the workers' rights movement, to be the only acceptable wage rate that should be permitted in any state, and many argue that all workers, regardless of the kind of work they perform, should be entitled to a living wage and that failing to provide at least this basic level of wages violates basic principles of human rights standards. Studies indicate that a majority of Americans support raising the minimum wage to $15, but support for such a measure is sharply divided along partisan lines. Opinion polls from 2020 and 2021 indicate that between 68 and 72 percent of those identifying as "conservative" oppose raising the minimum wage. This level of resistance is related to the long-standing claim that forced wage increases are "bad for business," though research does not generally support this claim.[10]

While increasing the minimum wage to $15 per hour will not be sufficient to guarantee a "living wage" for most Americans, and while such an increase might force some companies to either struggle or to reduce profit for investors/ownership, opinions on this issue reflect underlying beliefs about the value of human workers and their time. Some critics of minimum wage laws have argued that individuals earning the minimum wage or below that wage are responsible for their own fate, and that the work that they perform simply isn't valuable enough to justify a higher wage. Critics of this view argue that all workers, no matter their roles, should be afforded compensation sufficient not only to survive, but to advance in their lives. Ultimately, opinions on the minimum wage are less a matter of opting for a reasonable or proven economic strategy as they are expressions of the value that a person assigns to themselves and other workers struggling to earn a living in American companies.

Works Used

Baker, Dean. "CORRECTION: The Productivity Adjusted Minimum Wage Would Be $21.50 in 2020 and $23 in 2021." *CEPR*. 16 Mar. 2022. https://cepr.net/correction-the-productivity-adjusted-minimum-wage-would-be-21-50-in-2020-and-23-in-2021/.

Bloomenthal, Andrew, Somer Anderson, and Peter Rathburn. "Can a Family Survive on the US Minimum Wage?" *Investopedia*. 18 Mar. 2022. https://www.investopedia.com/articles/personal-finance/022615/can-family-survive-us-minimum-wage.asp.

DeSimone, Bailey. "From the Serial Set: The History of the Minimum Wage." *LOC*. Library of Congress. 3 Sept. 2020. https://blogs.loc.gov/law/2020/09/from-the-serial-set-the-history-of-the-minimum-wage/#:~:text=Serial%20Set%20Vol.-,No.,and%20Arbitration%20Act%20of%201894.

Dunn, Amina. "Most Americans Support a $15 Federal Minimum Wage." *Pew Research Center*. 22 Apr. 2021. https://www.pewresearch.org/fact-tank/2021/04/22/most-americans-support-a-15-federal-minimum-wage/.

"History of Federal Minimum Wage Rates Under the Fair Labor Standards Act, 1938–2009." *US Department of Labor*. https://www.dol.gov/agencies/whd/minimum-wage/history/chart.

"Living Wage Calculator." *Massachusetts Institute of Technology*. https://livingwage.mit.edu/.

"A Minimum Wage." *New Zealand Herald*. 5 July 1894. *National Library of New Zealand*. Moran,

Moran, William. *The Belles of New England: The Women of the Textile Mills and the Families Whose Wealth They Wove*. Macmillan, 2002.

Upmeyer, Linda. "Minimum Wage Levels—Let the States and Free Markets Decide." *Alec*. 7 June 2018. https://alec.org/article/minimum-wage-levels-let-the-states-and-free-markets-decide/.

Watson, Bruce. *Bread and Roses: Mills, Migrants, and the Struggle for the American Dream*. Penguin Books, 2005.

Notes

1. "A Minimum Wage," *New Zealand Herald*.
2. DeSimone, "From the Serial Set: The History of the Minimum Wage."
3. Moran, *The Belles of New England: The Women of the Textile Mills and the Families Whose Wealth They Wove*, p. 183.
4. Watson, *Bread and Roses: Mills, Migrants, and the Struggle for the American Dream*.
5. "History of Federal Minimum Wage Rates Under the Fair Labor Standards Act, 1938–2009," *US Department of Labor*.
6. Upmeyer, "Minimum Wage Levels—Let the States and Free Markets Decide."
7. Baker, "CORRECTION: The Productivity Adjusted Minimum Wage Would Be $21.50 in 2020 and $23 in 2021."
8. Bloomenthal, Anderson, and Rathburn. "Can a Family Survive on the US Minimum Wage?"
9. "Living Wage Calculator," *MIT*.
10. Dunn, "Most Americans Support a $15 Federal Minimum Wage."

Most Americans Support a $15 Federal Minimum Wage

By Amina Dunn
Pew Research Center, April 22, 2021

About six-in-ten U.S. adults (62%) say they favor raising the federal minimum wage to $15 an hour, including 40% who strongly back the idea. About four-in-ten (38%) say they oppose the proposal, according to a Pew Research Center survey conducted April 5-11.

The Biden administration and many congressional Democrats favor increasing the federal minimum wage to $15 an hour from the current rate of $7.25 an hour, but the proposal's fate in the Senate is uncertain. Some senators, including several Democrats, support a more modest increase in the wage.

62% of Americans support a $15 federal minimum wage; most opponents want a more modest increase

% who say they ____ raising the federal minimum wage to $15.00 an hour

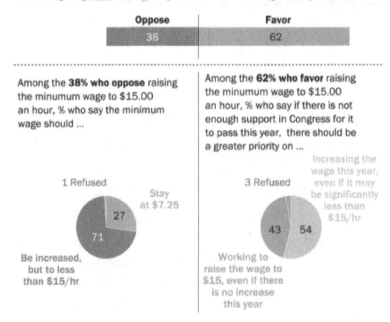

Note: No answer responses not shown.
Source: Survey of U.S. adults conducted April 5-11, 2021.

PEW RESEARCH CENTER

Among the public, those who back a $15 minimum wage are fairly divided over how to approach the issue if there is insufficient support in Congress for an increase to that amount this year. A narrow majority of these Americans (54%) say leaders should focus on passing an increase to the wage "even if it may be significantly less than $15 an hour," while 43% say the priority should be to work to raise the hourly minimum wage to $15 "even if no increase makes it into law this year."

Among those who oppose raising the minimum wage to $15 an hour, a substantial majority (71%) say the federal minimum wage should be increased, but that the standard should be less than $15 an hour; those who hold this view account for 27% of the overall public. Only one-in-ten Americans in all say that federal minimum wage should remain at the current level of $7.25 an hour.

Support for raising the minimum wage to $15 an hour is extensive across most demographic groups, according to the survey, which was conducted among 5,109 U.S. adults.

Black adults in particular stand out for their support: 89% favor raising the minimum wage to $15 an hour, including 73% who support the idea strongly.

Across most demographic groups, majorities favor raising federal minimum wage to $15 an hour

% who say they _____ raising the federal minimum wage to $15.00 an hour

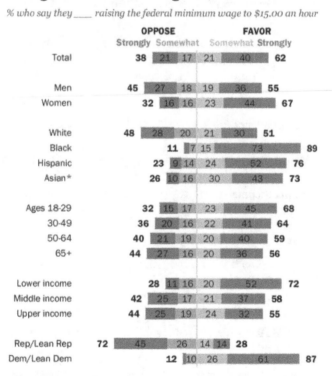

*Asian adults interviewed in English only.
Notes: White, Black, and Asian adults include those who report being one race and are not Hispanic. Hispanics are of any race. Family income tiers based on adjusted 2019 earnings. No answer responses not shown.
Source: Survey of U.S. adults conducted April 5-11, 2021.

PEW RESEARCH CENTER

About three-quarters of Hispanic (76%) and Asian Americans (73%) also favor raising the minimum wage to $15 an hour, with 52% of Hispanics and 43% of Asians
saying they strongly support the idea.

White adults, by contrast, are divided: 51% favor raising the minimum wage to
$15 an hour—including just 30% who strongly favor it—while 48% oppose it.

About seven-in-ten adults who live in lower-income households (72%) say they
favor raising the federal minimum wage to $15 an hour, including about half (52%)
who strongly favor such an increase. Smaller majorities of those in middle- (58%)
and upper-income households (55%) say they favor a $15 minimum wage.

There are sharp partisan differences in opinions. While 87% of Democrats and
Democratic-leaning independents say they favor increasing the wage to $15 an hour
(including 61% who strongly favor it), 72% of Republicans and GOP leaners oppose
the idea (including 45% who strongly oppose it).

People living in areas with higher minimum wages are more likely to say federal minimum should be $15 an hour

% who favor raising the federal minimum wage to $15.00 an hour

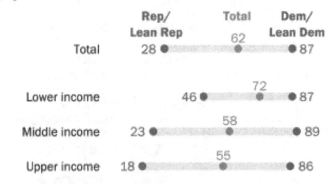

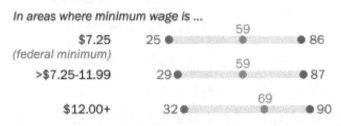

Note: Area minimum wage is usually set by state law. In cases where
the city or county sets a higher minimum wage, that is used instead.
Source: Survey of U.S. adults conducted April 5-11, 2021.

PEW RESEARCH CENTER

People living in areas where the state-level minimum wage is currently $12 or higher are more likely than others to say they favor a federal increase to $15 an hour. About seven-in-ten adults in these places (69%) favor raising the federal minimum wage to $15 an hour, compared with 59% of those living in places with a minimum wage of less than $12 an hour.

> **While 87% of Democrats and Democratic-leaning independents say they favor increasing the wage to $15 an hour, 72% of Republican and GOP leaners oppose the idea.**

While Democrats are largely united in their support for increasing the federal minimum wage to $15 an hour, Republicans' views differ by household income.

Lower-income Republicans (46%) are much more likely than middle- (23%) and upper-income Republicans (18%) to say they favor raising the federal minimum wage to $15 an hour. Still, a majority of lower-income Republicans (54%) say they oppose such an increase.

Similarly, Republicans who live in areas where the state minimum wage is $12 or higher are slightly more likely than those living in places where the $7.25 federal minimum wage applies to say they favor raising the federal minimum to $15 an hour (32% vs. 25%).

What Should Happen if Congress Lacks Support for a $15 Minimum Wage?

More than half of Americans who favor a $15 federal minimum wage (54%) say that if there is not enough congressional support for such an increase this year, Congress should prioritize increasing the wage even if the new wage is significantly less than $15.

These views differ by race and ethnicity, as well as by income. A majority of Black adults who favor a $15 standard (55%) say that if there is not sufficient support in Congress for that to pass, congressional leaders should continue to work for a $15 minimum wage even if no minimum wage increase becomes law this year. Half of Hispanic adults who back the $15 wage also express this view.

Demographic divides among backers of $15 minimum wage over next step if it lacks congressional support

*Among **the 62% of Americans who favor raising the federal minimum wage to $15 an hour**, % who say if there is not enough support in Congress for it to pass this year, there should be a greater priority on ...*

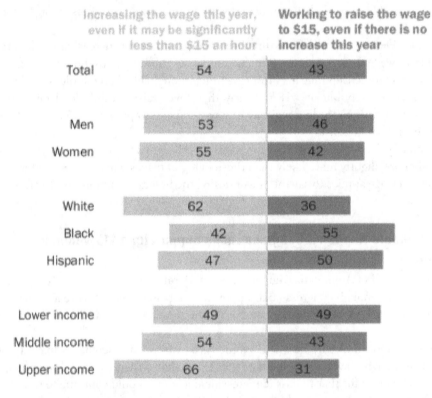

	Increasing the wage this year, even if it may be significantly less than $15 an hour	Working to raise the wage to $15, even if there is no increase this year
Total	54	43
Men	53	46
Women	55	42
White	62	36
Black	42	55
Hispanic	47	50
Lower income	49	49
Middle income	54	43
Upper income	66	31

Notes: White and Black adults include those who report being one race and are not Hispanic. Hispanics are of any race. Family income tiers based on adjusted 2019 earnings. No answer responses not shown.
Source: Survey of U.S. adults conducted April 5-11, 2021.

PEW RESEARCH CENTER

By contrast, 36% of White adults who favor a $15 minimum wage say Congress should keep pressing for that amount. A majority of White supporters of a $15 federal minimum wage, by contrast, say Congress should work for an increase in the minimum wage even if it is less than $15 an hour.

Lower-income adults who favor a $15 minimum wage are divided on the better approach if there is inadequate support in Congress for the proposal this year: 49% say congressional leaders should prioritize any raise to the minimum that can happen this year, while an identical 49% share say leaders should continue working until they pass legislation raising the wage to $15 an hour.

Among higher-income adults who support a $15 minimum wage, majorities say the priority for Congress should be to work to increase the minimum wage, even if the new wage is significantly less than $15 an hour.

Print Citations

CMS: Dunn, Amina. "Most Americans Support a $15 Federal Minimum Wage." In *The Reference Shelf: Income Inequality,* edited by Micah L. Issitt, 50–55. Amenia, NY: Grey House Publishing, 2022.

MLA: Dunn, Amina. "Most Americans Support a $15 Federal Minimum Wage." *The Reference Shelf: Income Inequality,* edited by Micah L. Issitt, Grey House Publishing, 2022, pp. 50–55.

APA: Dunn, A. (2021). Most Americans support as $15 federal minimum wage. In Micah L. Issitt (Ed.), *The Reference Shelf: Income inequality* (pp. 50–55). Amenia, NY: Grey House Publishing.

Six Reasons to Oppose a $15 Federal Minimum Wage

By Jarrett Skorup
The Hill, January 30, 2021

Just a decade ago, a mandatory $15-per-hour minimum wage seemed like a pipe dream—even liberal economists and The New York Times warned of negative effects. But a few large cities started enforcing it, and then it became part of the Democratic Party platform. It now stands a real chance of becoming federal law.

This would be a bad idea for six key reasons.

The trade-offs aren't worth it, suggests the bulk of the research. While the research over the effects of minimum wage hikes isn't as clear-cut as it used to be, the consensus of economists still is that they are a bad idea. A survey found a majority of economists oppose a $15 federal minimum wage. And the Congressional Budget Office (CBO) found it is likely to cost 1.7 million jobs with no corresponding increase in overall wages.

It won't help those in poverty. Many proponents of raising the minimum wage think it helps poor people, but, overall, it doesn't. Most people who earn low wages aren't living in poverty—in fact, most live in families earning more than the average U.S. income. That's because most are the second (or third or fourth) income earners in a family, not the primary one. Most people who live in poverty don't work at all, and only 10 percent of adults in poor households work full time. Even more liberal economists, and some proponents of minimum wage mandates, acknowledge a higher minimum wage isn't likely to affect poverty rates. A hike in the minimum wage won't help those in poverty; in fact, it is likely to make it harder for them to find a job, the real ticket out of poverty.

It is unlikely to raise wages for the lowest-paid workers. A higher wage mandate doesn't create wealth; it merely shifts it around. The CBO finds that a $15 minimum wage will raise wages for some workers, result in layoffs for others and be a net loss for income overall. The lowest-skilled workers tend to be the lowest-paid workers, and they'll suffer the most consequences. The American Enterprise Institute compared the earnings of low-wage workers in states that boosted their minimum wage with those that did not and found little or no difference in pay growth between the different sets of states. In other words, the earnings in low-pay jobs grew just as fast in states that did not raise their minimum wages as they did in states that did. Wages tend to rise because of broad-based economic growth, not government mandates.

It eliminates entry level jobs. The value of a minimum wage job isn't primarily the money—it's the experience and skills gained, the stepping stone to the next job, that's the real value. Raising the

> **Wages tend to rise because of broad-based economic growth, not government mandates.**

minimum wage limits the availability of these types of jobs, which means fewer people will get the opportunity to learn these important skills. This mostly harms low-skilled individuals and low-income households, the very people most in need of new employment opportunities.

It will raise prices for those who can afford it the least. Big businesses and high-end restaurants often support higher minimum wages. That may seem odd at first, but it makes sense when you consider their competitive environment. Big corporate firms can more easily absorb these mandated costs and can invest in new technologies that make them less dependent on human labor. The same cannot be said of the small businesses competing with these firms, so big businesses ultimately can benefit when governments raise costs.

It gets rid of key protections for workers. The current minimum wage law gives narrow exceptions to youths and people with disabilities because these government wage mandates harm these workers the most and they tend to be the first ones laid off or not hired altogether. Tipped workers—primarily servers and bartenders—also are currently allowed to count tips towards their salaries. The Biden plan would eliminate these provisions for tipped employees and those with disabilities, which likely means higher unemployment and lower wages overall for those workers.

Proponents of the $15 federal minimum wage see a simple problem ("People don't make enough money!") and pitch a simple solution ("Force employers to pay them more!"). But as the great economist Thomas Sowell has said, "There are no solutions; only trade-offs." For all public policy decisions, we need to consider the trade-offs—and for a $15 federal minimum wage mandate, they will leave us worse off.

Print Citations

CMS: Skorup, Jarrett. "Six Reasons to Oppose a $15 Federal Minimum Wage." In *The Reference Shelf: Income Inequality,* edited by Micah L. Issitt, 56–57. Amenia, NY: Grey House Publishing, 2022.

MLA: Skorup, Jarrett. "Six Reasons to Oppose a $15 Federal Minimum Wage." *The Reference Shelf: Income Inequality,* edited by Micah L. Issitt, Grey House Publishing, 2022, pp. 56–57.

APA: Skorup, J. (2021). Six reasons to oppose a $15 federal minimum wage. In Micah L. Issitt (Ed.), *The reference shelf: Income inequality* (pp. 56–57). Amenia, NY: Grey House Publishing.

Five Myths That Pervade the Minimum Wage Debate

By Jensen Ahokovi
Grassroot Institute of Hawaii, March 16, 2022

The vast majority of Hawaii residents support increasing the state's legal minimum wage on the grounds that it would help Hawaii's low-income workers better cope with the state's high cost of living.[1]

But that isn't what the vast majority of evidence indicates would happen.

The data is overwhelming that legally increasing a minimum wage anywhere negatively affects employment—and not necessarily in the short term. The results typically include job loss,[2] cutbacks in hours,[3] fewer benefits,[4] automation[5] and higher consumer prices.[6]

In other words, setting the legal wage rate higher than the present market rate isn't just about causing unemployment, but also triggering a range of effects, all of which negatively affect those whom the higher minimum wage is intended to help, primarily low-skilled and less-educated workers.

In the current Hawaii debate about whether to increase the state's minimum wage—from \$10.10 an hour to a higher amount still to be determined, most likely \$18 by some date in the near future—there are five prominent myths favoring the proposed increase that have been more persuasive to the public than the empirical data opposing it. Those are:

Myth: The research that won the 2021 Nobel Prize in economics proves that minimum wages do not reduce employment.

The 2021 Nobel Prize in economics was awarded to three economists—David Card, Joshua Angrist and Guido Imbens—but it was not for their research into the minimum wage. Rather, it was their use of "natural experiments" to deal with cause and effect in a way that resembles clinical trials.

As the Royal Swedish Academy of Sciences stated in its announcement of the award, "The key is to use situations in which chance events or policy changes result in groups of people being treated differently, in a way that resembles clinical trials in medicine."[7]

Card, in particular, was recognized for his contributions to "the labor market effects of minimum wages, immigration and education." The Academy mentioned his "studies from the early 1990s [that] challenged conventional wisdom, leading to new analyses and additional insights. The results showed, among other things, that increasing the minimum wage does not necessarily lead to fewer jobs."

The key phrase here is "not necessarily." In addition, Card's nearly 30-year-old minimum-wage research,[8] which he and co-author Alan P. Krueger revisited in 2000,[9] has been widely criticized.

For example, three years after Card and Krueger initially published their research, the Employment Policies Institute found that, "the data set used in the New Jersey study bears no relation to numbers drawn from the payroll records of the restaurants the New Jersey study claims to cover."[10]

EPI President Richard Berman went so far as to say, "The data base used in the New Jersey fast food study is so bad that *no credible conclusions* can be drawn from the report [original emphasis]."[11]

A year earlier, economists David Neumark and William Wascher had found that when looking at the actual payroll data of surveyed restaurants instead of the survey data used by Card and Krueger, "the New Jersey minimum wage increase led to a 4.6% decrease in employment in New Jersey."[12]

The minimum-wage debate continues, obviously.[13] But it is not true to say that Card's and Krueger's Nobel Prize-winning research "proved" that minimum wages do not reduce employment.

Myth: Minimum wages do not reduce employment.

Almost 80% of all published minimum-wage research in the U.S. since 1992 has concluded that employment elasticities are negative.[14]

What does that mean?

It means that—all things being equal—any increase in the minimum wage by a certain percentage results in unemployment. That is because, as economist Per Bylund has stated: "Minimum wage mandates above the present market wage … have only one direct effect: Jobs below that level are outlawed. Hence, any person on the job market with a productivity level below the minimum wage mandate, for whatever reason, will not be able to find a job."[15]

But again, this is not just about causing unemployment. For those who are already employed, there is the risk of being let go, or having their hours or benefits reduced, or eventually being replaced by automation—certainly nothing beneficial from the point of view of minimum-wage advocates.

Myth: Hawaii employment increased after the state minimum wage was increased.

Supporters of increasing Hawaii's minimum wage have argued employment continued to increase during previous periods after the rate was increased.[16] Since 1990, there have been four increases in Hawaii's minimum wage, the most recent being in 2015.

There are probably several ways to explain this, one being that local employment data reported by the U.S. Bureau of Labor Statistics accounts for only the number of employees and not hourly-wage determinants such as the number of hours worked.

Indeed, there is a significant body of evidence that indicates that minimum-wage increases do lead to reductions in hours worked by low-wage workers.[17]

To illustrate this issue, let's look at Hawaii's low-wage employment among food service workers, janitorial staff, personal care workers, cashiers and retail workers.[18] There is a great deal of variation in employment among these occupations relative to the years when the state minimum wage was increased, so it is not clear that increases in the minimum wage are correlated with the fluctuations in low-wage employment.[19]

> A better way forward would be to lower Hawaii's high cost of living, so the money we do have would buy more and, in effect, give everyone a raise.

This myth additionally mistakes correlation for causation. As noted by economist Wayne Liou with the Hawaii Department of Business, Economic Development and Tourism:

"Even though there is some growth in employment in the face of increases in the minimum wage, this could be due to a growing economy or higher demand for certain goods or services, such as those related to the tourism industry. If other occupations that are less likely to be affected by the minimum wage are growing at a faster rate than the occupations in the above figures, it would support the theory that minimum wages have a negative effect on employment."[20]

Myth: Minimum wages reduce poverty.

If minimum wages reduced poverty, we'd expect there to be at least a correlation between the minimum wage and the poverty rate. In reality, there is little evidence to suggest this is the case.

Cornell University economist Richard Burkhauser wrote in a 2014 paper: "Minimum-wage increases are not a very effective mechanism for reducing poverty. They are not related to decreases in poverty rates. They can cost some low-income workers their jobs. And most minimum-wage earners who gain from a higher minimum wage do not live in poor (or near-poor) families."[21]

In 2010, Burkhauser along with economist Joseph Sabia looked at state and federal minimum wage increases between 2003 and 2007 and found: "[Minimum-wage increases] had no effect on state poverty rates," and that "the working poor face a disproportionate amount of the job losses."[22]

Why is there little correlation between poverty reduction and minimum wages? It turns out that most minimum-wage workers are not poor.

For example, according to a 2017 report from the U.S. Government Accountability Office, 13% of workers earning between the federal minimum wage and $12 per hour were in poverty. Note that this wage range includes Hawaii's current state minimum wage of $10.10.[23]

However, one might rightfully counter and say that this data is misleading, considering that the federal and most state minimum wages are not indexed to inflation. But in his review of the available literature on minimum wages that are tied to inflation, Joseph Sabia wrote, "The only two studies that provide empirical evidence on the employment effects of indexed minimum wages find no statistically significant differences in the low-skilled employment effects of indexed versus non-indexed minimum wages."[24]

Myth: Minimum wages boost the economy.

The thought behind this myth is that if the minimum wage is increased, then minimum-wage workers will have more disposable income to spend on daily necessities. Moreover, if more people are spending, then that drives consumption, which subsequently drives the economy.

But it ain't necessarily so.

In 2015, economist Joseph Sabia produced the first comprehensive study into how minimum wages affects state-level gross domestic products. Sabia found that minimum wages actually contribute to declines in state GDPs rather than increases.[25]

In a separate review of the relevant literature, Sabia found that, "the existing empirical evidence suggests that minimum wage increases reduce or redistribute productivity rather than increase aggregate GDP."[26]

Conclusion

Clearly there is little reason or data to suggest that an increase in Hawaii's legal minimum wage would improve the lives of those it is intended to help.

A better way forward would be to lower Hawaii's high cost of living, so the money we do have would buy more and, in effect, give everyone a raise.

A good place to start for ideas on how to do that is the Grassroot Institute of Hawaii's "Road map to prosperity," issued in May 2020.

Suggestions in the report include reducing existing taxes and rejecting all proposed new ones; relying more on private contractors to help deliver public services; exempting food, medicines and healthcare providers and services from the state general excise tax; repealing or reforming the state's medical certificate-of-need laws; liberalizing zoning and land-use laws to encourage more housing; reforming the Jones Act, which restricts shipping competition to Hawaii; and more.[27]

Of course, no amount of state or county legislation is going to eliminate the federal government's constant devaluation of the dollar through inflation—as facilitated by the Federal Reserve, a spend-happy Congress and the president, whomever that might be at any particular time.

We can lower the cost of living and boost productivity, but unless America's monetary inflation can be stopped, the minimum-wage debate will continue, and probably regardless of whether we could somehow peg Hawaii's legal wage floor to inflation.

In fact, in the face of inflation, you could argue that leaving the minimum wage rate right where it is probably would help Hawaii's unskilled and less-educated workers more in the long run than a minimum-wage increase. That's because eventually it would make low-skilled and less-educated workers more employable,[28] thus expanding employment and giving those new entry-level workers their first opportunity to join the workforce and begin their economic ascent.

For now, we must realize that establishing a legal wage floor above the market rate is counterproductive, as validated by the law of supply and demand and the bulk of all existing relevant data.

Unfortunately, perceptions and passions often rule the day, even in the face of facts.

Notes

1. Andrew Gomes, "Hawaii residents strongly back minimum wage increase, poll finds," Honolulu Star-Advertiser, Feb. 9, 2022.
2. David Neumark and Peter Shirley, "Myth or Measurement: What Does the New Minimum Wage Research Say about Minimum Wages and Job Loss in the United States?" National Bureau of Economic Research, first published January 2021, revised May 2021, pp. 3-4.
3. Quiping Yu, Shawn Mankad and Masha Shunko, "Evidence of The Unintended Labor Scheduling Implications of The Minimum Wage," Social Science Research Network, June 16, 2021, pp. 14, 17-18.
4. Ibid, p. 14-16.
5. Grace Lordan, et al., "People Versus Machines: The Impact of Minimum Wages on Automatable Jobs," National Bureau of Economic Research, first published August 2017, revised January 2018, pp. 13-14.
6. Daniel Cooper, Marìa José Luengo-Prado and Jonathan A. Parker, "The Local Aggregate Effects of Minimum Wage Increases," Journal of Money, Credit and Banking, Vol. 52, No. 1, May 29, 2019, p. 21.
7. "Press release: The Prize in Economic Sciences 2021," The Royal Swedish Academy of Sciences, Oct. 11, 2021.
8. David Card and Alan P. Krueger, "Minimum Wages and Employment: A Case Study of the Fast Food Industry in New Jersey and Pennsylvania," National Bureau of Economic Research, Working Paper 4509, October 1993.
9. David Card and Alan P. Krueger, "Minimum Wages and Employment: A Case Study of the Fast Food Industry in New Jersey and Pennsylvania: Reply," American Economic Review, Vol. 90, No. 5, December 2000.
10. Richard B. Berman, "The Crippling Flaws in the New Jersey Fast Food Study," Employment Policies Institute, 2nd Edition, executive summary, April 1996.
11. Ibid.
12. David Neumark and William Wascher, "The Effect of New Jersey's Minimum Wage Increase on Fast-Food Employment: A Re-Evaluation Using Payroll Records," National Bureau of Economic Research, August 1995.
13. Neumark and Shirley, "Myth or Measurement: What Does the New Minimum Wage Research Say about Minimum Wages and Job Loss in the United States?"
14. Ibid, p. 3.

15. Per Bylund, "Does a Minimum Wage Reduce Poverty?" Mises Institute, Jan. 5, 2014. Note: By "productivity level," Bylund is referring to the fact that, according to economic theory, wages are determined by the marginal productivity of labor. There is no precise definition of "productivity" in this case, other than the mathematical definition being change in output divided by labor.

16. Kevin Dayton and Blaze Lovell, "House Approves Minimum Wage, Mauna Kea Bills After Emotional Floor Debate," March 9, 2022, which stated: "Rep. Jeanne Kapela ... said ... the last series of increases in the state minimum wage from 2014 to 2018 did not trigger any huge loss of jobs. ... In fact, the number of people employed by small businesses grew by 3% during those years, while the number of small businesses in Hawaii grew by 8%, she said."

17. Wayne Liou, "The Minimum Wage in Hawai'i: Labor Market Impacts," Research and Economic Analysis Division, Hawaii Department of Business, Economic Development & Tourism, January 2020, p. 9, Figure 4.

18. Per Bylund, "Does a Minimum Wage Reduce Poverty?" Mises Institute, Jan. 5, 2014. Note: By "productivity level," Bylund is referring to the fact that, according to economic theory, wages are determined by the marginal productivity of labor. There is no precise definition of "productivity" in this case, other than the mathematical definition being change in output divided by labor.

19. Ibid, p. 9, Figure 4.

20. Ibid, p .9.

21. Richard Burkhauser, "Why Minimum Wage Increases Are a Poor Way to Help the Working Poor," Institute of Labor Economics, June 2014, p.3. Note: Until 2016, the Institute of Labor Economics was known as the Institute for the Study of Labor. See: "IZA Institute of Labor Economics," Wikipedia, accessed March 7, 2022.

22. Joseph Sabia and Richard Burkhauser, "Minimum Wages and Poverty: Will a $9.50 Federal Minimum Wage Really Help the Working Poor?" Southern Economic Journal, Vol. 73, No. 3, January 2010, p. 592.

23. "Low-Wage Workers: Poverty and Use of Selected Federal Social Safety Net Programs Persist among Working Families," U.S. Government Accountability Office, Sept. 22, 2017 (publicly released Oct. 23, 2017).

24. Joseph Sabia, "Do minimum wages stimulate productivity and growth?" Institute of Labor Economics, December 2015, p. 7.

25. Joseph Sabia, "Minimum Wages and Gross Domestic Product," Contemporary Economic Policy, Vol. 33, Iss. 4, Jan. 23, 2015.

26. Joseph Sabia, "Do minimum wages stimulate productivity and growth?" Institute of Labor Economics, December 2015, p. 5.

27. "Road map to prosperity," Grassroot Institute of Hawaii, May 2020.

28. "10.2 The Effects of a Minimum Wage: Inflation and the Minimum Wage" Saylor Academy, accessed March 16, 2022.

Print Citations

CMS: Ahokovi, Jensen. "Five Myths That Pervade the Minimum Wage Debate." In *The Reference Shelf: Income Inequality,* edited by Micah L. Issitt, 58–64. Amenia, NY: Grey House Publishing, 2022.

MLA: Ahokovi, Jensen. "Five Myths That Pervade the Minimum Wage Debate." *The Reference Shelf: Income Inequality,* edited by Micah L. Issitt, Grey House Publishing, 2022, pp. 58–64.

APA: Ahokovi, J. (2022). Five myths that pervade the minimum wage debate. In Micah L. Issitt (Ed.), *The reference shelf: Income inequality* (pp. 58–64). Amenia, NY: Grey House Publishing.

Statement by President Joe Biden on $15 Minimum Wage for Federal Workers and Contractors Going into Effect

By Joe Biden
The White House, January 28, 2022

A job is about more than a paycheck. It's about dignity. When I was running for president, I said it was past time to increase the federal minimum wage to $15 an hour. Last year, I made a down payment on that pledge with Executive Orders directing my Administration to work toward ensuring that employees working on federal contracts and federal employees earned a $15 per hour minimum wage.

These directives go into effect this Sunday, meaning nearly 70,000 federal workers will immediately start to earn $15 an hour, and 300,000 employees of federal contractors will start to see a raise to $15 an hour reflected in their paychecks over the course of the year.

These are the customer service representatives who answer the phones to ensure that Americans get the health care they deserve; wildland firefighters who protect our forests and communities; custodial workers who keep our military bases clean and safe; nursing assistants who care for our veterans; and laborers who build and repair federal facilities. The workers that will disproportionately benefit from this pay increase are women, workers of color, and workers with disabilities.

This increase will provide those workers and their families a little more breathing room. And because we know that higher wages boost productivity and mean lower job turnover, these orders will allow the government to do its work better and faster.

> **A job is about more than a paycheck. It's about dignity.**

These workers benefiting from these actions are critical to the functioning of the federal government and of our nation, and I'm proud that their wages will begin to reflect that. I continue to urge Congress to raise the federal minimum wage to $15 an hour, so that American workers can have a job that delivers dignity.

Print Citations

CMS: Biden, Joe. "Statement by President Biden on $15 Minimum Wage for Federal Workers and Contractors Going into Effect." In *The Reference Shelf: Income Inequality,* edited by Micah L. Issitt, 65–66. Amenia, NY: Grey House Publishing, 2022.

MLA: Biden, Joe. "Statement by President Biden on $15 Minimum Wage for Federal Workers and Contractors Going into Effect." *The Reference Shelf: Income Inequality,* edited by Micah L. Issitt, Grey House Publishing, 2022, pp. 65–66.

APA: Biden, J. (2022). Statement by President Biden on $15 minimum wage for federal workers and contractors going into effect. In Micah L. Issitt (Ed.), *The reference shelf: Income inequality* (pp. 65–66). Amenia, NY: Grey House Publishing.

The Missing Piece of the Minimum Wage Debate

By Colleen Doody
The Washington Post, February 25, 2021

As part of his massive $1.9 trillion emergency pandemic relief plan, President Biden called on Congress to raise the federal minimum wage to $15 an hour from the current $7.25. Democratic senators are waiting for a ruling from the Senate parliamentarian on whether such a provision can be in the relief bill and debating whether to raise the minimum wage to $15 or some lower amount.

The debate over a minimum-wage increase has been fierce. Supporters claim raising the minimum wage would benefit women and people of color—the very demographics hurt the most by the coronavirus pandemic.

Yet opponents argue it would increase unemployment because higher wages would force small businesses, already under economic duress because of the pandemic, to lay off employees.

This conversation, however, ignores just what increasing the minimum wage does to the larger economy. To understand the intent of the federal minimum wage, it is necessary to look at the original minimum wage legislation—the 1938 Fair Labor Standards Act (FLSA), an enduring part of President Franklin D. Roosevelt's New Deal.

As with much New Deal legislation, the aim was to create what New Dealers called purchasing power. The basic idea: Raising wages would increase consumption, thus giving businesses the incentive to hire more workers. It worked, reminding us today that mandating higher wages doesn't just increase standards of living. It boosts the economy.

Many New Dealers believed the Great Depression was caused by underconsumption. Productivity among American manufacturers doubled during the 1920s while wages lagged. As American manufacturers churned out increasing numbers of consumer durables, particularly automobiles, consumer spending did not keep up. Businesses couldn't sell their inventories, and so they began cutting costs and laying off workers. The economy spiraled downward.

Advocates of increased purchasing power argued that raising wages would increase consumption, thus giving businesses the incentive to hire workers. Edward Filene, the founder of the Filene's department store chain and an advocate for boosting consumption, argued that "increased production demands increased buying." According to Filene, "the greatest total profits can be obtained only if the masses can and do enjoy a higher and ever higher standard of living. Mass production is production for the masses."

Roosevelt agreed. In his 1938 State of the Union address, he explained that when millions of workers receive "pay so low that they have little buying power" they were unable to "buy their share of manufactured goods." Raising wages would stimulate the national economy by allowing workers to purchase the goods and services they produced. Because the national economy depended on consumer spending, helping consumers buy would benefit the nation as a whole.

> **As with much New Deal legislation, mandating higher wages doesn't just increase standards of living, it boosts the economy.**

Minimum-wage legislation, Roosevelt argued, was thus "an essential part of economic recovery." Congress agreed and passed the 1938 Fair Labor Standards Act, which created the first federal minimum wage (25 cents per hour, to increase to between 30 and 40 cents per hour) and restricted the workweek to 44 hours. After Roosevelt signed the bill, he said in one of his fireside chats, "Without question it starts us toward a better standard of living and increases purchasing power to buy the products of farm and factory."

Along with stabilizing the economy to avoid the recurring economic downturns the nation suffered regularly between the 1870s and 1930s, a nationwide minimum wage would improve the quality of life for the poorest areas of the country. Communities where the average wages were low, Roosevelt pointed out, also had the "poorest educational facilities and the worst conditions of health" because their tax base was inadequate to support a functioning local government.

That was especially true for the South. The per capita income in Mississippi, for example, was $216 in 1940, compared with $676 in Michigan. At the same time, the life expectancy at birth in Mississippi was 60.7 years, while it was 63.4 years for men and 64.4 years for women in Michigan. The per capita income in South Carolina was $301 compared with $648 in Pennsylvania. The number of women in South Carolina who died during childbirth was more than twice the rate in Pennsylvania. The statistics certainly supported Roosevelt's assertion that low wages and poor health conditions went hand in hand. Not surprisingly, the FLSA had its greatest impact in the South, where 54 percent of the workers earning less than 30 cents per hour in 1939 were located.

Southern Democratic congressmen, whose business constituents embraced the region's low wages as a way to attract Northern businesses, objected to the law. They recognized that a federally mandated wage threatened legal segregation. Rep. Martin Dies (D-Tex.), for example, complained about the FSLA because "what is prescribed for one race must be prescribed for the others, and you cannot prescribe the same wages for the black man as for the white man."

To get the bill through Congress, Roosevelt caved to Southern segregationists. The Roosevelt administration modified the legislation to ensure it passed Congress, notably excluding farmworkers and domestic workers, two professions that were heavily African American, from its provisions. As a result of these Jim Crow policies, many Southern African Americans didn't earn the minimum wage. While Roosevelt sought to raise the living standard in the poorest region of the country, he was unwilling to challenge the system of legal segregation that kept Southern wages so low.

The FSLA applied only to employers involved in interstate commerce and so did not cover service employees, many of whom were women. As with other key New Deal laws like the Social Security Act, many women and minorities were therefore deprived of the legal protections the FLSA provided.

Despite its very real shortcomings, the federal minimum wage along with other New Deal programs helped lead to the doubling of inflation-adjusted income for the bottom 20th percentile of wage workers between the end of World War II and the mid-1970s. That increase went hand-in-hand with relatively widely shared national prosperity during this period.

However, since the 1970s, overall economic growth has decreased while the income gap has widened. Those at the very top have seen their income and wealth increase dramatically while those at the bottom have struggled to stay afloat.

These long-term issues have been exacerbated by the pandemic. According to the Bureau of Labor Statistics, 10.1 million people are unemployed, up from 5.7 million at the start of the pandemic. The weak job numbers for January appear to show the recovery slowing, even as coronavirus rates have decreased. And the unemployment rate for African Americans (9.2 percent) and Latinos (8.6 percent) remains far higher than for Whites (5.7 percent). Over 2 million women, particularly women in traditionally low-paying service jobs, have left the labor force in the past year. All of these troubling statistics point to the need for action.

In the current debate over the $15 minimum wage, it is important to consider the type of economy that is best for most Americans. Is the intent to increase purchasing power and expand the population of workers who can afford to buy the goods and services they produce, as the New Deal did? Or is the goal to maintain an economy that ensures the lowest-paid Americans can barely afford food and shelter?

The choice seems obvious.

Print Citations

CMS: Doody, Colleen. "The Missing Piece of the Minimum Wage Debate." In *The Reference Shelf: Income Inequality,* edited by Micah L. Issitt, 67–69. Amenia, NY: Grey House Publishing, 2022.

MLA: Doody, Colleen. "The Missing Piece of the Minimum Wage Debate." *The Reference Shelf: Income Inequality,* edited by Micah L. Issitt, Grey House Publishing, 2022, pp. 67–69.

APA: Doody, C. (2021). The missing piece of the minimum wage debate. In Micah L. Issitt (Ed.), *The reference shelf: Income inequality* (pp. 67–69). Amenia, NY: Grey House Publishing.

California's $15 Minimum Wage Debate Begins This Year: Debate on the Next Increase has Already Begun

By Ryan Golden
HR DIVE, February 24, 2022

In the world of labor and employment law, California is a bellwether. The state's legislative activity on HR issues such as pay, time off, discrimination and a host of other issues have spurred similar laws across the U.S.—and minimum wage laws are no exception.

In 2016, California became the first state to officially adopt a statewide minimum wage of $15 an hour implemented by incremental increase. This year is the first in which the state's large employers, defined as those with 26 or more employees, will need to comply with the $15 minimum. By 2023, small employers will need to do the same.

Several states would announce plans to increase their wages, and a handful will cross the $15 threshold in the coming years, according to the National Conference of State Legislatures. But California's law does not stop there. Beyond 2023, the state will adjust its minimum annually for inflation based on the national consumer price index for urban wage earners and clerical workers.

That last bit is important, as many local employers may not realize future increases are in store, said Lisa Charbonneau, associate at management-side firm Liebert Cassidy Whitmore.

Even with future inflation-related increases scheduled, however, California residents are already debating a new minimum wage threshold.

Worker advocates, led by activist and Blue Apron founding investor Joe Sanberg, have submitted a ballot initiative to increase the state's minimum wage to $18 an hour by 2025. If the initiative, titled the Living Wage Act of 2022, gains the necessary number of signatures from California voters, it could be put up for vote in November.

Proponents of the $18 minimum argue it is needed to help workers adjust to the rising cost of living in many of California's largest metropolitan areas. That trend explains, in part, why cities like Los Angeles have experienced high levels of homelessness, according to Victor Narro, project director at the UCLA Labor Center. Even the new minimum of $15 an hour is not sufficient for many workers to maintain their quality of life without needing to work multiple jobs, he told HR Dive in an interview.

"There is not one California worker who is making a good living on $15 an hour," Sanberg said in a press release announcing the beginning of signature gathering for the proposal. He added that essential workers and workers of color were particularly likely to be impacted by low wages; "That has to change."

Cost of living in selected California cities, percentage compared to national average

City	Cost of living
Anaheim	+32.6%
Bakersfield	-1.4%
Berkeley	+56.8%
Carlsbad	+34.4%
Fresno	-2.6%
Long Beach	+27.8%
Los Angeles	+41.1%
Sacramento	+7.4%
San Diego	+35.0%
San Francisco	+86.1%

SOURCE: Salary.com

Others are concerned about the challenges the higher threshold would place on California employers. Specifically, Charbonneau, who represents city and county employers in the state in labor negotiations, said that these entities may struggle to budget for future increases without implementing cost-saving measures or raising revenue.

"Cities and counties can't just pass the cost onto their customers like private companies can," Charbonneau said. "Their hands are somewhat tied."

But many employees of these municipal governments are represented by labor unions that, through collective bargaining, already participate in negotiating pay for members that tend to be higher than the state minimum wage, Narro said.

"That's what they do every year anyway," he continued. "They try to get more for their members."

Narro said the argument about potential negative impacts of an $18 minimum wage on municipal governments is one of many put forward by the business community to oppose minimum wage increases. He said California's economic success, notwithstanding past increases, bolsters advocates' side of the debate.

Similarly, Steve Smith, communications director for the California Labor Federation, an advocacy group for unions in the state, characterized the Living Wage Act proposal as modest; "We're not talking about a drastic increase from where we are now."

Additionally, municipal governments employ fewer minimum wage workers than private-sector employers do, Smith continued. "There may be some budgetary increase, but there doesn't seem to be anything that would cause municipal employers to need to raise more revenue."

Charbonneau agreed that unions in the state are typically successful at securing wages for members that exceed the minimum wage. But among mu-

> **Even the new minimum of $15 an hour is not sufficient for many workers to maintain their quality of life without needing to work multiple jobs.**

nicipal governments, those most likely to be impacted are temporary and part-time workers as well as workers who are hired to complete a particular assignment, she said. These workers typically see pay closer to the minimum.

Municipal employers in certain parts of the state already have struggled to attract talent, such as in Menlo Park, Santa Clara and other centers for California's technology sector. "You can't hire a police officer who will be able to live anywhere near the department he or she is working for," Charbonneau said. "It's a huge recruiting problem, and that goes all throughout city government."

So far, Charbonneau said employers in such areas have sought to draw talent by looking into other options, such as providing flexible schedules, remote work where possible, commuter benefits, subsidized home loans programs and other benefits.

Despite its economic success, California continues to see a large discrepancy between the high-income and low-income residents, Narro said, and he added that this difference cannot be entirely explained by wage levels alone.

Officials still need to create solutions that allow workers to find quality, affordable housing, Narro said, and even if wage increases are enacted, these increases may not amount to much without proper enforcement; "Otherwise, when you increase the minimum wage, all you do is increase wage theft."

Print Citations

CMS: Golden, Ryan. "California's $15 Minimum Wage Debate Begins This Year: Debate on the Next Increase Has Already Begun." In *The Reference Shelf: Income Inequality,* edited by Micah L. Issitt, 70–72. Amenia, NY: Grey House Publishing, 2022.

MLA: Golden, Ryan. "California's $15 Minimum Wage Debate Begins This Year: Debate on the Next Increase Has Already Begun." *The Reference Shelf: Income Inequality,* edited by Micah L. Issitt, Grey House Publishing, 2022, pp. 70–72.

APA: Golden, R. (2022). California's $15 minimum wage debate begins this year: Debate on the next increase has already begun. In Micah L. Issitt (Ed.), *The reference shelf: Income inequality* (pp. 70–72). Amenia, NY: Grey House Publishing.

3

The Taxation Dilemma

Chart by Wikideas1, via Wikipedia, CCO.

Corporate tax rates by state.

Corporate and Wealth Taxes and Income Inequality

In the 1760s, as the "patriot" independence movement was ramping up in the American colonies, a Massachusetts lawyer named James Otis is credited with coming up with the phrase, "taxation without representation is tyranny," meaning that it is unfair for a government to levy taxes on citizens, without affording those same citizens with any input into the structure and function of their government.[1] The association between "taxation" and "tyranny" became deeply ingrained in the American imagination and helped to create a culture uniquely resistant to the *idea* of governmental taxation, though few Americans have a deep understanding of the role that taxation plays in American life and culture.

The Redistribution of Resources

Despite its unsavory reputation, taxation is both necessary and essential in any advanced society. To see why this is the case, it is necessary to understand that a society is not a collection of independent individuals generating their own resources or making their own "money," it is more realistically a vast, complicated network of interdependent roles and jobs, none of which can exist without the others.

For one of many examples, consider Elon Musk, who became the world's wealthiest man in 2022. Musk made his fortune by starting a company that sells electric vehicles—named Tesla Motors in honor of famed European electrical pioneer Nicola Tesla. While the designs initially used by Tesla Motors were marginally original, the achievements attributed to the company could not have happened without the work of thousands of others. For one thing, all electric batteries are part of a lineage of electrical engineering innovation that stretches back to the 1800s and electric vehicles (thought primitive) actually preceded gas-driven vehicles in America. It wasn't until the petroleum industry dominated the nation's politics and economy that development of electric vehicles was largely abandoned.

Actually, making a Tesla (or any other vehicle) also depends on the participation of the hundreds of technicians and administrative personnel who actually design and build the vehicles—parts of the business that Musk himself and the other car industry CEO do not and could not do. Manufacturing a Tesla also depends on the availability of raw materials, which in turn depends on thousands of people working in mining and material engineering, and on logistical systems used to ship materials to manufacturing plants, where they can be used to make parts for eventual vehicles.

It is also true that no one would be purchasing Tesla vehicles without municipal electrical grids and the systems used to deliver electricity to consumers. The electric

. car industry took a long time to develop, in part, because municipalities lacked the robust power grids that would allow consumers to power their vehicles conveniently and effectively. These electrical systems that pump power into America's towns and cities are the products of decades of work by hundreds and thousands of laborers, engineers, and scientists, and depend on the operation of hydroelectric, gas, petroleum, and nuclear power plants that actually generate the electricity used to fill the batteries of an electric car. There would also be no automobile customers of any kind without a system of roads that make automobiles useful to have. There would be no roads without real-estate development. There would be no real-estate development without sewage and water systems.

The basic point is that the money that allowed Musk to become the world's wealthiest man did not come from Musk's efforts alone, but was collectively generated by thousands of people working in different jobs and sometimes very different fields, but whose efforts are *all* necessary for a company like Tesla to exist and to succeed. Not only did Musk not really *create* his own wealth, but he also cannot *maintain* this wealth without a system of infrastructure that allows people to enjoy the products that his company sells. This is true in every single industry, no matter its history or the specific products that each company makes or sells. All wealth, everywhere in the world, is based on the collective efforts of hundreds if not thousands of people. If we accept that all wealth is generated by collective efforts, it follows that there needs to be a way to redistribute the resources controlled by a society, to maintain the basic systems and infrastructure that allow that society to function, and also that allow companies like Tesla to operate and to "do business."

What are the essential components that allow a society to operate? Well, first there is the basic physical infrastructure, such as bridges, roads, tunnels, etc. This also includes the systems used to channel resources into homes and businesses, like electricity, petroleum products, and water. Taxes also pay for governmental institutions that exist to assist, protect, or defend members of the public, including police, emergency services, and military organizations. Taxation also funds what is perhaps the most important collective activity within any society; education, which is the system through which new generations are introduced to the knowledge gained by past generations. Education prepares individuals for various roles within their society and enables innovation and discovery essential to advancing society through technology, medicine, etc.

Tax Revenues

The tax revenues collected by governments are used in many different ways, but it is important for anyone who wants to be involved in the tax debate to understand that tax revenues are necessary to maintaining the public infrastructure that people in every city and state depend on. To achieve these goals, governments collect taxes based on the resources controlled by a person or family, and these taxes typically take three forms: income, wealth, and consumption.[2]

Income taxes are based on the amount of money that an individual earns through their work or investments, or the work of others in the case of chief executive officers

(CEOs) and stockholders. Both individuals and corporations are expected to pay income taxes to the federal government, while most states and many municipalities also collect taxes based on income.

Consumption taxes are based on consumer spending, and include familiar taxes like the sales tax charged on purchases in most states. There are other types of taxes levied on certain consumer products seen as having an exceptionally high cost in a society.

Wealth taxes are based on the amount of wealth that a person has and may include property taxes, which are assessed based on property or real estate that a person owns, as well as taxes on inheritance, estates, and gifts.[3]

All three forms of taxation are important to the function of America's municipalities, states, and the national government, but all three tax systems are also frequently controversial. Some absolutist antitax activists have gone as far as to refer to income and property tax as governmental "theft," and this view typically comes from the perception that people should be allowed to keep whatever they make. Such a perspective ignores that benefits that each individual accrues from living within a society that provides access to collective resources, like petroleum products, electricity, water, and food, and ignores the role other workers play in helping a person to accrue wealth and property. However, it is true that tax systems can be oppressive and unfair, largely because tax laws tend to be shaped by a society's wealthiest inhabitants, who then influence tax laws so as to benefit themselves (and consequently other wealthy individuals as well).

Two of the major debates within the broader debate over "income inequality" concern the taxation of America's wealthy elites and American corporations. Critics have argued that wealthy Americans and corporations pay too little in taxes because of unfair "tax loopholes" and other methods that are frequently used to avoid taxation, which both reduces the collective resources available for public welfare investment, like emergency services, education, and infrastructure, while also shifting the majority of the tax burden to middle-income earners who lack the economic power to avoid taxation, but also do not earn enough that taxation is no longer a serious concern or burden.

The Wealth Tax and Corporate Taxes

Consumption taxes are generally "regressive" taxes, which is a tax that is applied uniformly, and therefore impacts low-income consumers more than upper-income consumers. A person who earns $10 per day will experience a greater level of impact from paying an additional 6 percent on purchases than a person who earns $100 per day, and so any "flat" tax irrespective of a person's socioeconomic status tends to impact poorer people more than wealthier people, and is therefore called "regressive."[4] By contrast, income taxes and taxes on assets (wealth taxes) are generally "progressive," which means that the amount that a person pays is based on the amount that the person has or earns. Until the 1930s, all American taxes were essentially regressive, with individuals paying a similar percentage of their income whether they were nearly destitute or extraordinarily wealthy.

Since the introduction of progressive taxes, there have been two separate economic movements dominating American tax law. On the one hand, there are a number of wealthy Americans, allied legal/economic professionals, and conservative politicians who argue that the progressive tax system is unfair because wealthy individuals should not be forced to subsidize the lives of lower-income earners. This argument follows a more or less "libertarian" view, holding that individuals should be allowed to "keep" what they "earn." A similar argument says that taxation limits productivity and that by reducing taxation on the wealthy and corporations, the economy can become more productive, which will filter revenues to lower-income earners as well.

On the other hand, progressive activists and politicians argue that America's wealthy elite and corporations exploit the working class by offering jobs that do not provide a living wage and by exploiting the law to hoard wealth and resources that have not been privately generated and so should not be privately "owned." This allows corporate investors, and the wealthy, to retain an unfair share of the revenues generated by corporations and investments. Because all wealth is collectively generated and depends on the society that all workers expend effort to maintain, activists argue that corporations and wealthy individuals should be required to contribute more of their wealth to the general welfare, where those resources can be redistributed to compensate for the effort that all working Americans contribute to the collective productivity of the nation.[5]

In opinion polls, a significant majority of Americans, ranging from 60 to 70 percent support progressive taxation and believe that America's wealthy class should be taxed at a higher rate. However, opinion on this issue tends to be divided along partisan lines. Because the conservative movement is closely aligned with corporate and wealthy interests, those who support conservative politicians or groups are more likely to support limiting taxation on corporations and wealthy individuals.[6]

Writing in the *Christian Science Monitor*, Laurent Belsie summarized this debate and noted that in 1933, the *New York Times* reported that millionaire J. P. Morgan had been allowed to avoid income tax for two years. Eighty-eight years later, the website *ProPublica* reported that billionaire Jeff Bezos had likewise been able to manipulate the tax system to avoid paying income taxes, despite being one of the wealthiest people in the world. Belsie presents these two examples, separated by nearly a century, to demonstrate how the American tax system has remained skewed towards the interests of the wealthy for much of American history and little has changed despite repeated efforts to create a more progressive tax system.

The first concerted effort to make the American tax system more equitable came with the Revenue Act of 1935, passed under the Franklin D. Roosevelt Administration as part of the administration's "New Deal" programs. This wealth tax, instituted in 1935, imposed taxes of up to 75 percent on the wealthy, and was embraced by most of the public, because the nation was still suffering from the Great Depression, which led to massive levels of unemployment and poverty across the country. However, just two years after the Revenue Act passed, the system needed to be reformed because loopholes in the tax code had allowed millionaires, like J. P. Morgan, to avoid the increased taxes intended in the initial Revenue Act legislation.[7]

Between 1935 and 2022 there were many additional efforts to alleviate wealth inequality by instituting more progressive tax systems, but such efforts alternate with conservative-led tax reforms that typically reduce taxes on high-income Americans and large corporations. Additional changes to tax codes, both at the federal and the state level, also create systems that can be used by those with sufficient economic power, to further reduce their tax burdens. A study by economists Greg Leiserson and Danny Yagan of the Office of Management and Budget (OMB) showed, for instance, that people on the Forbes 400 list (of the wealthiest 400 people in America) paid an average of 8.2 percent in taxes, which is a lower rate than most middle-income Americans. For instance, the study provided the example of a first-year, single teacher, earning $40,154 per year, who rents an apartment and pays $2,400 in student loan debt per year, would pay an average of 11.7 percent. The researchers provide many other examples of situations in which middle-income earners would pay higher tax rates than millionaires and billionaires in the same states.[8]

A separate but related issue is corporate taxation, which involves the income and asset taxes that corporations must pay to the federal, state, and municipal governments each year. Corporate tax rates are perennially contentious in part because Americans have highly divided attitudes about how best to manage businesses in an effort to maintain American economic growth. Conservative politicians frequently argue that America should maintain low-levels of regulation on companies, and low tax rates, in order to provide companies with the capital necessary to continue to grow, which they argue will lead to more job availability and greater opportunities for income growth at all levels of society. The problem with this strategy is that it rarely works to generate growth for most Americans. In general, reducing corporate tax rates often leads to companies increasing revenue payouts to shareholders and increasing investments, but less often to expansion and an increase in job availability. This is because the availability of resources is not always the determining factor in whether or not a company has jobs available for workers. Corporate expansion and hiring depends on many different factors, only one of which is whether companies have sufficient revenues to afford new hires.

One of the most complicated and controversial aspects of the corporate tax system are the tax laws in place that allow corporations, especially large and wealthy corporations, to dramatically reduce their tax burdens. For instance, in 2022 *Axios* reported that nineteen of the largest companies in the United States were able to manipulate their tax reporting to pay less than 10 percent on corporate income in 2022, with many companies paying less than the average rate paid by individual taxpayers across the country. The companies that were able to avoid taxes or to pay vastly reduced taxes included brands like AT&T, Dow Inc., Charter Communications, General Motors, Ford Motor, MetLife, ExxonMobil, Chevron, and Bank of America.[9]

Conservative politicians and corporate lobbyists frequently argue that large corporations and the wealthy men and women who own stock in them, create American jobs and that affording these individuals and organizations the opportunity to retain a higher share of their annual profit will lead to expansion and further job growth, but this rarely turns out to be the case. More realistically, job growth is a function of fostering economic stability at the middle and lower levels of society. Studies have shown that new businesses account for much of the job growth that occurs in America, but also account for the majority of job losses as new companies are more fragile and vulnerable to closure within their first one to two years of operation.[10] When economic growth is strong among the working class and middle class, new businesses have more opportunities to grow and are less likely to close because of higher spending among the population. This combination of factors is one of the keys to creating sustained growth in the American job market. By contrast, cutting tax rates on large corporations contributes very little to overall job growth, and is a contributing factor in income inequality as reduced taxes on companies typically lead to higher pay for investors and upper management, but do not translate into higher pay or more jobs among the working class.

Corporate tax rates have become one of the key battlegrounds in the debate over income inequality, and it is a debate that has many of the same characteristics and largely the same structure that existed in the 1800s and 1900s. Then, as in the 2020s, opinions are largely divided between those who see low taxation as a way to stimulate business growth, and those who believe that corporations should contribute equally into the tax system, helping to find programs and to maintain infrastructure that corporations require to do business within the nation.

To Tax or Not to Tax

Opinions on taxation, in many ways, reflect underlying attitudes about one's place within society and the value of other people. Those who think more individualistically, emphasizing their own welfare over considerations of others, might be more likely to embrace low taxation as a key to their own financial future. Likewise, those who place little trust in governmental agents and agencies, may be less likely to approve of higher tax rates or new governmental tax initiatives. On the other hand, those who place less faith in the good will of the wealthy or corporations might approve of far higher tax rates on wealth and corporate earnings, believing that such polices are necessary to force corporations and the wealthy to pay their fair share into the system for the collective benefit. In general, those who believe in collective efforts and collective rewards are more likely to embrace higher taxes in return for subsidized services, like socialized medicine, publicly funded education systems, and other socioeconomic systems that draw upon collective revenues to spread the benefits of American productivity. Whether there is a more "correct" answer on how to tax the wealthy and corporations therefore depends on one's perspective and on how one chooses to prioritize and to place value on American workers.

Works Used

Allec, Logan. "What Are Taxes?" *The Balance*. 15 Dec. 2021. https://www.thebalance.com/what-are-taxes-5213316.

Atkinson, Robert D., and Michael Lind. "Debunking the Myth of Small Business Job Creation." *MIT Press*. 30 May 2019. https://thereader.mitpress.mit.edu/small-business-job-creation-myth/.

Beamer, Glenn. *Creative Politics: Taxes and Public Goods in a Federal System*. U of Michigan P, 1999.

Belsie, Laurent. "Taxes and the Rich: America's History of Favoritism and Crackdowns." *The Christian Science Monitor*. 21 June 2021. https://www.csmonitor.com/USA/Politics/2021/0621/Taxes-and-the-rich-America-s-history-of-favoritism-and-crackdowns.

Hanlon, Seth. "The Forbes 400 Pay Lower Tax Rates Than Many Ordinary Americans." *American Progress*. Center for American Progress. 7 Oct. 2021. https://www.americanprogress.org/article/forbes-400-pay-lower-tax-rates-many-ordinary-americans/#:~:text=According%20to%20the%20Tax%20Policy,0.5%20percent%20in%20excise%20taxes.

Hiltzik, Michael. *The New Deal: A Modern History*. Free Press, 2011.

Newport, Frank. "U.S. Public Opinion and Increased Taxes on the Rich." *Gallup*. 4 June 2021. https://news.gallup.com/opinion/polling-matters/350555/public-opinion-increased-taxes-rich.aspx.

"On This Day: 'No Taxation without Representation!'" *Constitution Center*. 7 Oct. 2021. https://constitutioncenter.org/blog/no-taxation-without-representation.

Peck, Emily. "These Companies Paid Little to No Taxes Last Year." *Axios*. 26 Apr. 2022. https://www.axios.com/2022/04/26/these-companies-paid-little-to-no-taxes-last-year.

Smith, Stephen. *Taxation: A Very Short Introduction*. Oxford UP, 2015.

Notes

1. "On This Day: 'No Taxation without Representation!'" *Constitution Center*.
2. Smith, *Taxation: A Very Short Introduction*.
3. Allec, "What Are Taxes?"
4. Beamer, *Creative Politics: Taxes and Public Goods in a Federal System*.
5. Belsie, "Taxes and the Rich: America's History of Favoritism and Crackdowns."
6. Newport, "U.S. Public Opinion and Increased Taxes on the Rich."
7. Hiltzik, *The New Deal: A Modern History*.
8. Hanlon, "The Forbes 400 Pay Lower Tax Rates Than Many Ordinary Americans."
9. Peck, "These Companies Paid Little to No Taxes Last Year."
10. Atkinson and Lind, "Debunking the Myth of Small Business Job Creation."

Why It's So Hard to Tax the Rich

By Monica Prasad
Politico, November 2, 2021

In the last few weeks, the Democrats have veered from one tax-the-rich plan to another. First there was President Joe Biden's suggestion to increase capital gains taxes for heirs, which disappeared over the summer. Sen. Ron Wyden's (D-Ore.) Billionaires Income Tax made it as far as a plan, but seems to have died the day it was born. The latest version is a surtax on millionaires, but it could easily meet the same fate as its predecessors by the time the deal is done.

Why is it so hard to tax the rich? After all, the idea behind progressive taxation is simple, even beautiful: Let the engine of capitalism roar and then have the winners compensate the losers. By taking care of those who lose out in the free-market melee, the winners ensure the losers won't want to destroy the system. What's more, taxing the wealthy is popular, with a majority of Americans telling pollsters that they think the wealthy don't pay their fair share. And economists have endorsed it, pointing out that the wealthy have benefited disproportionately from the economic growth of the last several decades, that taxes on the wealthy prevent unproductive dynasties from forming, and that the things those tax revenues are spent on, from child care to clean energy, can benefit the economy.

And yet Democrats can't find a way. They're not alone—in fact no country has yet managed to get enough money out of progressive taxation to fund a comprehensive system of social programs. European countries with generous social programs fund them by making everyone pay, not just the rich. As a result, in those countries social programs don't feel like charity or redistribution, but rather like insurance—something everyone pays for, and which everyone can access in times of need as a matter of right.

The United States has always rejected this broad-based approach to taxation, insisting on progressive taxation instead. On multiple occasions it has even been the American left, which in theory supports a more robust social system, that has undermined creating the European-style tax base needed to fund it. We do have a few programs that work on the insurance principle, like Social Security and Medicare, and it's not a coincidence that those are our most resilient programs. But the talk lately has been of redistribution rather than insurance because it's hard not to think that the wealthy, who have benefited so spectacularly over the last several decades, ought to shoulder more of the tax burden (and indeed, the European wealthy should too).

Examining the history of taxing the rich shows why it's hard, even when there is a compelling economic and moral argument for doing so.

Taxes on the rich increased dramatically during the First and Second

No country has yet managed to get enough money out of progressive taxation.

World Wars, but other than global catastrophes with mass casualties, nothing seems to produce the desperation that leads to broad, bipartisan consensus on raising taxes on the rich. Indeed, even a global catastrophe with mass casualties can't always do it, as the pandemic has shown, because low interest rates have made it easier for the government to borrow instead.

Where are Democrats in the tax hike fight? Thus, since the Second World War, the top marginal income tax rate for individuals has declined steeply, as Democrats came around to the position that cutting taxes for the wealthy stimulates the economy (under John F. Kennedy) and then Republicans came around to the position that deficits are not a big problem (under George. W. Bush, and because of Ronald Reagan). Even if you account for all of the loopholes in the 1950s tax code, the effective tax rate for the top 1 percent — that is, the taxes they actually pay — is considerably lower now than it was at mid-century. In fact, in 2018, one study found that the top 400 billionaires were, for the first time in history, actually paying a lower tax rate than the bottom 50 percent of families.

A few recent U.S. presidents have successfully raised taxes on the rich, but those efforts didn't pay off politically. Under Bill Clinton's administration the top marginal tax rate rose very slightly in 1993, but it did not help Clinton in the 1994 midterms. Under Barack Obama tax rates for the wealthy went up in 2013 — and then the 2014 midterm elections produced the largest gains for Republicans in the Senate since the 1980s, and in the House since the 1930s. The midterm defeats were not caused by the tax increases, but increasing taxes on the rich didn't help either Clinton or Obama. Although polls always show majorities favorable to taxing the rich, people don't seem to vote based on that issue.

The awareness that taxing the rich doesn't gain votes must be part of what makes moderate Democrats cautious. And because the rich can pay people to figure out how to legally violate the spirit of the law—an old standby is to find ways to turn income into things that don't get taxed as highly, like capital gains, and a newer trick is to borrow against your assets so you don't have to sell them and incur taxes at all—it takes a complex administrative machinery to stay ahead of them. Wyden's wealth tax plan, which received support from over a hundred organizations, would have run into questions about whether it violated the constitutional requirement that direct taxes be proportional to a state's population. It would also have required new procedures for valuing people's wealth. It's difficult to value assets as it is; you can guess how much a painting is worth but how do you really know until you try to sell it? And valuing those assets in the middle of an adversarial exchange between government and taxpayer is even harder, which may be why most of the countries that have attempted wealth taxation have ended it. It's not impossible, and nothing says we have to restrict ourselves to what has happened in the past. But it is a big push on an issue on which notional support in polls does not translate into electoral support.

In the absence of desperate need or strong political support, is there any way to tax the rich? Raising capital gains taxes remains an appealing option. Getting rid of the home mortgage interest deduction is another.

And as it happens, there is one option that would not require any complex new administrative procedures, and that has actually been tried recently, and has been shown to work—but it's Democrats who are standing in the way.

Other than Clinton and Obama, the other president who successfully raised taxes on the rich was Donald Trump. His tax cut of 2017, which was mostly a giveaway to the wealthy, included one provision that actually raised their taxes instead—the cap on deductions for state and local taxes, or SALT. This is a deduction that, all analysts agree, is shockingly regressive. It benefits only 9 percent of taxpayers, and most of the benefits go to the wealthy. As scholars have argued, it underpins systemic racism. It essentially forces the less wealthy to subsidize the local public services the rich purchase through higher state and local taxes. By putting a cap on it, Trump and the Republican Congress actually raised taxes for the wealthy. (They also put a limit on the home mortgage interest deduction, which also amounts to raising taxes on the wealthy, but because they raised the standard deduction the end result was to make the mortgage deduction even more regressive.)

Republicans have wanted to get rid of SALT for a long time, as it benefits the wealthy in blue states the most. These are the states where state and local taxes are the highest. As political maneuvering it's brilliant, because it forces Democrats into a position of deciding between their principles of taxing the rich and their political wishes to protect their constituents.

In that battle, principles aren't standing much of a chance. Senate Majority Leader Chuck Schumer and a coalition of Democrats from blue states have even argued for repealing Trump's cap, even though the benefits of that repeal would go almost entirely to the richest quintile, and even though that would be an even bigger giveaway to the wealthy than Trump's entire tax cut.

It's Joe Manchin and Krysten Sinema who have drawn the ire of progressives. But Schumer and allies have been so devastatingly and quietly effective that somehow there is not much complaint that they have been lobbying for what amounts to a tax cut for rich Democrats. Indeed, they have been so invisibly effective that completely getting rid of the deduction is not on the table, despite the fact that even with the cap the deduction benefits the wealthy the most. Perhaps the easiest and simplest way of raising taxes on the rich—by getting rid of this deduction—is not even being proposed.

Why has it been so hard for Democrats to find a way to tax the rich? Because those rich people live in the blue states.

Print Citations

CMS: Prasad, Monica. "Why It's So Hard to Tax the Rich." In *The Reference Shelf: Income Inequality,* edited by Micah L. Issitt, 82–85. Amenia, NY: Grey House Publishing, 2022.

MLA: Prasad, Monica. "Why It's So Hard to Tax the Rich." *The Reference Shelf: Income Inequality,* edited by Micah L. Issitt, Grey House Publishing, 2022, pp. 82–85.

APA: Prasad, M.. (2021). Why it's so hard to tax the rich. In Micah L. Issitt (Ed.), *The reference shelf: Income inequality* (pp. 82–85). Amenia, NY: Grey House Publishing.

Corporate Taxes Are Wealth Taxes

By David Leonhardt
The New York Times, April 8, 2021

The main cause of the radical decline in tax rates for very wealthy Americans over the past 75 years isn't the one that many people would guess. It's not about lower income taxes (though they certainly play a role), and it's not about lower estate taxes (though they matter too).

The biggest tax boon for the wealthy has been the sharp fall in the corporate tax rate.

In the 1950s, '60s and '70s, many corporations paid about half of their profits to the federal government. The money helped pay for the U.S. military and for investments in roads, bridges, schools, scientific research and more. "A dirty little secret," Richard Clarida, an economist who's now the vice chairman of the Federal Reserve, once said, "is that the corporate income tax used to raise a fair amount of revenue."

Since the mid-20th century, however, politicians of both political parties have supported cuts in the corporate-tax rate, often under intense lobbying from corporate America.

The cuts have been so large—including in President Donald Trump's 2017 tax overhaul—that at least 55 big companies paid zero federal income taxes last year, according to the Institute on Taxation and Economic Policy. Among them: Archer-Daniels-Midland, Booz Allen Hamilton, FedEx, HP, Interpublic, Nike and Xcel Energy.

"Right now, the U.S. raises less corporate tax revenue as a share of economic output than almost all other advanced economies," Alan Rappeport and Jim Tankersley of *The Times* write.

The justification for the tax cuts has often been that the economy as a whole will benefit—that lower corporate taxes would lead to company expansions, more jobs and higher incomes. But it hasn't worked out that way. Instead, economic growth has been mediocre since the 1970s. And incomes have grown even more slowly than the economy for every group except the wealthy.

The U.S. raises less corporate tax revenue as a share of economic output than almost all other advanced economies.

The American economy turns out not to function very well when tax rates on the rich are low and inequality is high.

Corporate Taxes Are Wealth Taxes

Corporate taxes are such an important part of the overall taxes paid by the wealthy because much of their holdings tend to be stocks. And as the owners of companies, they are effectively paying corporate taxes. Most of their income doesn't come through a salary or bonus; it comes from the returns on their wealth.

"In effect, the only sizable tax for these billionaires is the corporate tax they pay through their firms," Gabriel Zucman, an economist and tax specialist at the University of California, Berkeley, told me. "The main reason why the U.S. tax system was so progressive before the 1980s is because of heavy taxes on corporate profits."

President Biden is now trying to reverse some (but by no means all) of the decline in corporate taxes. His plan would raise the corporate tax rate, punish companies that move profits overseas and introduce a rule meant to prevent companies from paying zero taxes, among other things. The money would help pay for his infrastructure plan. "It's honest, it's fair, it's fiscally responsible, and it pays for what we need," Biden said at the White House yesterday.

Experts and critics are already raising legitimate questions about his plan, and there will clearly be a debate about it. Biden said he was open to compromises and other ideas.

But one part of the criticism is pretty clearly inconsistent with the facts: The long-term decline in corporate taxes doesn't seem to have provided much of a benefit for most American families.

Print Citations

CMS: Leonhardt, David. "Corporate Taxes Are Wealth Taxes." In *The Reference Shelf: Income Inequality,* edited by Micah L. Issitt, 86–87. Amenia, NY: Grey House Publishing, 2022.

MLA: Leonhardt, David. "Corporate Taxes Are Wealth Taxes." *The Reference Shelf: Income Inequality,* edited by Micah L. Issitt, Grey House Publishing, 2022, pp. 86–87.

APA: Leonhardt, D. (2021). Corporate taxes are wealth taxes. In Micah L. Issitt (Ed.), *The reference shelf: Income inequality* (pp. 86–87). Amenia, NY: Grey House Publishing.

What's in the New Global Tax Agreement?

By Daniel Bunn and Sean Bray
Tax Foundation, April 7, 2022

In recent years, countries have been debating significant changes to international tax rules that apply to multinational companies. Following a July 2021 announcement by countries involved in negotiations at the Organisation for Economic Co-Operation and Development (OECD), in October there was a further agreement on an outline for the new tax rules by more than 130 jurisdictions.

Large companies would pay more taxes in countries where they have customers and a bit less in countries where their headquarters, employees, and operations are. Additionally, the agreement sets up the adoption of a global minimum tax of 15 percent, which would increase taxes on companies with earnings in low-tax jurisdictions.

Governments are now in the process of developing implementation plans and turning the agreement into law.

The OECD proposal follows an outline that has been under discussion since 2019. There are two "pillars" of the reform: Pillar 1 changes where large companies pay taxes (impacting roughly $125 billion in profits); Pillar 2 includes the global minimum tax (increasing tax revenues by an estimated $150 billion, globally).

Pillar 1 contains "Amount A" which would apply to companies with more than €20 billion in revenues and a profit margin above 10 percent. For those companies, a portion of their profits would be taxed in jurisdictions where they have sales; 25 percent of profits above a 10 percent margin may be taxed. After a review period of seven years, the €20 billion threshold may fall to €10 billion.

Amount A is a limited redistribution of tax revenue from countries that currently tax large multinationals based on the location of their operations to countries where those companies have customers. U.S. companies are likely to be a large share of the companies in scope of this policy.

The U.S. could lose tax revenue because of this approach. However, U.S. Treasury Secretary Yellen has previously written that she believes Amount A would be roughly revenue neutral for the U.S. For this to be true, the U.S. would need to collect significant revenue from foreign companies or from U.S. companies that sell to U.S. customers from foreign offices.

Recent draft rules outline where companies will pay taxes under Amount A. The rules include approaches for identifying the final consumer even when a company is selling to another business in a long supply chain. The draft rules also allow companies to use macroeconomic data on consumer spending to allocate their taxable profits.

Pillar 1 also contains "Amount B" which provides a simpler method for companies to calculate the taxes on foreign operations such as marketing and distribution.

The agreement sets up the adoption of a global minimum tax of 15 percent, which would increase taxes on companies with earnings in low-tax jurisdictions.

Pillar 2 is the global minimum tax. It includes three main rules and then a fourth rule for tax treaties. These rules are meant to apply to companies with more than €750 million in revenues. Model rules were released in December 2021.

The first is a "domestic minimum tax" which countries could use to claim the first right to tax profits that are currently being taxed below the minimum effective rate of 15 percent.

The second is an "income inclusion rule," which determines when the foreign income of a company should be included in the taxable income of the parent company. The agreement places the minimum effective tax rate at 15 percent, otherwise additional taxes would be owed in a company's home jurisdiction.

The income inclusion rule would apply to foreign profits after a deduction for 8 percent of the value of tangible assets (like equipment and facilities) and 10 percent of payroll costs. Those deductions would be reduced to 5 percent each over a 10-year transition period.

Because the Pillar 2 rules rely primarily on financial accounting data there will be differences from tax calculations. These book/tax differences mean that the Pillar 2 rules account for timing differences by focusing on deferred tax assets which can include net operating losses and capital allowances. However, those deferred tax assets are required to be valued at the 15 percent minimum tax rate.

Like other rules that tax foreign earnings, the income inclusion rule will increase the tax costs of cross-border investment and impact business decisions on where to hire and invest around the world—including in domestic operations.

The third rule in Pillar 2 is the "under-taxed profits rule," which would allow a country to increase taxes on a company if another related entity in a different jurisdiction is being taxed below the 15 percent effective rate. If multiple countries are applying a similar top-up tax, the taxable profit is divided based on the location of tangible assets and employees.

Together, the domestic minimum tax, the income inclusion rule, and the under-taxed payments rule create a minimum tax both on companies that are investing abroad and on foreign companies that are investing domestically. They are all tied to the minimum effective rate of at least 15 percent, and they would apply for each jurisdiction where a company operates.

The fourth Pillar 2 rule is the "subject to tax rule," meant to be used in a tax treaty framework to give countries the ability to tax payments that might otherwise only face a low rate of tax. The tax rate for this rule would be set at 9 percent.

For Pillar 1 to work well, it would be simpler if all countries adopt the rules in the same fashion. This would avoid companies having to deal with multiple approaches across the globe. The outline mentions a streamlined system that might require a sort of clearinghouse for Amount A payments and credits alongside a dispute resolution mechanism.

Pillar 2 is more optional. The outlined version of Pillar 2 is more like a template rather than a requirement for countries to adopt exactly what is described. If enough countries adopt the rules, though, then much of corporate profits across the globe would face a 15 percent effective tax rate.

Both Pillar 1 and Pillar 2 represent major changes to international tax rules, and the outline suggests that the changes should be put in place by 2023. The outline specifically states that digital services taxes and similar policies will need to be removed as part of implementing Pillar 1. The U.S. Trade Representative has negotiated with some countries that have digital services taxes to ensure a smooth transition. Countries would have to write new laws, adopt new tax treaty language, and repeal some policies that conflict with the new rules.

The United States is exploring changes to its own, unique approach, but it is currently unclear if or when those changes will be adopted. Though the Biden administration has supported the global agreement, it may be challenging to get Congress to follow through on implementing these policies.

The Build Back Better legislation which included changes to partially align Global Intangible Low-Tax Income to the income inclusion rule has failed to pass Congress. Even the changes to GILTI proposed in Build Back Better did not rely on financial accounting rules, which is the approach of the Pillar 2 model rules.

President Biden's most recent budget assumes the Build Back Better legislation does pass and adds a new domestic minimum top-up tax which would apply in cases where a foreign jurisdiction uses an under-taxed profits rule to tax U.S. companies. It is not yet clear whether Congress will take up these additional proposals from President Biden.

Tax treaty ratification requires 67 votes in the Senate, which will make adoption of Pillar 1 challenging if there is not broad bipartisan support for the new rules.

On the other side of the Atlantic, the European Union (EU) is also debating the rules and implementation timelines. The package will require unanimous agreement among the 27 EU member states in the Council of the EU. However, unanimity has proven elusive.

On March 15th, finance ministers failed to reach a unanimous agreement on Pillar 2. Sweden, Poland, Malta, and Estonia all objected. By the next meeting, on Tuesday, technical compromises relieved Swedish, Maltese, and Estonian objections. However, Poland once again vetoed the agreement on the grounds that EU's legislative process should link Pillars 1 and 2.

Even though it was rejected, it is important to note that the compromise proposal would have given member states until the end of 2023 to implement the Pillar 2 rules.

To date, the European Commission has only produced a proposal on Pillar 2. This is primarily because the details of Pillar 1 are still being negotiated at the OECD level. A proposal to implement Pillar 1 is expected in the summer.

The agreement represents a major change for tax competition, and many countries will be rethinking their tax policies for multinationals in light of it. However, with both the U.S. and EU hitting roadblocks in their respective legislative processes, it is unclear when or even if the agreement will be implemented. If implementation fails, a return to a world of distortive European digital services taxes and retaliatory American tariffs could be on the horizon.

Print Citations

CMS: Bunn, David, and Sean Bray. "What's in the New Global Tax Agreement?" In *The Reference Shelf: Income Inequality,* edited by Micah L. Issitt, 88–91. Amenia, NY: Grey House Publishing, 2022.

MLA: Bunn, David, and Sean Bray. "What's in the New Global Tax Agreement?" *The Reference Shelf: Income Inequality,* edited by Micah L. Issitt, Grey House Publishing, 2022, pp. 88–91.

APA: Bunn, D., & Bray, S. (2022). What's in the new global tax agreement? In Micah L. Issitt (Ed.), *The reference shelf: Income inequality* (pp. 88–91). Amenia, NY: Grey House Publishing.

Democrats Struggle with Plan to Tax Dynastic Wealth

By Brian Faler
Politico, June 8, 2021

A bid by Democrats to go after dynastic wealth would also hit some people who'd never be confused for the jet set, and that is causing major headaches for lawmakers.

They want to end a longstanding provision in the tax code that enables the rich to pass assets on to heirs tax free by forgiving capital gains taxes on things like company stock and land when people die.

The trouble is their plan would also hurt other, more average Americans: farmers, small business owners, people who are well off but not extremely wealthy and even a few people who don't necessarily make all that much money.

While they'd be a small share of those affected, those people represent an outsized political problem for Democrats.

"They're fine catching really high-income people, but they don't want to catch my Aunt Jo," says Rick Grafmeyer, a former top tax aide in Congress now at the firm Capitol Tax Partners.

It's an example of how Democrats will face a whole new set of challenges even if they end negotiations with Republicans and go it alone with their plans for another big-spending package.

Democrats want to fund a big chunk of their spending package by curbing the nearly century-old provision, sometimes called the Angel of Death loophole and technically known by the clunky term "stepped up basis at death." Along with a related plan to raise capital gains rates on millionaires, it is projected to raise more than $300 billion over 10 years.

But the idea is running into intense opposition, with even some Democrats uncomfortable with the proposal. Last week, House Agriculture Chair David Scott (D-Ga.) called the administration's plan "untenable."

At issue is a plan to require a lot more people to pay taxes when they die—something only the very wealthy currently have to worry about.

They're subject to the estate tax, which is a levy on the transfer of wealth to their heirs. Republicans have been loosening the tax for years, which now only kicks in once a single filer has more than $11.7 million in assets. Just a couple thousand taxpayers typically pay it each year.

Democrats are not proposing to tinker with the estate tax, but their bid to end the capital gains exemption would amount to creating a new tax due at death.

Here's How It Would Work

Normally, when someone sells an asset, like a stock, they have to pay the capital gains tax on any growth in its value. So if someone sells a stock for $100, and it originally cost them $25, they pay tax on the $75 difference.

But a different set of rules apply when someone dies: the starting point for calculating the tax—known as the "basis"—is increased, or stepped up, to current values. So the heir receiving the stock originally purchased at $25 would only owe taxes on any appreciation beyond its current $100 value.

The provision has been part of the tax code for nearly a century though it is widely considered unfair by tax experts, in part because it can allow the wealthy to escape taxes on huge fortunes.

For instance, if Jeff Bezos were to sell all of his Amazon stock while he is alive, he'd owe taxes on all the appreciation since the founding of the company. But if he simply waits until he dies, that tax would evaporate, even if his heirs sell the stock the next day.

"It's a loophole for the American aristocracy," said Sen. Chris Van Hollen (D-Md.).

Now, the Biden administration wants to require people to pay taxes on the appreciation of unsold assets when they die.

To avoid hitting average Americans, it would give people a $1 million-per-person exemption, along with a $250,000 per-person housing allowance. Couples would get twice that.

The Treasury Department says fewer than a half-percent of taxpayers would be subject to the tax—a tiny share overall, though still be a big increase compared to the number now subject to the estate tax.

In some ways, it would be a throwback to the 1970s, before Republicans began relaxing the estate tax. In 1976, when the estate tax kicked in when people had assets worth more than $60,000, almost 8 percent of everyone who died paid it. By comparison, fewer than 0.1 percent of decedents today pay the estate tax.

Advocates of Biden's plan got a boost Tuesday when ProPublica reported that Bezos, Tesla Founder Elon Musk and others at the pinnacle of the earnings ladder have paid little or no income taxes even as the value of their unrealized capital gains soared.

To shield itself politically, the administration is proposing special rules for two of the most politically important groups that would be affected by its plan: farmers and small businesses.

Farmers worry about having to pay tax on land that's been appreciating for decades while small business owners are concerned about being able to hand down their companies to children.

While farms and small businesses would lose the step-up treatment, the administration is proposing to allow them to postpone paying the resulting tax until their business or farm is sold or ceases to be family-owned and operated. Details such as which family members would count would be worked out by Congress.

But the influential American Farm Bureau Federation is rejecting the administration's attempt at compromise—which will put Democrats from rural areas in a tough spot. The National Federation of Independent Business, another group with clout, is similarly opposed.

> **Along with a related plan to raise capital gains rates on millionaires, it is projected to raise more than $300 billion over 10 years.**

"No exemption or carve out is better than current law," says Courtney Titus Brooks, NFIB's senior manager of federal government relations. Small business owners "would still have a tremendous tax liability hanging over them."

Those aren't the only politically sensitive groups that could be hit by the plan.

It could also affect people who are well-to-do but not extremely wealthy. Think of someone who has owned a home for 30 years in a high-cost city like Washington, D.C. If they also have a vacation home and a stock portfolio swelled by the recent runup on Wall Street, they could find themselves on hook for the tax.

"This isn't just affecting the Jeff Bezos's of the world or the folks in the Hamptons or the people in Malibu," said Kenneth Van Leeuwen, who runs Van Leeuwen & Company, a financial planning firm in Princeton, New Jersey.

There would also be a small number of people with incomes below $400,000 who would be subject to the tax—even though the administration has said it won't raise taxes on people making less than that—because they are sitting on a pile of unrealized capital gains.

It could be someone who never earned more than, say, $80,000 during their working lives, but who purchased shares in their companies through employee stock option programs that have been growing in value for decades. The Tax Policy Center figures 2 percent of decedents who made less than $400,000 could be liable for the tax.

"It seems inevitable that some people with incomes under $400,000 are going to be affected," said Robert McClelland, a senior fellow with the group.

Speaking on condition of anonymity, a Treasury official said that would not violate the administration's pledge because if someone had enough unrealized gains at the time of their death to owe the tax, then that person, by definition, would have made more than $400,000.

Jonathan Blattmachr, a longtime estate tax lawyer who supports Democrats' plans, says its critics are focusing on the wrong people.

While the tax would technically be paid by the person who died, in reality, he says, it would be borne by their heirs—because they're the ones who are still alive.

"The person who bought the Tesla stock is never going to pay the tax if he doesn't sell it during his lifetime—you're not hurting him," he said. "It's the heirs who will pay."

And he would not feel badly for them.

They are merely "the lucky winners of the sperm lottery—who were born into a wealthy family who will inherit a tremendous amount of money for nothing they did."

Print Citations

CMS: Faler, Brian. "Democrats Struggle with Plan to Tax Dynastic Wealth." In *The Reference Shelf: Income Inequality,* edited by Micah L. Issitt, 92–95. Amenia, NY: Grey House Publishing, 2022.

MLA: Faler, Brian. "Democrats Struggle with Plan to Tax Dynastic Wealth." *The Reference Shelf: Income Inequality,* edited by Micah L. Issitt, Grey House Publishing, 2022, pp. 92–95.

APA: Faler, B. (2021). Democrats struggle with plan to tax dynastic wealth. In Micah L. Issitt (Ed.), *The reference shelf: Income Inequality* (pp. 92–95). Amenia, NY: Grey House Publishing.

The Truth About Income Inequality

By David R. Henderson
Reason, February, 2020

"The issue of wealth and income inequality, to my mind, is the greatest moral issue of our time," said presidential candidate Sen. Bernie Sanders (I–Vt.). Former Secretary of Labor Robert Reich claims that "great wealth amassed at the top" will cause us to lose democracy. To fight economic inequality, presidential candidate Sen. Elizabeth Warren (D–Mass.) is calling for a 2 percent annual tax on household net worth between $50 million and $1 billion and a 3 percent tax on net worth above $1 billion.

Language like that and proposals like Warren's make increasing inequality sound like a crisis. But they misread the situation and misdiagnose the underlying problems.

On a global scale, inequality is declining. While it has increased within the United States, it has not grown nearly as much as people often claim. The American poor and middle class have been gaining ground, and the much-touted disappearance of the middle class has happened mainly because the ranks of the people above the middle class have swollen. And while substantially raising tax rates on higher-income people is often touted as a fix for inequality, it would probably hurt lower-income people as well as the wealthy. The same goes for a tax on wealth.

Most important: Not all income inequality is bad. Inequality emerges in more than one way, some of it justifiable, some of it not. Most of what is framed as a problem of inequality is better conceived as either a problem of *poverty* or a problem of *unjustly acquired wealth*.

Measuring Inequality

First, though, let's look at how much inequality there is. The Congressional Budget Office (CBO) produced a report in November 2018 on the growth of household income in each of five quintiles. Between 1979 and 2015, average real income for people in the top fifth of the population rose by 101 percent, while it rose for people in the bottom quintile by "only" 32 percent. For the middle three quintiles, average real income increased by 32 percent as well.

Or at least those are the numbers if you ignore the effects of taxes and direct government transfers. But you really shouldn't leave those out: If you're debating whether to increase taxes on the rich and transfers to the poor, it seems important to take into account the taxation and safety net already in place. Once the CBO researchers subtracted taxes and added welfare, Social Security, and so on, the picture changed dramatically for the lowest quintile: Income rose by 79 percent. (For the middle three quintiles, it increased by 46 percent. For the highest quintile, it went up by 103 percent—slightly more than before, probably thanks to Ronald Reagan's and George W. Bush's tax cuts.)

The above data on real income growth actually understate the growth of income for each quintile. When the CBO compares incomes over time, it measures inflation using the Consumer Price Index (CPI). But many economists have concluded that the CPI overstates inflation by not sufficiently adjusting for new products, improvements in quality, changes in the mix of goods and services purchased, and shifts in where consumers buy their goods. (The latter factor is sometimes called "the Walmart effect," but that term is arguably dated. Maybe we should call it "the Amazon effect" instead.)

Stanford economist Michael Boskin estimates that the CPI overstates inflation by 0.8 to 0.9 percentage points a year. That's small for any given year, but over time it doesn't just add up—it compounds up. If you go with the conservative estimate of 0.8 percentage points and adjust the CBO's after-tax, after-transfer data accordingly, the top quintile's average real income between 1979 and 2015 increased by 168 percent and the bottom quintile's average real income increased by 136 percent.

That's still an increase in income inequality, of course. But it's not an inequality increase in which the poor and near-poor are worse off. They're much better off. Everyone is.

And those numbers don't do complete justice to how much better off we are. Donald J. Boudreaux, an economist at George Mason University, has compared the prices of items you could have bought from a Sears catalog in 1975 with prices for similar items in 2006. He shows that with the average wage in 2006, you would have to spend far less time working to earn enough to buy the items than you would have had to spend in 1975. Moreover, he notes, the 2006 items are almost always of much higher quality. Who wants a 1975 TV? In 2010, my local Goodwill wouldn't even accept a working 1999 TV. And those awful primitive cellphones everyone had in 1975? Oh, wait.

I asked Boudreaux to update his data to 2019. Since 2013, he told me, the "time cost" of his chosen goods has fallen by another 30 percent.

I should note that while most consumer goods have been getting cheaper, education, housing, and health care have become more expensive. Interestingly, these are all areas in which governments have had a substantial influence on prices. In education, state and local governments have almost a monopoly; in housing, governments on the West Coast and in the Northeast have so restricted new construction that supply has not kept up with demand, causing prices to explode; and in health care, extensive regulation and subsidization have driven up the cost, though not always the price, of health care. (The difference is that the price to the consumer is often low because insurance and government subsidies hide the true cost, which is often high.)

On a global level, meanwhile, inequality is *declining*—and it's likely to fall further.

Economists measure inequality with something called the Gini coefficient. A coefficient of 100 would mean that one person gets all the income while everyone else gets nothing; a coefficient of zero would mean complete equality. In a 2015 study published by the Peterson Institute for International Economics, Tomas Hellebrandt of the Bank of England and Paolo Mauro of the International Monetary Fund tracked the global Gini coefficient from 2003 and 2013. During that time it fell from 69 to 65, thanks to rapid economic growth in lower-income countries—not just India and China but also sub-Saharan Africa. Hellebrandt and Mauro project that by 2035 it will have declined to 61.

What About Mobility?

Often when we look at income inequality, we do it by comparing income "quintiles." That is, we ask how much better or worse the richest fifth of the population did over a span of time vs. the second-richest, the middle, the second-poorest, and the poorest fifths. But it's important to keep in mind that there is substantial mobility from one quintile to another, even over just a few years. In a 2015 report for the Census Bureau, Carmen DeNavas-Walt and Bernadette D. Proctor concluded that "57.1 percent of households remained in the same income quintile between 2009 and 2012, while the remaining 42.9 percent of households experienced either an upward or [a] downward movement across the income distribution."

That's important to remember when considering the frequently stated worry that the middle class is disappearing. The middle class is getting smaller—but it's disappearing, for the most part, because it's moving *up*.

Now, it matters how we define the middle class. If the middle class is defined as the middle three income quintiles, then in 2018 it consisted of households with income between $25,600 and $130,000. In 1967, the middle three quintiles had income ranging from $19,726 to $54,596 (in 2018 dollars). The people in the middle, in other words, are considerably richer than their counterparts a half century ago.

Of course, defining the middle class that way means that exactly 60 percent of households will always qualify. That seems too broad. American Enterprise Institute economist Mark Perry, on his blog *Carpe Diem*, defines the middle class more narrowly to include any household with an income, in 2018 dollars, of between $35,000 and $100,000. In 1967, he notes, 54 percent of households were in that category; by 2018, that was down to 42 percent. That wasn't because they slipped; it was because they rose. In 1967, only 9.7 percent of U.S. households had income of $100,000 or more (in 2018 dollars). By 2018, that percentage had more than tripled to 30.4 percent.

And remember that this calculation adjusts for inflation using the CPI, and the CPI overstates inflation. So in some ways, the improvements are even greater than Perry's data suggest. On the other hand, the numbers arguably overstate the progress for people who live in coastal California, other urban parts of the West Coast, and the coastal northeastern United States, where the cost of housing has skyrocketed thanks to barriers erected by local and state governments.

On a related note: It's important to distinguish the concepts of *inequality* and *poverty*. The distinction seems obvious, yet even some economists confuse the two. In 2015, for example, University of Oregon economist Mark Thoma, author of the popular *Economist's View* blog, wrote: "Recent research…from UCLA›s Fielding School of Public Health provides evidence that income inequality is associated with inequality in health. In particular, lower income is associated with 'high levels of stress, exhaustion, cardiovascular disease, lower life expectancy and obesity.'"

> **Most of what is framed as a problem of inequality is better conceived as either a problem of poverty or a problem of *unjustly acquired wealth*.**

Notice that Thoma subtly jumps from "income inequality" to "lower income." Absolute real incomes certainly could be plausibly connected to health, but that's a separate question from how well off someone is relative to others. It's hard to believe that if group A's real income increases by a large percent but group B's income increases by an even larger percent, group A's health would worsen.

The 1 Percent

One reason so many people worry about income inequality is that they believe the share of income that accrues to the top 1 percent has increased dramatically. This became a hot issue during Bill Clinton's run for the presidency in 1992, and President Barack Obama harped on it repeatedly during his years in office. French economist Thomas Piketty's influential 2014 bestseller, *Capital in the Twenty-First Century*, also put a lot of emphasis on this assertion.

Piketty and the Berkeley economist Emmanuel Saez have estimated that, for the United States between 1979 and 2015, the top 1 percent's share of pretax income (including capital gains) increased from 9.0 percent to 20.3 percent. But in a 2018 paper, economists Gerald Auten of the U.S. Treasury Department and David Splinter of the congressional Joint Committee on Taxation came to a very different conclusion. To get a better measure of income, they accounted for all of national income, including unreported income, retirement income missing from tax returns, and income due to changes in the tax base that resulted from the Tax Reform Act of 1986. Their conclusion: Between 1979 and 2015, the share of pretax income going to the top 1 percent rose from 9.5 percent to 14.2 percent, and the share of after-tax, after-transfer income rose even less, from 7.2 percent to 8.5 percent.

Who's right? Piketty and Saez have moved in Auten and Splinter's direction with a more complete accounting for income. Their new approach found that the top 1 percent's share rose from 9.1 percent in 1979 to 15.7 percent in 2014. Half of the remaining difference between Piketty/Saez and Auten/Splinter is due to how the pairs handle underreported business income. Piketty and Saez assume that underreported income is proportional to reported business income, whereas Auten and Splinter assume that lower-income business owners disproportionately under-report. Auten has been at Treasury since 1987, which makes me inclined to trust his instincts here, but you can decide for yourself.

In any case, one thing that is clear from the data is that the higher your income, the higher the percent of your income you pay to Washington. In 2015, according to a recent study from the Tax Foundation, people in the lowest quintile paid 1.5 percent of their income in federal taxes, on average; the second quintile paid 9.2 percent; the middle quintile, 14.0 percent; the fourth quintile, 17.9 percent; and the highest quintile, 26.7 percent. Those in the top 1 percent paid a whopping 33.3 percent. This includes all federal taxes: income taxes, taxes for Social Security and Medicare, corporate income taxes, and excise taxes.

That means that whenever there is a large federal tax cut, those in the top quintile will almost certainly get a much bigger benefit, both in dollars and as a percentage of their income, than other quintiles. This is especially true when most or all of the cut is in the individual income tax, because that tax is disproportionately paid by higher-income people. But do they get a bigger cut as a percentage of their federal tax burden? For the George W. Bush 2001, 2002, and 2003 tax cuts and the Donald Trump 2017 tax cuts, the answer has been no.

Because of Bush's tax cuts, people in the second-lowest quintile in 2004 saw a 17.6 percent cut in their income taxes, the biggest percentage tax cut of any quintile. The middle quintile's cut was 12.6 percent, the second-highest quintile's cut was 9.9 percent, and the highest quintile's cut was slightly more than 11 percent.

Similarly, the 2017 Trump cuts reduced taxes most, percentage-wise, for the second-lowest quintile, cutting their taxes by 10.3 percent. The middle quintile got an 8.7 percent cut; the second-highest quintile, a 7.5 percent cut; the top quintile, a 6.7 percent cut; and the top 1 percent, a 4.6 percent cut. The lowest quintile had its taxes cut by 7.3 percent—it's hard to cut taxes for a quintile whose members mostly don't pay them.

Many people who worry about income inequality want to tax higher-income people more. Given what economists know about the harmful effects from raising already high marginal tax rates even higher, tax increases could certainly reduce measured inequality—because they would cause higher-income people to reduce their taxable income by working less, by taking more pay in the form of untaxed fringe benefits, or by investing more in municipal bonds, whose interest is not taxable by the feds. Of course, none of this would make lower-income people better off. Indeed, to the extent that higher taxes discourage capital accumulation, they slow the growth of worker productivity. One of the main ways to increase worker productivity is to increase the amount of capital per worker. With a slower growth rate of capital, worker productivity will grow more slowly—and so will real wages. This makes lower-income people worse off than they would have been.

Piketty recognizes that higher tax rates won't yield much additional tax revenue. In his 2014 magnum opus, he wrote that when a government "taxes a certain level of income or inheritance at a rate of 70 or 80 percent, the primary goal is obviously not to raise additional revenue (because these high brackets never yield much)." Instead, he argued, the goal is to "put an end to such incomes and large estates."

Because of limited space, I have focused on income inequality rather than wealth inequality. I will point out, though, that a tax on wealth—proposed both by Piketty and by Warren—would reduce the incentive to invest in capital, decreasing worker productivity and, therefore, workers' wages.

Two Kinds of Inequality

When is a growth in inequality justified, and when is it not? Consider two opposite cases: an innovator and a seeker of privilege.

In 1949, Robert McCulloch introduced the 3-25, a one-man chainsaw weighing only 25 pounds. This revolutionized forestry. A friend of mine, now in his late 80s, told me that when he was a teenager, his father made him cut wood for a whole winter of heating a large house. When my friend found out about the 3-25, he used his own allowance to buy one. It changed his life.

McCulloch made a lot of money with his chainsaw. But everyone who bought a 3-25 wanted it. It's likely that almost all of them got a large benefit from the purchase. McCulloch got richer, and so did his customers, who were able to save huge amounts of time and effort. Eventually, competitors produced their own chainsaws to compete with McCulloch's—products that were better, cheaper, or both.

That increased the benefits to consumers while reducing the profits to McCulloch. Still, he made a lot—enough that his innovation almost certainly increased income inequality, by raising McCulloch's income far above most other people's.

Now consider a story in which someone used political power to make himself and his wife very wealthy. In 1942, a young congressman from Texas had a net worth of approximately zero. But by 1963, when he became president of the United States, Lyndon Johnson and his wife had a net worth of about $20 million, a large part of which could be attributed to a license from the Federal Communications Commission (FCC) to operate the radio station KTBC in Austin, Texas.

During the 1964 presidential campaign, Johnson claimed that his wife had turned an asset she bought for $17,500 into a property worth millions by working hard. Not quite. *Lyndon* had worked hard—at using his political influence as a congressman. Before his wife acquired it, KTBC›s owners had spent years trying to get the FCC›s permission to sell the station. On January 3, 1943, Lady Bird Johnson filed her application to buy it, and just 24 days later, the owners were suddenly allowed to sell. That June, the future first lady applied for permission to operate for more hours a day and at a much better part of the AM band. She received permission a month later.

While all this was happening, the FCC was under attack by a powerful congressman, Eugene Cox, who wanted to cut the FCC's budget to zero. Lyndon Johnson strategized secretly with an FCC official named Red James and used his influence with House Speaker Sam Rayburn to deflect the attack. James later admitted that he had recommended to Lady Bird that she apply for the license.

Over the subsequent decades, the FCC didn't just clear an easy path when her radio station (and, later, a television station as well) needed an application approved. When a competitor wanted to make a move, the agency would put regulatory barriers in its way. In this manner, Lady Bird's company came to dominate Austin broadcasting.

So here we have two examples of income and wealth inequality increasing. In the first case, inequality increased because a man's company introduced a product that made the lives of those who bought it substantially better, raising their real incomes. In the second case, inequality increased because a politician used his influence to get monopolistic privileges from a federal agency, making the politician wealthier and lowering the real incomes of people in the Austin area.

There are at least two reasons to think differently about these two cases. The first is that McCulloch's actions improved others' well-being in addition to his own, while the Johnsons' actions benefited themselves at the expense of others. The second is why McCulloch's actions had those benevolent social effects and Johnson's didn't. McCulloch's wealth—and the benefits to his customers—were rooted in voluntary transactions in the marketplace. The Johnsons' wealth was rooted in raw political power.

There is a third possible source of wealth for the very rich: inheritance. Some people inherit wealth from fortunes like McCulloch's, and some inherit it from fortunes like the Johnsons'. The important question, as far as I'm concerned, is how the money is initially acquired. But in any event, the long-term importance of inheritance in American inequality is overstated. In the May 2013 *American Economic Review*, Steven Kaplan of the University of Chicago and Joshua Rauh of Stanford analyzed the fortunes of the superwealthy. They found that only 32 percent of people on the *Forbes* 400 list in 2011 had come from very rich families—down from 60 percent in 1982. Moreover, 69 percent of the 400 had started their own business. In short, a majority of those who made fortunes *made* fortunes. Maybe they made it the McCulloch way, maybe they made it the Johnson way, or maybe it was a mix. But they didn›t simply rely on their parents.

The Real Problem Isn't Inequality

The word inequality sparks thoughts of the very rich and the very poor. But data on the degree of inequality tell us nothing about the degree of poverty or the lives of the poor. Inequality can grow even while the poor and almost everyone else are becoming better off. Indeed, in the last half-century, while U.S. income inequality grew, the poor and the middle class became substantially better off. And the even better news is that global income inequality has fallen and is likely to fall even further.

Great wealth, meanwhile, is a problem only to the extent that it is unjustly extracted. Government favoritism to politically powerful people may increase income and wealth inequality, as it did in the case of Lyndon Johnson and his wife. But it is the government favoritism, not inequality per se, that is the true problem.

The Important Role of Work

Many people, including many economists, who worry about income inequality overlook the role of work. You might imagine that the rich are generally idle while the poor work their fingers to the bone. But that's not the full picture.

The Department of Commerce's Census Bureau gathers data annually on characteristics of the five income quintiles. One thing that changes very little from year to year is the number of workers per household.

The data for 2018 are no exception. Each quintile that year was made up of 25.7 million households. For the lowest quintile, 16.2 million households had no one working at all during 2018. For the highest quintile, by contrast, only 1.1 million households had no one working. How many households in the bottom quintile had two earners? Only 1.1 million, or 4.3 percent of the total number of households. For the top quintile, 14.1 million households, or 54.7 percent of the total, had two earners. Not surprisingly, therefore, the average number of workers per household in the bottom quintile was 0.4, while the average number for households in the top quintile was 2.1.

The lesson seems clear for people who want to avoid being in the bottom quintile: Try your hardest to get a job year-round. Fortunately, that is relatively easy in the current economy, with its less than 4 percent unemployment rate. To further improve your chances, get married to—or just live with—someone else who works year-round as well.

Print Citations

CMS: Henderson, David R. "The Truth About Income Inequality." In *The Reference Shelf: Income Inequality,* edited by Micah L. Issitt, 96–103. Amenia, NY: Grey House Publishing, 2022.

MLA: Henderson, David R. "The Truth About Income Inequality." *The Reference Shelf: Income Inequality,* edited by Micah L. Issitt, Grey House Publishing, 2022, pp. 96–103.

APA: Henderson, D. R. (2020). The truth about income inequality. In Micah L. Issitt (Ed.), *The reference shelf: Income inequality* (pp. 96–103). Amenia, NY: Grey House Publishing.

4
Causes and Effects

Photo by Paul Stein, www.flickr.com, via Wikipedia, CC BY-SA 2.0.

The 2011 Occupy Wall Street protest was one of the most visible effects of income inequality and led to other protest movements over the next decade.

Social and Economic Factors Influencing Income Inequality

Economists and social scientists have identified many different factors influencing wealth and income inequality in America. Beyond the influence of tax rates and political spending, other factors that influence income inequality include the availability and strength of advocacy groups for workers and technological changes that influence supply and demand in the labor market.

Unionization and Worker's Rights

One of the major factors impacting workers in the United States is the relative strength and participation in worker's advocacy groups, such as labor unions and other professional organizations. Labor unions have been part of the United States from the very beginning and evolved from the trade unions that existed in England prior to colonization. These early guilds and trade organizations afforded workers in certain fields with opportunities to meet and network, and members of trade groups were able to offer assistance to other members in finding job opportunities and avoiding employment problems. As European colonists came to the United States, some of the same trade organizations were reestablished for colonial workers. Many of the workers organizations changed to better reflect the differences between the European and American labor markets. One example is the Freemasons, which served as a professional organization for stoneworkers in the early years of the republic, but later moved away from workers' rights and became a popular social club for American men.

The basic economic philosophy of the US free-market system is that competition between companies will, over the longer term, lead to a stronger and more innovative economic environment. Supporters of this system have long argued that competition ultimately leads to better prices for consumers, as companies compete to offer the best price, and better conditions/pay for workers, as companies compete to attract potential employees. In practice, competition alone is typically insufficient to create favorable conditions for workers. For one thing, workers in a specific field might only have a few options for employment in that field within a specific area. To find alternative employment, an employee might have to migrate to a new area, or a new state, which is a financial burden that not all workers could surmount. A lack of local diversity in employment therefore means that competition might not do much to directly improve conditions for workers in a specific labor market. To make matters worse, for most of American history it was legal for owners of companies to work together to fix wage rates, such that workers had absolutely no option of moving to a new company for higher wages. Further, competition only improves conditions for workers when employers are competing with one another to *attract* workers, which means that there must be more jobs than there are available workers. When there are more workers than *jobs*, employers can offer substandard wages, because desperate workers will be more likely to endure exploitation by company owners in order to avoid poverty and unemployment.[1]

In the absence of competitive pressures, the job market in the United States has always been highly exploitative and rarely beneficial for laborers. Workers in many industries are forced to accept unlivable wages and must devote as many hours of their lives as possible to work simply to sustain themselves and their families without much in the way of potential to advance, accrue savings, or build equity. One of the ways that workers have been able to combat exploitative policies and practices has been to join with other workers to increase their collective bargaining power, and this is the role that trade's organizations and labor unions have played in American history. An influential labor union that succeeds in attracting most or all of the potential workers for a certain field, in a certain area, can gain the power to force employers in that industry to improve conditions for workers, or to increase pay. If employers refuse to negotiate or to accede to the demands of the union, unions can stage strikes or boycotts, which are in essence financial penalties on companies that refuse to negotiate with their workforce. Companies then have the option of trying to find workers who will fill vacancies without working with the union, or must negotiate with union leadership to end the union's strikes or other actions against the company.[2]

The first labor strike in America also predated unification and statehood, with a group of Polish artisans going on strike in 1619 in the Jamestown Colony, protesting unfair treatment and a lack of political representation.[3] During the Industrial Revolution of the mid-to-late 1800s and early 1900s, demand for workers was high, but the constant influx of immigrants also meant that competition alone did not guarantee livable wages and acceptable workplace conditions. In the early to mid-1800s, dozens of labor unions formed across the United States, protesting low wages and unsafe conditions in the nation's many factories. Though American business owners and allied politicians cooperated maintain the exploitative system that came to characterize American working life, unions played an essential role in earning needed wage increases for workers, and were active also in the hard-fought campaign to include women in the workplace, to end exploitative child labor, and to mandate basic sanitation and safety measures. Modern laws prohibiting child labor, discrimination among employers, and protecting workers from on-the-job injuries can all be traced to the collective bargaining power of unions.

In the 1980s, President Ronald Reagan's "new conservative" movement established a much closer relationship between the Republican Party and American businesses, and drove a wedge between conservative Americans and the nation's labor unions. Over the decades that followed, membership in the unions declined and this led to a subsequent decline in union power and influence. A number of economic studies indicate that the decline in union membership between the 1980s and 2020s has been associated with an overall decline in economic equality and income gains among the working and middle class. Without the power of collective bargaining, and the threat of collective action, workers' wages have been based almost entirely on corporate policy. A 2019 study, for instance, showed that the percentage of income going to the top 10 percent of earners in America has increased from 33 percent in 1977 to 45.8 percent in 2019–20.[4]

Political propaganda has created the impression among many Americans that unions are often corrupt, do little for workers, and are frequently linked to organized crime. These misconceptions continue to discourage workers from seeking out professional organizations, and this limit the power that workers command to improve their pay and conditions. There are a number of examples, from the 2010s and 2020s, of efforts to unionize in some of America's largest and most familiar companies, like the Starbucks coffee chain and Amazon, that have generated controversy in American pop culture. Representatives of Amazon and Starbucks have argued that the unions will drive a wedge between workers and management and may lead to layoffs and reduced job opportunities, but there is little evidence that unionization would result in slow growth for either company. Supporters of unionization argue that it is especially important for workers in large-scale companies like Starbucks and Amazon to have the advantage of collective bargaining because large and wealthy companies have little in the way of competition and are not motivated to increase costs by affording workers with better benefits or pay unless forced to do so under threat of collective action against the companies.

Automation and Outsourcing

Other factors that greatly impact income fairness and equality in America are the ongoing process of automation and the outsourcing of labor. Automation occurs when a company adopts technology that replaces the jobs once done by human workers, while outsourcing involves employers contracting individuals in other areas to complete work that was once completed by local workers. Automation and outsourcing both have the effect of reducing the availability of jobs for local workers, which increases competition for jobs, and allows employers to offer reduced wages or, at least, to avoid offering higher wages, better benefits, or cost-of-living increases.

Automation is a process that has been ongoing in the United States since the early 1800s, with the introduction of the first semiautomated manufacturing systems in the textile industry. Large automated milling machines that were introduced into the factory mills of the 1800s were capable of enabling just a few workers to complete the work that once required a team of workers specializing on different parts of the textile manufacturing process. Automation was controversial in the 1800s, with workers calling the process a violation of human rights, but because automating various types of work saved companies on the cost of labor, corporations eagerly embraced automation as it developed. In the twentieth century, the pace of automation greatly increased thanks to the introduction and spread of robotics, which allowed for the creation of the first truly automatic manufacturing machines in many different manufacturing fields, including the automotive industry.

Over the years automated systems have replaced human workers in many different fields and in different ways. Receptionists and clerks, for instance, were replaced by digital, automated telephone and answering systems, while metal workers in many different manufacturing fields were replaced by automated welding machines. Entire factories once staffed by hundreds of workers have been converted almost entirely to automated assembly lines, where only a few workers and technicians are needed to ensure that the system runs smoothly.

Controversy over automation was most apparent in the 1980s and 1990s, which was when hundreds of American jobs were initially being converted to mechanical automation, but the pace of automation has not slowed. A report from business analyst McKinsey Global, issued in 2021, indicated that 45 million Americans, nearly a quarter of the workforce, work in jobs vulnerable to replacement through automation and would likely be replaced in their work by 2030.[5] The most recent dimension of the automation debate concerns the development of AI or artificial intelligence (AI) systems which, while not truly "intelligent" are capable of performing work that once required human thought processes. Experts in the tech fields have warned that AI systems could mean the automation of jobs like digital coding and computer programming will accelerate as AI systems become more advanced.[6]

In a related vein, globalization, defined as the increasing economic and political integration and overlap between nations, has made it possible for more and more companies in the United States to utilize foreign workers, often in struggling economies, as a way to reduce labor costs. Most Americans are likely familiar with the fact that many companies, especially large-scale national companies, hire workers living and working elsewhere in the world to manage customer service and tech support, or to manufacture products or parts for products that are sold in the United States. Outsourcing works for companies by allowing companies to hire workers in developing or struggling economies in which American dollars have higher value in comparison to purchasing power.

For instance, a tech support worker in India makes an average of ₹ 18,896 per month when employed by the Amazon corporation, which is roughly equivalent to $243.89 in US dollars. Whereas a salary of $243.89 per month is insufficient for an American to afford even basic living expenses anywhere in the United States, this is considered a slightly below-average salary in much of India, outside of the major and wealthier urban enclaves. Coupled with high competition for jobs across much of India, the low-average wages offered by Amazon are competitive in the Indian semiskilled labor market, but not in the United States. The company therefore saves on expenditures by allowing Indian workers to manage much of the company's technical support services handled over the telephone or via digital communication. Likewise, many American companies attempt to increase profitability by allowing workers in developing economies to handle tasks that would cost far more if those same jobs were given to American workers.

Supporters of automation and outsourcing argue that companies have a duty to their shareholders to maximize profit and that saving on expenses is one way of maximizing profit. It has also been argued that saving on expenditures allows companies to offer lower prices to consumers, and so that consumers also benefit from automation and outsourcing. Critics argue that companies could reduce corporate salaries and stockholder payouts, in order to free up the resources needed to hire American workers instead of investing in cost-saving mechanization or outsourcing jobs to struggling economies.

In general, Americans are fearful of automation and most Americans believe that automation and outsourcing will have more negative than positive effects for American society. In polls, nearly three quarters of Americans believe that automation specifically will increase inequality between the rich and the poor. However, about a third of Americans believe that automation could also create new job opportunities for American workers and some polls indicate that between 30 to 40 percent of Americans are optimistic that automation might make American culture more efficient, economically and professionally.[7]

While Americans are skeptical and at times hostile towards the familiar process of companies replacing American workers in one way or another, economists and sociologists have proven through detailed study and analysis that automation and worker replacement has been and remains a contributing factor to economic inequality in America. Ultimately, any factor that reduces the number of jobs available to American workers is a detriment to workers seeking employment, but also increases the power of companies by increasing the demand for jobs, while simultaneously reducing supply. With the American population continuing to grow, meaning that more and more Americans are searching for work, this imbalance in supply and demand means that companies needn't offer attractive wages to workers, but can instead count on desperation within the workforce to fill roles in their companies.

Complicated Equations

There are many different factors influencing patterns of wealth and inequality in American society and this makes it extremely difficult if not impossible to identify the key strategies that might be effective in reducing inequality or in helping those at lower ends of the society to reach economic stability or affluence. While it is clear that certain factors, like automation and the capability/willingness of workers to organize and work together, can have a dramatic impact on income levels and so also on economic equity, all of these factors become important only if Americans, as a whole or at least in the majority, prioritize these issues and make income inequality a top political and voting priority.

Works Used

Carey, Kevin. "Do Not Be Alarmed by Wild Predictions of Robots Taking Everyone's Jobs." *Slate*. 31 Mar. 2021. https://slate.com/technology/2021/03/job-loss-automation-robots-predictions.html.

Flemming, Sean. "A Short History of Jobs and Automation." *We Forum*. World Economic Forum. Sep 3, 2020. https://www.weforum.org/agenda/2020/09/short-history-jobs-automation/.

Geiger, A. W. "How Americans See Automation and the Workplace In 7 Charts." *Pew Research Center*. 9 Apr. 2019. https://www.pewresearch.org/fact-tank/2019/04/08/how-americans-see-automation-and-the-workplace-in-7-charts/.

Graafland, Johan. *Ethics and Economics: An Introduction to Free Markets, Equality and Happiness*. Routledge, 2022.

Greenhouse, Steven. *Beaten Down, Worked Up*. Anchor Books, 2019.

Grizzard, Frank E., and D. Boyd Smith. *Jamestown Colony: A Political, Social, and Cultural History*. ABC-CLIO, 2007.

Shierholz, Heidi. "Working People Have Been Thwarted in Their Efforts to Bargain for Better Wages by Attacks on Unions." *Economic Policy Institute*, Aug. 2019. https://www.epi.org/publication/labor-day-2019-collective-bargaining/.

Notes

1. Graafland, *Ethics and Economics: An Introduction to Free Markets, Equality, and Happiness*.
2. Greenhouse, *Beaten Down, Worked Up*.
3. Grizzard and Smith, *Jamestown Colony: A Political, Social, and Cultural History*, pp. 171–72.
4. Shierholz, "Working People Have Been Thwarted in their Efforts to Bargain for Better Wages by Attacks on Unions."
5. Carey, "Do Not Be Alarmed by Wild Predictions of Robots Taking Everyone's Jobs."
6. Flemming, "A Short History of Jobs and Automation."
7. Geiger, "How Americans See Automation in the Workplace In 7 Charts."

Automation Is Not to Blame for the Growth of Income Inequality

Robert D. Atkinson
ITIF, August 10, 2021

For at least four decades, wages have grown more slowly for less-educated workers than workers with more education, although the gap is often exaggerated. But to be sure, income growth has not been as broad-based as it was in the post-war period. The key question is why?

Many neoclassical economists have laid the blame on technological change, arguing first that it was biased in favor of workers with more skills. If more workers would just go to college, all would be well.

But this "skill-biased technological change" (SBTC) argument never made sense because the growth in inequality among workers with a college degree was higher than between workers with and without college. As the Economic Policy Institute points out, "The flat or declining 50/10 wage gap in the 30 years after 1987 is inconsistent with the skills-gap narrative, since middle-wage workers who have more education than low-wage workers have not reaped a growing advantage since then." (The 50/10 wage gap refers to the average wages of workers in the 50th income percentile vs. those in the 10th percentile.)

The newest flavor of the "blame technology" argument is that automation has caused inequality. This is a much more dangerous argument. In contrast to the SBTC argument that logically led policies to get more people to go to college, the automation argument leads to destructive policies to limit automation and productivity growth, such as robot taxes.

The biggest proponent of this claim is economist Daron Acemoglu, who argues that the growth in income inequality is due to automation impacting lower-wage jobs more than higher-wage jobs and leading to excess lower-wage workers relative to labor demand. But this notion is even more flawed than the original SBTC argument.

First, Acemoglu points to data showing the increase in divergence of wage growth by education starting in 1981. I wonder what could have started in 1981? Could it have been the rise of the Reagan revolution and the weakening of unions, the increase in low-skill immigration, and minimum wage stagnation?

What's even more illogical about blaming automation for slow wage growth among the less educated is that labor productivity after 1981 was, for the most part, quite low. Automation, including routine tasks, was much higher in the 1950s and 60s when inequality had declined.

Acemoglu also looks at average wage growth for each education group to show growth in inequality. But this overlooks the enormous growth of the top 5 percent of earners, making it look like the lower growth among non-college degree workers is due to education. As EPI notes, there has been dramatic growth in the 95/50 wage gap.

Policymakers should instead support accelerated automation so employers can afford to pay their workers more.

Perhaps the most problematic for this automation argument is that the skill composition of U.S. jobs has not significantly changed over the past two decades. The demand for lower-skill jobs has not materially changed. Jobs requiring a college degree or more stayed constant at 22 percent of all jobs from 1998 to 2008, while jobs requiring only short-term or moderate-term on-the-job training decreased slightly from 53 percent to 51 percent; hardly a dramatic drop in demand for low-skilled workers. At the same time the growth of less-educated workers from immigration has been significant. Foreign-born Americans with less than a college degree went from 9 million in the mid-1970s to 37 million in 2018.

So if we want to boost the wages of the bottom half of the labor market, rather than limit automation, policymakers should instead support accelerated automation so employers can afford to pay their workers more. Instituting an investment tax credit for new machinery would be a great start, but absent that, preserving the ability of all firms to expense equipment investment in the first year for tax purposes would also be a big help.

At the same time, policymakers should require all employers, big and small, to provide health insurance and paid vacation and family leave for their workers. In addition, we need to significantly increase the minimum wage, and at the same time, limit low-skill immigration, while enabling unions to organize workers more effectively.

In short, if we want growth with opportunity, we need more tech and automation, not less.

Print Citations

CMS: Atkinson, Robert D. "Automation Is Not to Blame for the Growth of Income Inequality." In *The Reference Shelf: Income Inequality*, edited by Micah L. Issitt, 113–114. Amenia, NY: Grey House Publishing, 2022.

MLA: Atkinson, Robert D. "Automation Is Not to Blame for the Growth of Income Inequality." *The Reference Shelf: Income Inequality*, edited by Micah L. Issitt, Grey House Publishing, 2022, pp. 113–114.

APA: Atkinson, R. D. (2021). Automation is not to blame for the growth of income inequality. In Micah L. Issitt (Ed.), *The reference shelf: Income inequality* (pp. 113–114). Amenia, NY: Grey House Publishing.

Artificial Intelligence Has Caused a 50% to 70% Decrease in Wages—Creating Income Inequality and Threatening Millions of Jobs

By Jack Kelly
Forbes, June 18, 2021

The middle and working classes have seen a steady decline in their fortunes. Sending jobs to foreign countries, the hollowing out of the manufacturing sector, pivoting toward a service economy and the weakening of unions have been blamed for the challenges faced by a majority of Americans.

There's an interesting, compelling and alternative explanation. According to a new academic research study, automation technology has been the primary driver in U.S. income inequality over the past 40 years. The report, published by the National Bureau of Economic Research, claims that 50% to 70% of changes in U.S. wages, since 1980, can be attributed to wage declines among blue-collar workers who were replaced or degraded by automation.

Artificial intelligence, robotics and new sophisticated technologies have caused a wide chasm in wealth and income inequality. It looks like this issue will accelerate. For now, college-educated, white-collar professionals have largely been spared the fate of degreeless workers. People with a postgraduate degree saw their salaries rise, while "low-education workers declined significantly." According to the study, "The real earnings of men without a high-school degree are now 15% lower than they were in 1980."

Much of the changes in U.S. wage structure, according to the paper, were caused by companies automating tasks that used to be done by people. This includes "numerically-controlled machinery or industrial robots replacing blue-collar workers in manufacturing or specialized software replacing clerical workers."

Artificial intelligence systems are ubiquitous. AI-powered digital voice assistants share everything you want to know just by asking it a question. Instead of a live person addressing a problem, a corporate chatbot forces you to engage with it. The technology is remarkable. It helps diagnose cancer and health issues. Banks use sophisticated software to check for fraud and bad behaviors. Driverless automobiles, newsfeeds, social media and job applications are all controlled by AI.

The World Economic Forum (WEF) concluded in a recent report, "A new generation of smart machines, fueled by rapid advances in AI and robotics, could potentially replace a large proportion of existing human jobs." Robotics and AI will cause a serious "double-disruption," as the pandemic pushed companies to fast-track the deployment of new technologies to slash costs, enhance productivity and be less reliant on real-life people. The WEF asserts automation will slash about 85 million jobs by 2025. In a dire prediction, WEF said, "While some new jobs would be created as in the past, the concern is there may not be enough of these to go round, particularly as the cost of smart machines falls over time and their capabilities increase."

Management consulting giant PriceWaterhouseCoopers reported, "AI, robotics and other forms of smart automation have the potential to bring great economic benefits, contributing up to $15 trillion to global GDP by 2030." However, it will come with a high human cost. "This extra wealth will also generate the demand for many jobs, but there are also concerns that it could displace many existing jobs."

Concerns of new technologies disrupting the workforce and causing job losses have been around for a long time. On one side, the argument is automation will create new and better jobs and erase the need for physical labor. The counterclaim is that people without the appropriate skills will be displaced and not have a home in the new environment.

Amazon, Google, Microsoft, Apple, Zoom and other tech giants greatly benefited financially during the pandemic. The virus outbreak accelerated trends, including choosing technology over people. There's still a need for humans. For example, although Amazon invested heavily in automation for its warehouses, the online retail giant still needed to hire over 300,000 workers during the pandemic. This brings up another important overlooked issue: the quality of a job. Proponents of AI say that there's nothing to worry about, as we've always successfully dealt with new technologies. You may have a job, but what is the quality of it?

To remain relevant, you will have to learn new skills to stay ahead of the curve. *Bloomberg* reported, "More than 120 million workers globally will need retraining in the next three years due to artificial intelligence's impact on jobs, according to an IBM survey." The amount of individuals who will be impacted is immense.

The world's most advanced cities aren't ready for the disruptions of artificial intelligence, claims Oliver Wyman, a management consulting firm. It is believed that over 50 million Chinese workers may require retraining, as a result of AI-related deployment. The U.S. will be required to retool 11.5 million people in America with skills needed to survive in the workforce. Millions of workers in Brazil, Japan and Germany will need assistance with the changes wrought by AI, robotics and related technology.

For those who may be left behind, there's a call for offering a universal basic income (UBI). This idea gained national attention when it became a major part of Democratic candidate Andrew Yang's 2020 presidential campaign. Yang's policy was to lift people out of poverty or help them through rough patches with a guaranteed monthly income. Supporters say it gives people needed financial security to find good jobs and avoid debt. Critics have argued free money would be a disincentive to work, creating a society dependent on the state.

According to a Wells Fargo research report, robots will eliminate 200,000 jobs in the banking industry within the next 10 years. This has already adversely impacted highly paid Wall Street professionals, including stock and bond traders. These are the people who used to work on the trading floors at investment banks and trade securities for their banks, clients and themselves. It was a very lucrative profession until algorithms, quant-trading software and programs disrupted the business and rendered their skills unnecessary—compared to the fast-acting technology.

> **The U.S. will be required to retool 11.5 million people in America with skills needed to survive in the workforce.**

There is no hiding from the robots. Well-trained and experienced doctors will be pushed aside by sophisticated robots that can perform delicate surgeries more precisely and read x-rays more efficiently and accurately to detect cancerous cells that can't be readily seen by the human eye.

Truck and cab drivers, cashiers, retail sales associates and people who work in manufacturing plants and factories have and will continue to be replaced by robotics and technology. Driverless vehicles, kiosks in fast-food restaurants and self-help, quick-phone scans at stores will soon eliminate most minimum-wage and low-skilled jobs.

The rise of artificial intelligence will make even software engineers less sought after. That's because artificial intelligence will soon write its own software, according to Jack Dorsey, the tech billionaire boss of Twitter and Square. That will put some beginner-level software engineers in a tough spot. When discussing how automation will replace jobs held by humans, Dorsey told Yang on an episode of the Yang Speaks podcast, "We talk a lot about the self-driving trucks and whatnot." He added, "[AI] is even coming for programming [jobs]. A lot of the goals of machine learning and deep learning is to write the software itself over time, so a lot of entry-level programming jobs will just not be as relevant anymore."

When management consultants and companies that deploy AI and robotics say we don't need to worry, we need to be concerned. Companies—whether they are McDonald's, introducing self-serve kiosks and firing hourly workers to cut costs, or top-tier investment banks that rely on software instead of traders to make million-dollar bets on the stock market—will continue to implement technology and downsize people, in an effort to enhance profits.

This trend has the potential to adversely impact all classes of workers. In light of the study's spotlight on the dire results of AI, including lost wages and the rapid growth in income inequality, it's time to seriously talk about how AI should be managed before it's too late.

Print Citations

CMS: Kelly, Jack. "Artificial Intelligence Has Caused a 50% to 70% Decrease in Wages—Creating Income Inequality and Threatening Millions of Jobs." In *The Reference Shelf: Income Inequality,* edited by Micah L. Issitt, 115–118. Amenia, NY: Grey House Publishing, 2022.

MLA: Kelly, Jack. "Artificial Intelligence Has Caused a 50% to 70% Decrease in Wages—Creating Income Inequality and Threatening Millions of Jobs." *The Reference Shelf: Income Inequality,* edited by Micah L. Issitt, Grey House Publishing, 2022, pp. 115–118.

APA: Kelly, J. (2021). Artificial intelligence has caused a 50% to 70% decrease in wages—Creating income inequality and threatening millions of jobs. In Micah L. Issitt (Ed.), *The reference shelf: Income inequality* (pp. 115–118). Amenia, NY: Grey House Publishing.

How to Solve AI's Inequality Problem

By David Rotman

MIT Technology Review, April 19, 2022

The economy is being transformed by digital technologies, especially in artificial intelligence, that are rapidly changing how we live and work. But this transformation poses a troubling puzzle: these technologies haven't done much to grow the economy, even as income inequality worsens. Productivity growth, which economists consider essential to improving living standards, has largely been sluggish since at least the mid-2000s in many countries.

Why are these technologies failing to produce more economic growth? Why aren't they fueling more widespread prosperity? To get at an answer, some leading economists and policy experts are looking more closely at how we invent and deploy AI and automation—and identifying ways we can make better choices.

In an essay called "The Turing Trap: The Promise & Peril of Human-Like Artificial Intelligence," Erik Brynjolfsson, director of the Stanford Digital Economy Lab, writes of the way AI researchers and businesses have focused on building machines to replicate human intelligence. The title, of course, is a reference to Alan Turing and his famous 1950 test for whether a machine is intelligent: Can it imitate a person so well that you can't tell it isn't one? Ever since then, says Brynjolfsson, many researchers have been chasing this goal. But, he says, the obsession with mimicking human intelligence has led to AI and automation that too often simply replace workers, rather than extending human capabilities and allowing people to do new tasks.

For Brynjolfsson, an economist, simple automation, while producing value, can also be a path to greater inequality of income and wealth. The excessive focus on human-like AI, he writes, drives down wages for most people "even as it amplifies the market power of a few" who own and control the technologies. The emphasis on automation rather than augmentation is, he argues in the essay, the "single biggest explanation" for the rise of billionaires at a time when average real wages for many Americans have fallen.

Brynjolfsson is no Luddite. His 2014 book, coauthored with Andrew McAfee, is called *The Second Machine Age: Work, Progress, and Prosperity in a Time of Brilliant Technologies*. But he says the thinking of AI researchers has been too limited. "I talk to many researchers, and they say: 'Our job is to make a machine that is like a human.' It's a clear vision," he says. But, he adds, "it's also kind of a lazy, low bar.'"

In the long run, he argues, far more value is created by using AI to produce new goods and services, rather than simply trying to replace workers. But he says that for businesses, driven by a desire to cut costs, it's often easier to just swap in a machine than to rethink processes and invest in technologies that take advantage of AI to expand the company's products and improve the productivity of its workers.

Recent advances in AI have been impressive, leading to everything from driver-less cars to human-like language models. Guiding the trajectory of the technology is critical, however. Because of the choices that researchers and businesses have made so far, new digital technologies have created vast wealth for those owning and inventing them, while too often destroying opportunities for those in jobs vulnerable to being replaced. These inventions have generated good tech jobs in a handful of cities, like San Francisco and Seattle, while much of the rest of the population has been left behind. But it doesn't have to be that way.

Daron Acemoglu, an MIT economist, provides compelling evidence for the role automation, robots, and algorithms that replace tasks done by human workers have played in slowing wage growth and worsening inequality in the US. In fact, he says, 50 to 70% of the growth in US wage inequality between 1980 and 2016 was caused by automation.

That's mostly before the surge in the use of AI technologies. And Acemoglu worries that AI-based automation will make matters even worse. Early in the 20th century and during previous periods, shifts in technology typically produced more good new jobs than they destroyed, but that no longer seems to be the case. One reason is that companies are often choosing to deploy what he and his collaborator Pascual Restrepo call "so-so technologies," which replace workers but do little to improve productivity or create new business opportunities.

At the same time, businesses and researchers are largely ignoring the potential of AI technologies to expand the capabilities of workers while delivering better services. Acemoglu points to digital technologies that could allow nurses to diagnose illnesses more accurately or help teachers provide more personalized lessons to students.

Government, AI scientists, and Big Tech are all guilty of making decisions that favor excessive automation, says Acemoglu. Federal tax policies favor machines. While human labor is heavily taxed, there is no payroll tax on robots or automation. And, he says, AI researchers have "no compunction [about] working on technologies that automate work at the expense of lots of people losing their jobs."

But he reserves his strongest ire for Big Tech, citing data indicating that US and Chinese tech giants fund roughly two-thirds of AI work. "I don't think it's an accident that we have so much emphasis on automation when the future of technology in this country is in the hands of a few companies like Google, Amazon, Facebook, Microsoft, and so on that have algorithmic automation as their business model," he says.

> **Government, AI scientists, and Big Tech are all guilty of making decisions that favor excessive automation—federal tax policies favor machines.**

Backlash

Anger over AI's role in exacerbating inequality could endanger the technology's future. In her new book *Cogs and Monsters: What Economics Is, and What It Should Be*, Diane Coyle, an economist at Cambridge University, argues that the digital economy requires new ways of thinking about progress. "Whatever we mean by the economy growing, by things getting better, the gains will have to be more evenly shared than in the recent past," she writes. "An economy of tech millionaires or billionaires and gig workers, with middle-income jobs undercut by automation, will not be politically sustainable."

Improving living standards and increasing prosperity for more people will require greater use of digital technologies to boost productivity in various sectors, including health care and construction, says Coyle. But people can't be expected to embrace the changes if they're not seeing the benefits—if they're just seeing good jobs being destroyed.

In a recent interview with MIT Technology Review, Coyle said she fears that tech's inequality problem could be a roadblock to deploying AI. "We're talking about disruption," she says. "These are transformative technologies that change the ways we spend our time every day, that change business models that succeed." To make such "tremendous changes," she adds, you need social buy-in.

Instead, says Coyle, resentment is simmering among many as the benefits are perceived to go to elites in a handful of prosperous cities.

In the US, for instance, during much of the 20th century the various regions of the country were—in the language of economists—"converging," and financial disparities decreased. Then, in the 1980s, came the onslaught of digital technologies, and the trend reversed itself. Automation wiped out many manufacturing and retail jobs. New, well-paying tech jobs were clustered in a few cities.

According to the Brookings Institution, a short list of eight American cities that included San Francisco, San Jose, Boston, and Seattle had roughly 38% of all tech jobs by 2019. New AI technologies are particularly concentrated: Brookings's Mark Muro and Sifan Liu estimate that just 15 cities account for two-thirds of the AI assets and capabilities in the United States (San Francisco and San Jose alone account for about one-quarter).

The dominance of a few cities in the invention and commercialization of AI means that geographical disparities in wealth will continue to soar. Not only will this foster political and social unrest, but it could, as Coyle suggests, hold back the sorts of AI technologies needed for regional economies to grow.

Part of the solution could lie in somehow loosening the stranglehold that Big Tech has on defining the AI agenda. That will likely take increased federal funding for research independent of the tech giants. Muro and others have suggested hefty federal funding to help create US regional innovation centers, for example.

A more immediate response is to broaden our digital imaginations to conceive of AI technologies that don't simply replace jobs but expand opportunities in the sectors that different parts of the country care most about, like health care, education, and manufacturing.

Changing Minds

The fondness that AI and robotics researchers have for replicating the capabilities of humans often means trying to get a machine to do a task that's easy for people but daunting for the technology. Making a bed, for example, or an espresso. Or driving a car. Seeing an autonomous car navigate a city's street or a robot act as a barista is amazing. But too often, the people who develop and deploy these technologies don't give much thought to the potential impact on jobs and labor markets.

Anton Korinek, an economist at the University of Virginia and a Rubenstein Fellow at Brookings, says the tens of billions of dollars that have gone into building autonomous cars will inevitably have a negative effect on labor markets once such vehicles are deployed, taking the jobs of countless drivers. What if, he asks, those billions had been invested in AI tools that would be more likely to expand labor opportunities?

When applying for funding at places like the US National Science Foundation and the National Institutes of Health, Korinek explains, "no one asks, 'How will it affect labor markets?'"

Katya Klinova, a policy expert at the Partnership on AI in San Francisco, is working on ways to get AI scientists to rethink the ways they measure success. "When you look at AI research, and you look at the benchmarks that are used pretty much universally, they're all tied to matching or comparing to human performance," she says. That is, AI scientists grade their programs in, say, image recognition against how well a person can identify an object.

Such benchmarks have driven the direction of the research, Klinova says. "It's no surprise that what has come out is automation and more powerful automation," she adds. "Benchmarks are super important to AI developers—especially for young scientists, who are entering en masse into AI and asking, 'What should I work on?'"

But benchmarks for the performance of human-machine collaborations are lacking, says Klinova, though she has begun working to help create some. Collaborating with Korinek, she and her team at Partnership for AI are also writing a user guide for AI developers who have no background in economics to help them understand how workers might be affected by the research they are doing.

"It's about changing the narrative away from one where AI innovators are given a blank ticket to disrupt and then it's up to the society and government to deal with it," says Klinova. Every AI firm has some kind of answer about AI bias and ethics, she says, "but they're still not there for labor impacts."

The pandemic has accelerated the digital transition. Businesses have understandably turned to automation to replace workers. But the pandemic has also pointed to the potential of digital technologies to expand our abilities. They've given us research tools to help create new vaccines and provided a viable way for many to work from home.

As AI inevitably expands its impact, it will be worth watching to see whether this leads to even greater damage to good jobs—and more inequality. "I'm optimistic we can steer the technology in the right way," says Brynjolfsson. But, he adds, that will mean making deliberate choices about the technologies we create and invest in.

Print Citations

CMS: Rotman, David. "How to Solve AI's Inequality Problem." In *The Reference Shelf: Income Inequality,* edited by Micah L. Issitt, 119–123. Amenia, NY: Grey House Publishing, 2022.

MLA: Rotman, David. "How to Solve AI's Inequality Problem." *The Reference Shelf: Income Inequality,* edited by Micah L. Issitt, Grey House Publishing, 2022, pp. 119–123.

APA: Rotman, D. (2022). How to solve AI's inequality problem. In Micah L. Issitt (Ed.), *The reference shelf: Income inequality* (pp. 119–123). Amenia, NY: Grey House Publishing.

Can Labor Unions Help Close the Black-White Wage Gap?

By Natalie Spievack
Urban Institute, February 1, 2019

After nearly half a century of declining union membership, collective bargaining may be primed for a comeback. Given the convergence of four factors—rising income inequality, favorable public perceptions of unions, a new Democratic House majority, and likely presidential runs by several progressive candidates—legislation to ease barriers against union organization may soon gain traction.

This growing interest in strong unions is understandable in light of the well-documented link between declining union membership and rising income inequality. Less emphasized, however, is the relationship between unions and *racial* inequality.

A 2012 study found that if unionization rates remained at their 1970s level—when African American workers were more likely than white workers to be union members—black-white weekly wage gaps would be nearly 30 percent lower among women and 3 to 4 percent lower among men. Research also consistently finds that racial wage gaps are smaller among union members than among nonunion members.

This evidence shows that a rebound in union membership could reduce the racial wage gap that has been growing since 1979.

How Unions Transitioned from Excluding African Americans to Elevating Their Wages

Unions weren't always a positive force for black workers. In 1935, when the National Labor Relations Act gave workers the legal right to engage in collective bargaining, less than 1 percent of all union workers were black. Union formation excluded agricultural and domestic workers, occupations predominantly held by black workers, and largely left black workers unable to organize.

By the late 1960s and early 1970s, unions began to integrate. The manufacturing boom brought large numbers of black workers north to factories, the civil rights movement focused increasingly on economic issues, and the more liberal Congress of Industrial Organizations organized black workers.

In 1973, unionization rates among black men were over 40 percent, while rates among white men were between 30 and 40 percent. And by the late 1970s, almost one in four black women —nearly double the share of white women—belonged to a union.

As Unions Declined, the Racial Wage Gap Expanded

The steep decline in unionization rates among workers of all racial and ethnic groups over the past four decades has occurred in tandem with rising racial wage inequality. In 1983, 31.7 percent of black workers and 23.3 percent of the entire workforce were unionized. In 2017, those numbers had fallen to 12.6 percent and 10.7 percent, respectively (largely because of global competition, deindustrialization, and the passage of right-to-work laws in several states).

Meanwhile, from 1979 to 2016, average hourly earnings of black men in the US fell from 80 percent of white male earnings to 70 percent of white male earnings. For black women, average earnings fell from near parity with white women to 82 percent of white female earnings.

Strong unions play a role in the racial wage gap largely because of black workers' overrepresentation in labor market sectors that have higher rates of union membership. Union jobs pay, on average, 16.4 percent higher wages than do nonunion jobs because of workers' ability to bargain collectively for higher pay, more transparent hiring and promotion policies, and heavier regulation of grievance procedures.

Recent research also finds that union membership delivers a larger wage premium to black workers than to white workers. Hourly wages for black union workers are 14.7 percent higher than those of their nonunion counterparts, while white unionized workers make 9.6 percent higher hourly wages than do nonunionized white workers.

The impact of increased unionization on racial equality could extend beyond hourly wage increases. A 2016 study found that black union workers are 17.4 percentage points more likely than nonunion workers to have employer-provided health insurance and 18.3 percentage points more likely to have an employer-sponsored retirement plan, advantages that are even greater among workers with no high school degree.

Higher union membership also narrows the racial wealth gap by supplying a larger wealth dividend to nonwhite workers than to white workers. The increase in earnings, benefits, and employment stability afforded by union membership translates to a higher likelihood of homeownership and larger contributions to 401(k) plans. Between 2010 and 2016, the median wealth of nonwhite union members was nearly five times greater than that of their nonunion counterparts, while the median wealth of white union members was only 39 percent greater than that of white nonunion workers.

> **Union jobs pay, on average, 16.4 percent higher wages than nonunion jobs because of workers' ability to bargain collectively.**

Research and history provide a compelling case for the role of strong unions in furthering economic progress for African Americans and in reducing economic inequality among all Americans. That's why conversations about the importance of unions should be not only class based but racially conscious.

Print Citations

CMS: Spievack, Natalie. "Can Labor Unions Help Close the Black-White Wage Gap?" In *The Reference Shelf: Income Inequality,* edited by Micah L. Issitt, 124–126. Amenia, NY: Grey House Publishing, 2022.

MLA: Spievack, Natalie. "Can Labor Unions Help Close the Black-White Wage Gap?" *The Reference Shelf: Income Inequality,* edited by Micah L. Issitt, Grey House Publishing, 2022, pp. 124–126.

APA: Spievack, N. (2019). Can labor unions help close the black-white wage gap? In Micah L. Issitt (Ed.), *The reference shelf: Income inequality* (pp. 124–126). Amenia, NY: Grey House Publishing.

Don't Expect Unions to Make a Comeback

By Nick Gillespie and Regan Taylor
Reason, April 15, 2022

Big Labor supporters like President Joe Biden are cheering the first successful vote to unionize workers at an Amazon facility, in this case, an 8,000-worker warehouse in Staten Island, New York. The effort was spearheaded by a couple of best friends who built support on TikTok, among other places. "Amazon, here we come," promised the president at a recent union rally.

The *New York Times* gleefully called it "one of the most significant labor victories in a generation" and indicative of "an era of rising worker power." Former *Times* labor reporter Steven Greenhouse called it "by far the biggest, beating-the-odds David versus Goliath unionization win I've seen" in 25 years of reporting.

But the Staten Island story is overshadowed by other colossal unionization failures, including attempts to organize other Amazon warehouses, such as in Bessemer, Alabama, where last year 71 percent voted against joining the Retail, Wholesale, and Department Store Union, which lost about a quarter of its members from 2002 to 2019.

It's proven so hard for unions to gain a toehold at Amazon because it's actually a pretty good place to work. If we are indeed in a time of "rising worker power," that's because of incredibly low unemployment rates and historically high job vacancies giving the rank and file more leverage than ever to negotiate more pay and better conditions.

For its part, Amazon has consistently increased its wages and benefits to attract and retain workers, especially during the pandemic, when it went on a hiring spree. It set a minimum wage of $15 an hour back in 2018 and last year boosted its starting wage to $18, while also offering health insurance, reimbursement for college courses, and signing bonuses of up to $3,000. More than anything else, those sorts of perks explain the overwhelming failure of unionization efforts. For the second year in a row, LinkedIn named Amazon the top company to work at if you want to "grow your career."

It's not just Amazon, either. The main reason that unions in the private sector have been fading for decades isn't that there are union-busting Pinkertons terrorizing organizers but because of the changing nature of work and the willingness of employers to offer better terms. Unions flourished during the era of assembly lines and standardization, when schedules were rigid and outputs, employees, and even customers were expected to be identical. As everything in our lives becomes more personalized, it only makes sense unions would fade, which is exactly what's happened.

In 2021, just 6 percent of private sector workers were unionized, down from 17 percent in 1983. Unions are even losing clout in the public sector. After peaking at 39 percent in 1994, unionization among federal, state, and local employees is down to 34 percent and shows little sign of turning around.

> **Perks explain the overwhelming failure of unionization efforts.**

If K-12 teachers are any indication, the decline is explained by unions' inability to increase starting salaries. While unions such as the National Education Association and the American Federation of Teachers successfully lobby for health insurance and retirement benefits, the inflation-adjusted average starting salaries for teachers have actually declined from a decade ago. Why keep paying dues to a union that isn't delivering to younger teachers who are more interested in money now rather than promises down the road?

Labor organizers are turning to the federal government for help in strong-arming workers to rejoin their ranks. The Protecting the Right to Organize (PRO) Act would abolish "right to work" laws that keep unions from forcing nonmembers to pay dues in 27 states. But the PRO Act, which would reclassify millions of independent contractors as employees, has no chance of passing an evenly divided Senate, especially in a midterm election year where the Democrats are already expected to lose big in both houses.

Biden can come after Amazon, Starbucks, and any other public or private sector employer all he wants, but it's unlikely he—or any other politician or labor organizer—is going to be able to turn around a decades-long decline in union membership.

The biggest problem for unions, it turns out, is that workers are making real progress without them.

Print Citations

CMS: Gillespie, Nick, and Regan Taylor. "Don't Expect Unions to Make a Comeback." In *The Reference Shelf: Income Inequality,* edited by Micah L. Issitt, 127–128. Amenia, NY: Grey House Publishing, 2022.

MLA: Gillespie, Nick, and Regan Taylor. "Don't Expect Unions to Make a Comeback." *The Reference Shelf: Income Inequality,* edited by Micah L. Issitt, Grey House Publishing, 2022, pp. 127–128.

APA: Gillespie, N., & Taylor, R. (2022). Don't expect unions to make a comeback. In Micah L. Issitt (Ed.), *The reference shelf: Income inequality* (pp. 127–128). Amenia, NY: Grey House Publishing.

House Gives Green Light to Staffer Unionization

By Katherine Tully-McManus and Eleanor Mueller
Politico, May 10, 2022

The House voted Tuesday to allow close to 10,000 of its employees to bargain collectively and form unions, the biggest expansion of congressional staffer rights in three decades.

The move comes amid a swelling tidal wave of grievances from staff, along with efforts by leadership and lawmakers to stem burnout and brain drain among employees who serve vital roles in the legislative branch, including serving constituents, conducting oversight of federal agencies and drafting legislation.

The resolution codifies House employees' right to organize and bargain collectively, including aides in personal offices, district offices and committee staff. The measure expands rights already given to other workers in the Legislative Branch, including Capitol Police, the Library of Congress and professional tour guides.

"It's just outrageous that our own staffers had to wait 26 years after collective bargaining rights were afforded to everybody else on Capitol Hill," said Rep. Andy Levin (D-Mich.), who introduced the resolution in February. "This is the temple of our democracy, and if workers don't have their rights here, it's kind of hollow to say that we're standing up for the rights of people everywhere."

"Our job here is to shut up and pass a law that gives people their rights," he added.

House leaders have long been aware of abysmal staff retention, low pay and other factors that drive staffers off Capitol Hill, or deter applications in the first place. But 2021 saw the highest rate of staff turnover in more than 20 years, a reflection of the destabilizing effects of the pandemic and the toll that frequent threats and the Jan. 6 insurrection have taken on staff.

Lawmakers have ramped up efforts to improve the Hill as a workplace in recent years. The Select Committee on the Modernization of Congress has zeroed in on staff recruitment and retention, along with diversity. House Majority Leader Steny Hoyer (D-Md.) and Democratic Caucus Chair Hakeem Jeffries (D-N.Y.) made a successful push to increase individual office budgets by 20 percent in a recent spending bill, providing funding for possible pay raises. On Friday, Speaker Nancy Pelosi announced a minimum pay rate of $45,000 for House employees, which kicks in on Sept. 1.

The measure providing collective bargaining rights does not need Senate approval, as it only applies to operations within the House. And a flurry of organizing, at least in Democratic offices, is already expected in the coming days and weeks, even before the Office of Congressional Workplace Rights issues official guidance on a hugely complicated process.

The Congressional Workers Union top priorities include securing more competitive compensation, establishing standard vacation and paid leave policies, and improving workplace culture.

Many questions remain about the size and scope of bargaining units, as well as who would qualify as management or would otherwise be ineligible. Individual bargaining units—and each congressional office could have its own—will make those decisions and delineations. Like most workplace operations on Capitol Hill, there may not be a blanket answer.

Chiefs of staff and other senior aides have received guidance from the Office of House Employment Counsel on unionization, warning those senior staffers against having any discussions with other employees. Doing so could be interpreted as interfering with staff unionization, the attorneys warned.

John D. Uelmen, the Office of Congressional Workplace Rights general counsel, told lawmakers in March there could be as many as 500 "employing offices" in the House. But those could band together to cooperate. The OCWR told House lawmakers on April 5 that their offices would need an additional $500,000 and two more full-time employees to support unionization in the House.

A group of 12 aides may jump-start the process—they launched the Congressional Workers Union in February, despite no official collective bargaining protections on the books. They kept their organizing committee anonymous, but they now have the House's protection from retaliation and firing for discussing unionization.

"We can't retain the talent, we can't retain the representation that we need to actually meet the needs of the American people," said a member of the union's organizing committee, granted anonymity to speak candidly. "Right now, we're seeing a brain drain from Congress to the powerful special interests who seek to influence it, because those powerful special interests can afford to pay their employees enough that congressional staffers are incentivized to leave."

In an interview Tuesday before the vote, members of the Congressional Workers Union organizing committee underscored how they view the vote and subsequent bargaining process as a test of "whether our bosses are capable and willing to walk the walk when it comes to workers' rights in their own workplaces."

"The public is really watching to see if they're able to walk the walk and whether they're aware of the importance of upholding their values in their offices—or if Congress is really above the laws it creates," one of the members of the group said.

Unionizing efforts have gained unexpected momentum in the last several months, spurred by a historically tight labor market, outspoken staffers and an uncommonly pro-union White House. The Biden administration has been aggressive in its support for organized labor, sending Cabinet members to picket lines and even recently inviting union members to the White House, and workers across the country have felt more empowered as employers struggle to fill jobs.

There was a 57 percent increase nationwide in the number of petitions to hold a union election in the first half of fiscal 2022, according to the National Labor Relations Board—1,174, compared to 748 during the first half of fiscal 2021. Some of those drives, such as at Starbucks and Amazon, had the outspoken support of Democratic leaders, the Congressional Workers Union pointed out.

"It would be pretty hard" for lawmakers who have supported private-sector unionizing efforts to vote down a union in the House, another one of the group's members said. "It should be one of the easiest votes they've ever had to take."

The Congressional Workers Union is not the only group poised to hit the ground running; the Congressional Progressive Staff Association is preparing to give its members support when they try to organize their own offices. And they were ready for the vote Wednesday, hosting a pizza party to watch the House floor together.

The Congressional Workers Union outlined its top priorities Tuesday, including securing more competitive compensation, establishing standard vacation and paid leave policies and improving workplace culture.

"But the No. 1 thing is helping workers, through this process, to have a voice in their workplace," another member of the group's organizing committee said. "We hope that our bosses are ready to come to the bargaining table prepared to really give us conditions that will make material improvements."

And it's not just about creating better working conditions; for some, it's about creating a culture that welcomes diverse backgrounds in the nation's Congress. Historically, Capitol Hill has a reputation for hiring wealthy and politically connected young people to climb the ladder—the people who could afford to pay D.C. rent while earning low pay. Meanwhile, staff of color or without generational wealth were excluded or left behind.

Pelosi acknowledged that diversity was a key motivator for the establishment of a pay floor for House staff. She touted that it would "open the doors to public service for those who may not have been able to afford to do so in the past. This is also an issue of fairness, as many of the youngest staffers working the longest hours often earn the lowest salaries."

"We're looking forward to ... workers really being empowered to bring their grievances to their bosses, and to be able to have a say in their workplace conditions without fear of retaliation," one member of the Congressional Workers Union said.

Print Citations

CMS: Tully-McManus, Katherine, and Eleanor Mueller. "House Gives Green Light to Staffer Unionization." In *The Reference Shelf: Income Inequality*, edited by Micah L. Issitt, 129–132. Amenia, NY: Grey House Publishing, 2022.

MLA: Tully-McManus, Katherine, and Eleanor Mueller. "House Gives Green Light to Staffer Unionization." *The Reference Shelf: Income Inequality*, edited by Micah L. Issitt, Grey House Publishing, 2022, pp. 129–132.

APA: Tully-McManus, K., & Mueller, E. (2022). House gives green light to staffer unionization. In Micah L. Issitt (Ed.), *The reference shelf: Income inequality* (pp. 129–132). Amenia, NY: Grey House Publishing.

Weakened Labor Movement Leads to Rising Economic Inequality

By Heidi Shierholz
Economic Policy Institute, January 27, 2020

The basic facts about inequality in the United States—that for most of the last 40 years, pay has stagnated for all but the highest paid workers and inequality has risen dramatically—are widely understood. What is less well-known is the role the decline of unionization has played in those trends. The share of workers covered by a collective bargaining agreement dropped from 27 percent to 11.6 percent between 1979 and 2019, meaning the union coverage rate is now less than half where it was 40 years ago.

Research shows that this de-unionization accounts for a sizable share of the growth in inequality over that period—around 13–20 percent for women and 33–37 percent for men. Applying these shares to annual earnings data reveals that working people are now losing on the order of *$200 billion per year* as a result of the erosion of union coverage over the last four decades—with that money being redistributed upward, to the rich.

The good news is that restoring union coverage—and strengthening workers' abilities to join together to improve their wages and working conditions in other ways—is therefore likely to put at least $200 billion per year into the pockets of working people. These changes could happen through organizing and policy reform. Policymakers have introduced legislation, the Protecting the Right to Organize (PRO) Act, that would significantly reform current labor law. Building on the reforms in the PRO Act, the Clean Slate for Worker Power Project proposes further transformation of labor law, with innovative ideas to create balance in our economy.

How is it that de-unionization has played such a large role in wage stagnation for working people and the rise of inequality? When workers are able to join together, form a union and collectively bargain, their pay goes up. On average, a worker covered by a union contract earns 13.2 percent more than a peer with similar education, occupation and experience in a non-unionized workplace in the same sector. Furthermore, the benefits of collective bargaining extend well beyond union workers. Where unions are strong, they essentially set broader standards that non-union employers must match in order to attract and retain the workers they need and to avoid facing an organizing drive. The combination of the direct effect of unions on their members and this "spillover" effect to non-union workers means unions are crucial in fostering a vibrant middle class—and has also meant that as unionization has eroded, pay for working people has stagnated and inequality has skyrocketed.

Unions also help shrink racial wage gaps. For example, black workers are more likely than white workers to be represented by a union, and black workers who are in unions get a larger boost to wages from being in a union than white workers do. This means that the decline of unionization has played a significant role in the expansion of the black–white wage gap.

The share of workers covered by a collective bargaining agreement dropped from 27 percent to 11.6 percent between 1979 and 2019.

But isn't the erosion of unionization because workers don't want unions anymore? No—survey data show that in fact, a *higher* share of non-union workers say they would vote for a union in their workplace today than did 40 years ago. Isn't the erosion of unionization due to the shifts in employment from manufacturing to service-producing industries? No again—changing industry composition explains only a small share of the erosion of union coverage.

What has caused declining unionization? One key factor is fierce corporate opposition that has smothered workers' freedom to form unions. Aggressive anti-union campaigns—once confined to the most anti-union employers—have become widespread. For example, it is now standard, when workers seek to organize, for their employers to hire union avoidance consultants to coordinate fierce anti-union campaigns. We estimate that employers spend nearly $340 million per year hiring union avoidance advisers to help them prevent employees from organizing.

And though the National Labor Relations Act (NLRA) makes it illegal for employers to intimidate, coerce or fire workers in retaliation for participating in union-organizing campaigns, the penalties are grossly insufficient to provide a meaningful disincentive for such behavior. This means employers often engage in illegal activities, such as threatening to close the worksite, cutting union activists' hours or pay, or reporting workers to immigration enforcement authorities if employees unionize. In at least 1 in 5 union elections, employers are charged with illegally firing workers involved in organizing.

In the face of these attacks on union organizing, policymakers have egregiously failed to update labor laws to balance the system. Fundamental reform is necessary to build worker power and guarantee all workers the right to come together and have a real voice in their workplace.

Restoring the right to representation on the job will likely put at least $200 billion in the pockets of working families each year, reducing income inequality and racial wage gaps, building a vibrant middle class and creating an economy that works for all, not just the privileged few.

Print Citations

CMS: Shierholz, Heidi. "Weakened Labor Movement Leads to Rising Economic Inequality." In *The Reference Shelf: Income Inequality,* edited by Micah L. Issitt, 133–135. Amenia, NY: Grey House Publishing, 2022.

MLA: Shierholz, Heidi. "Weakened Labor Movement Leads to Rising Economic Inequality." *The Reference Shelf: Income Inequality,* edited by Micah L. Issitt, Grey House Publishing, 2022, pp. 133–135.

APA: Shierholz, H. (2020). Weakened labor movement leads to rising economic inequality. In Micah L. Issitt (Ed.), *The reference shelf: Income inequality* (pp. 133–135). Amenia, NY: Grey House Publishing.

Unions Help Reduce Disparities and Strengthen Our Democracy

Economic Policy Institute, April 23, 2021

Unions improve wages and benefits for all workers, not just union members. They help reduce income inequality by making sure all Americans, and not just the wealthy elite, share in the benefits of their labor.

Unions also reduce racial disparities in wages and raise women's wages, helping to counteract disparate labor market outcomes by race and gender that result from occupational segregation, discrimination, and other labor market inequities related to structural racism and sexism.

Finally, unions help win progressive policies at the federal, state, and local levels that benefit all workers. And conversely, where unions are weak, wealthy corporations and their allies are more successful at pushing through policies and legislation that hurt working people. A strong labor movement protects workers, reduces disparities, and strengthens our democracy.

Unions Lower Inequality

By bringing workers' collective power to the bargaining table, unions are able to win better wages and benefits for working people—reducing income inequality as a result. As seen in Figure A, there was less income inequality in the decades following World War II than there is today. Not coincidentally, union membership was at its highest rate in 1945, just as the war was ending. But as union strength steadily declined—particularly after 1979—income inequality got worse, and it is now at its worst point since the Great Depression.

As union membership declines, income inequality increases

Union membership and share of income going to the top 10%, 1917–2019

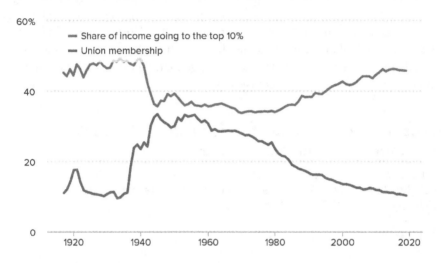

Source: Reproduced from Figure A in Heidi Shierholz, *Working People Have Been Thwarted in Their Efforts to Bargain for Better Wages by Attacks on Unions*, Economic Policy Institute, August 2019.

Economic Policy Institute

FIGURE A

Deunionization depressed the wages of middle-wage earners but had little impact on high-wage earners and therefore greatly increased wage inequality between these two groups. For instance, deunionization explains a third of the growth of the wage gap between high- and middle-wage earners over the 1979–2017 period.[1]

The erosion of collective bargaining is the second largest factor that suppressed wage growth and fueled wage inequality over the last four decades—only excessive unemployment had a larger impact.[2] When unions are strong, they set wage standards for entire industries and occupations; they make wages more equal within occupations; and they close pay gaps between white workers and workers of color. The reasons unions are such a major force for equality are set out more fully below.

Unions Raise Wages for Both Union and Nonunion Workers

While union workers receive higher wages than nonunion workers, nonunion workers also benefit immensely from the presence of unions. This raises wages for working people and reduces wage inequality. We explain below.

Union workers earn more than nonunion workers. On average, a worker covered by a union contract earns 10.2% more in hourly wages than someone with similar education, occupation, and experience in a nonunionized workplace in the same sector.[3]

When union density is high, *nonunion* **workers benefit from higher wages.** When the share of workers who are union members in an industry or occupation is relatively high, as it was in 1979, wages of nonunion workers are higher than they would otherwise be. For example, had union density remained at its 1979 level, weekly wages of nonunion men in the private sector would be 5% higher (that's an additional $2,704 in earnings for year-round workers), while weekly wages for nonunion men in the private sector without a college education would be 8%, or $3,016 per year, higher.[4] Figure B shows how much more nonunion workers would earn had union density remained the same, by gender. Figure C shows the numbers for nonunion workers without a college degree.

Drop in union membership has taken $52 weekly out of nonunion working men's wages

Additional weekly wages that nonunion private-sector workers would earn had the share of workers in a union (union density) remained the same as in 1979, by gender, 1979–2013 (2013 dollars)

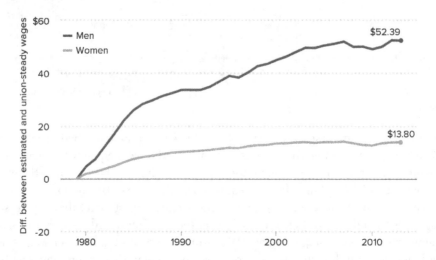

Notes: Sample restricted to nonunion full-time workers in the private sector ages 16 to 64.

Source: Adapted from Figure C in Jake Rosenfeld, Patrick Denice and Jennifer Laird, *Union Decline Lowers Wages of Nonunion Workers*, Economic Policy Institute, August 2016. Data points are authors' compilations from the Current Population Survey (CPS) May Supplement microdata and CPS Outgoing Rotation Group microdata.

Economic Policy Institute

FIGURE B

Drop in union membership has taken $58 weekly out of the wages of nonunion working men without a college degree

Additional weekly wages that nonunion private-sector workers without a college degree would earn had the share of workers in a union (union density) remained the same as in 1979, by gender, 1979–2013 (2013 dollars)

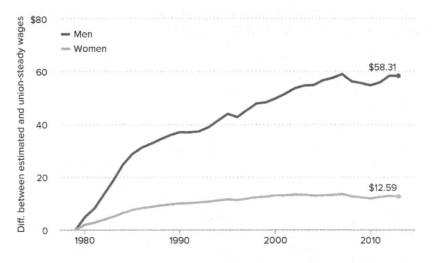

Notes: Sample restricted to nonunion full-time workers in the private sector ages 16 to 64.

Source: Adapted from Figure D in Jake Rosenfeld, Patrick Denice, and Jennifer Laird, *Union Decline Lowers Wages of Nonunion Workers*, Economic Policy Institute, August 2016. Data points are authors' compilations from the Current Population Survey (CPS) May Supplement microdata and CPS Outgoing Rotation Group microdata.

Economic Policy Institute

FIGURE C

In states where unions are strong, wages are higher for workers—union and nonunion alike. Wages are lower in states with low union density compared with states with high union density—$1,121.70 a week versus $942.70 a week in 2020.[5]

Unions bring living wages to low-wage jobs. Unions have transformed once-low-wage jobs in hospitality, nursing, and janitorial services into positions with living wages and opportunities for advancement. For example, after unionizing, dishwashers in Las Vegas hotels made $4 per hour more than the national average for that job, and they were offered excellent benefits. In Houston, a 2006 first-ever union contract for 5,300 janitors resulted in a 47% pay increase and an increase in guaranteed weekly hours of work.[6]

If unionization hadn't eroded, wages for the middle class would be much higher. Recent research examining the direct effect on wages of union workers and the spillover effect on wages of nonunion workers has demonstrated that the median worker's wages would have been much higher, and inequality between middle- and high-wage workers much lower, had there not been an erosion of collective bargaining. For instance, the "typical" or median worker would have earned $1.56 more, a 7.9% increase (0.2% annually), in 2017 had unionization not declined since 1979 (Figure D). This translates to an equivalent gain of $3,250 for a full-time, full-year worker.[7]

Median hourly wage, actual and without eroded collective bargaining, 1979–2017 (2020 dollars)

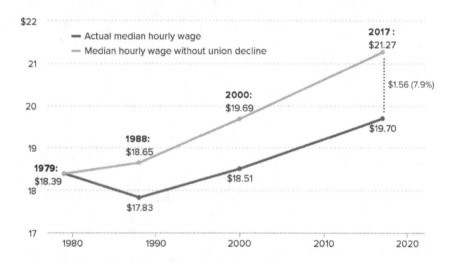

Note: Totals may not sum due to rounding.

Source: EPI analysis of unpublished tabulations from Thomas Lemieux (2021) using model in Fortin, Lemieux, and Lloyd (2021).

Economic Policy Institute

FIGURE D

Unions Help Raise Wages for Women and Reduce Racial Economic Disparities

Unions have played an essential role in narrowing gender and racial/ethnic pay gaps. Here's how.

Unions help raise women's pay. Hourly wages for women represented by unions are 4.7% higher on average than for nonunionized women with comparable characteristics.[8]

Unions raise wages in the female-dominated service occupations. Union-represented workers in service occupations (which include food service and janitorial services) make 52.1% more in wages than their nonunion counterparts. These occupations are disproportionately held by women.[9]

Unions help reduce racial economic disparities. Black and Hispanic workers get a larger boost from unionization than their white counterparts. Black workers—both men and women—are more likely than white workers to be covered by collective bargaining, and the wage boost they get from being covered by collective bargaining is 13.1%, above the 10.2% average wage boost for unionized workers overall. The result of this union wage premium—how much more union workers earn than comparable nonunion workers—is that collective bargaining lifts wages of Black workers closer to those of their white counterparts. Hispanic workers have slightly lower union coverage than white workers but have a much higher union wage advantage (an 18.8% boost in pay) and thus wage gaps between Hispanic workers and their white counterparts are also smaller because of collective bargaining.[10]

The phenomenon that unions narrow the Black–white wage gap isn't new. Starting in the mid-1940s, Black workers began to be more likely to be in unions and to have a larger union premium than white workers.[11] This means that the decline of unionization has played a significant role in the expansion of the Black–white wage gap in recent decades and that increasing unionization is a crucial step in reversing those trends.[12]

Unions Support Strong Families with Better Benefits and Job Protections

Union workers are more likely to be covered by employer-provided health insurance. More than nine in 10 workers—95%—covered by a union contract have access to employer-sponsored health benefits, compared with just 68% of nonunion workers. When adjustments are made for other characteristics that may affect benefits coverage—such as sector (public or private), industry, region, employee status (full- or part-time), and establishment size—union workers are 18.3% more likely to be covered.[13]

Union employers contribute more to workers' health care benefits. Union employers providing health insurance pay 77.4% more (per hour worked) toward their employees' health coverage (providing better benefits for a greater share of workers) than comparable nonunion employers. Occupations with higher-than-average union impact on employer-provided health care include transportation, services, construction, extraction, and installation/maintenance/repair.[14]

Union workers have greater access to paid sick days. More than nine in 10 workers—93%—covered by a union contract have access to paid sick days, compared with 75% of nonunion workers. Almost all union workers—98%—in state and local government have paid sick days, compared with 86% of their nonunion peers. In the private sector, 88% of union workers have paid sick days, compared with 74% of their nonunion peers.[15]

Union workers are more likely to have paid vacation and holidays. In the private sector, 91% of workers covered by a union contract get paid vacation and paid holidays, whereas 78% of nonunion workers get paid vacation and 79% get paid holidays. For workers overall (in both the private and public sectors), 81% of union workers get paid holidays, while 78% of nonunion workers do.[16]

Employers contribute more to paid vacation and holidays for union workers than for nonunion workers. Union employers contribute 11.4% more toward paid vacation and holidays for their workers than do comparable non-union employers. Industries and occupations with higher-than-average employer contributions toward paid vacation and holidays include production, transportation, office and administrative support, service occupations, and construction.[17]

> **Deunionization explains a third of the growth of the wage gap between high- and middle-wage earners over the 1979–2017 period.**

Unions provide due process, protecting workers from arbitrary dismissal. Private employment in every state except for Montana is generally "at will," meaning employers are free to dismiss workers for almost any reason, except for reasons specified by law (e.g., on account of race, religion, disability, or other identities that are protected classes). Union contracts typically have provisions that require employers to have a proper, documented, performance-related reason for disciplining or dismissing a worker ("just cause") and generally the worker has a chance to improve performance before the employer moves to dismiss the worker. Collective bargaining agreements also typically include a grievance and arbitration process to allow workers and the union to challenge unfair discipline or terminations.

Union workers have more input into the number of hours they work. Almost half (46%) of nonunion workers say they have little or no input into the number of hours they work each week, compared with less than a quarter (22%) of union workers.[18]

Union workers get more advance notice of their work schedules. More than one in three workers (34.4%) who belong to a union get at least a week's advance notice of their work schedules, whereas less than one in four nonunion workers (23.2%) do. (These calculations exclude workers whose schedules never change.)[19]

Unions Are Good for Workers' Retirement Security

Ninety-four percent of union workers participate in a retirement plan (of any kind), compared with 67% of nonunion workers.[20] Union employers (when adjustments are made for various employer characteristics) are 22.5% more likely to offer an employer-provided retirement plan and, on average, to spend 27.7% more on retirement plans than do comparable nonunion employers.[21]

Unions Boost Civic Participation

Unions communicate with their members about issues and candidates to make sure workers have information when they go to the polls on Election Day. Union members' voter turnout is significantly higher than the general public's. A study of union members finds they are 12 percentage points more likely to vote than voters who are not in a union.[22] Other research shows that voter turnout is higher in states with greater levels of unionization (Figure E).

Voter turnout in elections is higher in states with greater levels of union representation

Average voter turnout in top and bottom 10 states by average union density, 1989–2020

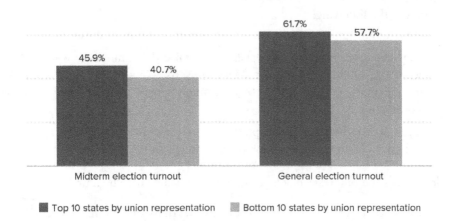

Midterm election turnout   General election turnout

■ Top 10 states by union representation   ▨ Bottom 10 states by union representation

Note: Top 10 states with the highest share of union workers are New York, Hawaii, Alaska, Washington, Michigan, New Jersey, Illinois, California, Rhode Island, and Minnesota. Bottom 10 states with the lowest share of union workers are South Dakota, Louisiana, Arizona, Mississippi, Virginia, Arkansas, Georgia, Texas, South Carolina, and North Carolina.

Source: EPI analysis of 1989–2020 Current Population Survey, Outgoing Rotation Group (CPS-ORG) data for all workers ages 16 and older; United States Elections Project, State Turnout Rates, 1986–2020.

Economic Policy Institute

FIGURE E

Conversely, turnout is lower in states that have adopted anti-worker "right-to-work" legislation. Right-to-work laws undermine unions' ability to collect "fair share fees" from workers whose interests they represent. Fair share fees cover the costs of bargaining, contract administration, and grievance processes that unions are required by law to undertake on behalf of all (union and nonunion) members of a collective bargaining unit. Without fair share fees, union power degrades quickly—which is exactly what anti-union employers want. According to research by Columbia University professor Alex Hertel-Fernandez and his colleagues, the passage of right-to-work laws reduced voter turnout by 2% in presidential elections. This is not insignificant considering that in right-to-work states Michigan and Wisconsin, the losing candidate lost by less than 1 percentage point in the 2016 election.[23]

Moreover, according to these authors, the state policy agenda becomes more anti-worker in states that adopt right-to-work laws. Right-to-work states are less likely to have minimum wages above the federal minimum wage, more likely to preempt local (city or county) minimum wages, and less likely to have prevailing wage laws.

Unions Are Key Supporters of Progressive Policies That Help All Workers

Unions have been a key part of efforts to pass laws that provide economic security, strong communities, and dignity on the job for all workers. The labor movement helped pass and defend the Occupational Safety and Health Act, the Civil Rights Act, the Social Security Act, Medicare and Medicaid, and numerous other laws benefiting all workers and their communities.

Consider the following:

- State minimum wages are lower in states with low union density.

- The states that have passed legislation to raise their minimum wage to $15 per hour (including California, Massachusetts, New Jersey, and New York) are among the states with the highest union density and the strongest labor movements.

- Cities and states that have adopted paid sick days laws, fair scheduling laws,[24] and other progressive legislation have strong labor movements.

Table 1 shows the progressive policies that exist in states with high union density.

States with high union density have progressive policies that benefit all workers

State	Union coverage in 2020	Policies adopted			
		$15 minimum wage	Paid sick leave	Paid family leave	Fair workweek laws
New York	23.6%	X	X	X	
Rhode Island	19.1%		X	X	
Washington	18.6%		X	X	
Connecticut	18.4%	X	X	X	
New Jersey	17.7%	X	X	X	
California	17.6%	X	X	X	
Oregon	17.2%		X	X	X
Michigan	16.6%		X		
Maryland	14.2%	X	X	X	
Vermont	13.8%		X		
Massachusetts	12.9%	X	X	X	
District of Columbia	9.5%	X	X	X	

Note: States with a given policy are indicated by X. The District of Columbia is included in the table even though it is not a state.

Sources: EPI analysis of 2020 Current Population Survey Outgoing Rotation Group (CPS-ORG) data for all workers age 16 and older; Economic Analysis and Research Network (EARN) and the National Employment Law Project, *A State Agenda for America's Workers*, December 2018; Economic Policy Institute, *Minimum Wage Tracker*, last updated January 2021.

Economic Policy Institute

TABLE 1

Notes

1. Lawrence Mishel, *The Enormous Impact of Eroded Collective Bargaining on Wages*, Economic Policy Institute, April 8, 2021.

2. Lawrence Mishel and Josh Bivens, *Identifying the Policy Levers Generating Wage Suppression and Wage Inequality* [working title]. Economic Policy Institute, forthcoming May 2021.

3. "Union Wage Premium by Demographic Group, 2011," Table 4.33 in Lawrence Mishel et al., *The State of Working America, 12th Edition*, an Economic Policy Institute book (Ithaca, N.Y.: Cornell Univ. Press, 2012), updated with 2020 microdata from the Current Population Survey Outgoing Rotation Group (CPS-ORG).

4. These estimates look at what wages would have been in 2013 had union density remained at its 1979 levels. Union density is the share of workers in similar industries and regions who are union members. For the typical nonunion man working year-round in the private sector, the decline in private-sector union density since 1979 has led to an annual wage loss of $2,704 (2013 dollars). For the 40.2 million nonunion men working in the private sector, the total loss is equivalent to $109 billion annually. The effects of union decline on the wages of nonunion women are not as substantial because women were not as likely to be unionized as men were in 1979. See Jake Rosenfeld, Patrick Denice, and Jennifer Laird, *Union Decline Lowers Wages of Nonunion Workers: The Overlooked Reason Why Wages Are Stuck and Inequality Is Growing*, Economic Policy Institute, August 2016.

5. EPI analysis of Bureau of Labor Statistics Current Population Survey Outgoing Rotation Group (CPS-ORG) 2020 microdata. Wages are the average of the median weekly wage by state, for the top and bottom 10 states by union coverage.

6. Matt Vidal and David Kusnet, *Organizing Prosperity: Union Effects on Job Quality, Community Betterment, and Industry Standards*, Economic Policy Institute and UCLA Institute for Research on Labor and Employment, 2009; C. Jeffrey Waddoups, "Wages in Las Vegas and Reno: How Much Difference Do Unions Make in the Hotel, Gaming, and Recreation Industry?" *UNLV Gaming Research & Review Journal* 6, no. 1 (2001).

7. Lawrence Mishel, *The Enormous Impact of Eroded Collective Bargaining on Wages*, Economic Policy Institute, April 2021.

8. "Union Wage Premium by Demographic Group, 2011," Table 4.33 in Mishel at al., *The State of Working America, 12th Edition*, an Economic Policy Institute book (Ithaca, N.Y.: Cornell Univ. Press, 2012), updated 2020 microdata from the Current Population Survey Outgoing Rotation Group (CPS-ORG) microdata.

9. Data are unadjusted for factors such as demographics and employer size. Data are as of March 2017 and are drawn from EPI analysis of Bureau of Labor Statistics, "Table 4. Median Weekly Earnings of Full-Time Wage and Salary Workers by Union Affiliation, Occupation, and Industry" (news release), last

modified January 22, 2021. In 2020, women made up 57.0% of those employed in service occupations, but only 46.8% of all workers employed in 2020 (Bureau of Labor Statistics, "Household Data, Annual Averages, Employed Persons by Occupation, Sex, Age" [data table], data from the Current Population Survey). Service occupations include protective service, food preparation and serving, health care support, building and grounds cleaning and maintenance, and personal care and service.

10. EPI analysis of Bureau of Labor Statistics Current Population Survey Outgoing Rotation Group (CPS-ORG) 2020 microdata. The regression analysis producing this estimate controlled for education, experience, gender, race, citizenship status, geographic division, industry, and occupation.

11. Henry S. Farber, Daniel Herbst, Ilyana Kuziemko, and Suresh Naidu, "Unions and Inequality over the Twentieth Century: New Evidence from Survey Data," National Bureau of Economic Research Working Paper no. 24587, published April 2021 in the *Quarterly Journal of Economics*, https://doi.org/10.1093/qje/qjab012.

12. Valerie Wilson and William M. Rodgers III, *Black–White Wage Gaps Expand with Rising Wage Inequality*, Economic Policy Institute, September 2016.

13. Bureau of Labor Statistics, Employee Benefits in the United States, "Table 2. Medical Care Benefits: Access, Participation, and Take-Up Rates, March 2020," in *Employee Benefits in the United States—March 2020*, published September 24, 2020.

14. Data are as of March 2017 and come from Tables 2 and 6 in Bureau of Labor Statistics, "Employee Benefits in the United States—March 2017" (news release), U.S. Department of Labor, July 21, 2017.

15. Bureau of Labor Statistics, Employee Benefits in the United States, "Table 6. Selected Paid Leave Benefits: Access, March 2020," in *Employee Benefits in the United States—March 2020*, published September 24, 2020.

16. Bureau of Labor Statistics, Employee Benefits in the United States, "Table 6. Selected Paid Leave Benefits: Access, March 2020," In *Employee Benefits in the United States—March 2020*, published September 24, 2020.

17. Data are as of March 2017 and come from Tables 2 and 6 in Bureau of Labor Statistics, "Employee Benefits in the United States—March 2017" (news release], U.S. Department of Labor, July 21, 2017.

18. EPI analysis of the 2016 General Social Survey Quality of Worklife and Work Orientations supplements. "Union worker" here refers to workers who said they belonged to a union.

19. EPI analysis of the 2016 General Social Survey Quality of Worklife and Work Orientations supplements. Respondents were asked whether they or their spouses belong to a union.

20. Bureau of Labor Statistics, Employee Benefits in the United States, "Table 1. Retirement Benefits: Access, Participation, and Take-Up Rates, March 2020," in *Employee Benefits in the United States—March 2020*, published September 24, 2020.

21. Adjusted data are based on analysis of fourth-quarter 1994 Employment Cost Index microdata as presented in Table 4.35 in Lawrence Mishel et al., *The State of Working America, 12th Edition*, an Economic Policy Institute book (Ithaca, N.Y.: Cornell Univ. Press, 2012), and drawn from Brooks Pierce, "Compensation Inequality," U.S. Department of Labor Statistics Working Paper no. 323, 1999.

22. Sean McElwee, "One Big Reason for Voter Turnout Decline and Income Inequality: Smaller Unions," *American Prospect*, January 30, 2015.

23. James Feigenbaum, Alexander Hertel-Fernandez, and Vanessa Williamson, "Right-to-Work Laws Have Devastated Unions—and Democrats," *New York Times*, March 8, 2018.

24. Fair scheduling laws provide workers with greater stability, predictability, and flexibility in their work schedules.

Print Citations

CMS: Economic Policy Institute. "Unions Help Reduce Disparities and Strengthen our Democracy." In *The Reference Shelf: Income Inequality*, edited by Micah L. Issitt, 136–147. Amenia, NY: Grey House Publishing, 2022.

MLA: Economic Policy Institute. "Unions Help Reduce Disparities and Strengthen our Democracy." *The Reference Shelf: Income Inequality*, edited by Micah L. Issitt, Grey House Publishing, 2022, pp. 136–147.

APA: Economic Policy Institute. (2021). Unions help reduce disparities and strengthen our democracy. In Micah L. Issitt (Ed.), *The reference shelf: Income inequality* (pp. 136–147). Amenia, NY: Grey House Publishing.

5
Solutions and Strategies

Photo by Office of Sen. Bernie Sanders, via Wikipedia.

Several solutions have been proposed for ending income inequality, including corporate tax increases and more unionization. Above Senator Bernie Sanders at a minimum-wage rally in 2017.

Can Income Inequality Be Solved?

Are there any effective solutions for addressing income inequality? In the political sphere, possible solutions to this problem tend to fall along partisan lines, but what are the views of experts in related fields? Across academia and public service, there are many different views about how best to tackle income inequality, ranging from massive tax and legal reforms to investing in new industries to create better, more lucrative job opportunities for workers.

Addressing Big-Picture Problems

Many experts studying income inequality have argued that one of the foremost goals must be to address major, largely scale social and economic factors impacting income stability. For instance, economic experts have produced a wealth of data demonstrating the many ways that the COVID-19 pandemic had a destabilizing impact on the global economy. According to data collected by the International Monetary Fund (IMF), the COVID-19 pandemic forced more than 120 million people into poverty due to loss of income and medical care costs. Globally, more than 6 million died of COVID-19 between 2020 and 2022 and more than 527 million contracted the disease. Millions of families lost primary earners and many American industries lagged in productivity as workers necessarily turned their attention to mortal and personal matters. Many who contracted and recovered from COVID-19 faced serious medical bills and many went into debt or lost savings and stability after they or immediate family members contracted the disease.[1]

Beyond the specific health and economic challenges of COVID-19, medical debt and medical costs are a major impediment to financial stability for many Americans. This is especially true for women, who tend to have higher levels of medical expenses, and for working class and poor families, for whom even relatively moderate levels of medical debt can significantly reduce financial stability.[2] Census Bureau data from 2020 and 2021 also indicated that nearly 20 percent of Americans could not afford medical care "right away," when suffering from some potential illness or ailment and were forced to accrue medical debt when seeking medical care. Nearly a quarter of Americans carried some level of medical debt, which decreases revenues available for other household expenses and can contribute to pushing individuals into poverty or bankruptcy.[3] Given how common medical debt has become in American culture, economic experts have argued that helping people to manage or eliminate medical care costs and debt could be one of the major keys to reducing income inequality.

Policies and Priorities

The resources that flow into and out of any society represent the totality of resources available to members of that society, at any level. What determines "fairness" within a society often comes down to the way that the revenues "earned" by a company are distributed. For instance, chief executive officer (CEO) C. Douglas McMillon of the Walmart Corporation earned $22,000,000 per year, compared to an annual employee salary of $24,960. This represents one of the largest gaps between executive and employee wages in the United States, but the company's broader impact on local markets also contributes to the problem.[4] Walmart specializes in general goods and groceries, which means it competes with a wide variety of business offering either general goods (similar to what Walmart offers) or offering goods that fall into one of the categories of goods that Walmart offers. Studies have shown that the opening of a Walmart within a community has a negative impact on small grocers, general stores, and many other businesses. Further, because of Walmart's size and purchasing power, the company can easily outcompete smaller competitors and this leads to an overall reduction in job and income potential for individuals living in that area.

Without competition for employees, Walmart is then able to engage in a cost-saving measure that economists call "monopsony," which happens when an employer has few competitors and so can suppress wages to below the minimum competitive level within a certain market. Walmart and other large chain stores then essentially offer similar wage levels, because they don't need to compete with one another for laborers as there are more laborers than jobs. Overall, this means lower, unsustainable wages for workers and the sole beneficiaries in such a system are upper-level executives and ownership investors in the large corporations that monopolize American communities across the country.[5]

The Walmart example demonstrates the importance of economic policy in combating income inequality. Many economic activists have suggested that large companies, like Walmart, must have revenues taken from them through higher tax rates, so that these revenues can essentially be redistributed among the workforce, as Walmart and other large companies have demonstrated an unwillingness to independently redistribute wealth by lowering corporate salaries and stockholder payouts in favor of increasing wages and benefits for employees. There are many different ways that the federal government and local governments can alter the redistribution of resources by implementing new laws mandating higher salaries, especially for larger corporations, or by enacting tax reforms that eliminate tax rebates and force companies to pay more into the tax system.

However, laws aimed at forcing the redistribution of resources aren't effective unless policies are also put into place to help low-income and middle-income Americans to keep more of the money they earn, which might then be available for reinvestment in other types of equity. Increasing taxes on corporations, for instance, will work best as a way to redistribute wealth if coupled with policies providing tax incentives for individuals at other levels of the income spectrum.

Predistribution of Resources

Tax and wage policies are ways of redistributing resources that are generated by companies, and so ultimately come from consumer spending, but experts warn that it is equally important to create ways to create a more equitable distribution of wealth from the start, before wealth and resources become concentrated among the largest corporations and wealthiest earners. Addressing the "predistribution" of wealth, to create a more equitable distribution of resources from the start, is a more difficult task as policies typically lag behind innovation and technological development, but economists and experts in income inequality warn that it is especially important for policy makers to pay attention to developing trends in technology and the digital economy to affect a more even distribution of wealth among the current and future generations.[6]

To provide one example, consider the way that larger corporations have been able to utilize "data mining" to collect and monetize data from consumers. Technologies to effectively mine and utilize consumer data are typically available only to larger corporations and smaller competitors are largely cut out of the digital data economy. Policies that allow smaller companies to utilize consumer data or that limit the capabilities of larger companies to profit from the collection of data might be used to foster a more competitive digital marketplace, which benefits consumers by encouraging competitive pricing and competitive wages for workers. Policies limiting corporate revenues, earnings, or expansion are often criticized as tyrannical or as a form of bureaucratic "overreach," but economists have long argued that the American free-market system only benefits consumers and workers when sufficient competition exists in the marketplace. Unless wealthy and powerful corporations are prevented from utilizing their wealth and power to limit competition, competition will remain limited and this leads to higher prices for consumers and lower wages and benefits for workers.

Governments at every level can also help to encourage a more even distribution of resources by enacting policies that help developing companies and entrepreneurs to access and utilize innovative and emerging technologies. Such measures might include systems to reform patents or to further public investment in important consumer technologies, which can lower the cost of implementing new technologies for companies, by keeping prices low. In essence, the basic goal is to create a more democratic process in terms of accessing and taking advantage of technological systems, creating more affordable innovation that benefits a larger share of companies and competitors.

Another way that laws and policies can help to affect a more egalitarian distribution of wealth is by helping laborers follow demand. Financial and logistical challenges prevent many workers and their families from relocating or accessing labor markets that are more favorable, and corporations take advantage of this by offering substandard wages to workers who are essentially lacking opportunities. Government policy can facilitate a higher level of labor movement by providing tax breaks and subsidies for employees who move to new areas seeking better employment opportunities. Further, policies can provide access to educational and trade programs aimed at helping workers to train for new jobs. Subsidies, tax benefit programs, and state-funded employment programs can help to shift workers away from declining fields, like coal mining or lumber harvesting, and towards jobs that are more relevant in the current and future economic environment.[7]

Education and Investment

While governmental policies can be used to help current workers find new roles and opportunities, it is equally true that investment in education for children and adolescents is key to combating income inequality over the longer term. Modern careers and future careers will depend more on digital literacy and an understanding of digital tools and technology and so training in these kills can be emphasized in the educational system at various levels. Such programs might be funded, in part, through government revenues derived from taxes levied on corporations, such that the redistribution of corporate wealth is used to prepare workers for the next generation of jobs and opportunities.[8]

Educational investment is certainly key to helping to end the cycle of income inequality, but it has proven difficult for America's towns and cities to increase investment in the educational system because of resistance among those in the population who feel that educational revenues have not been well used, or who believe that the educational system would be more effective if educational institutions operated more like businesses, competing for funding as businesses compete for consumer attention. This viewpoint fueled the growth of the private school system and also the more recent "charter school" system, which typically involves a blend of public and private investment, but research has also shown that the proliferation of private and charter schools has encouraged higher levels of income inequality by perpetuating economic educational inequities.[9] Whatever system is utilized, tax revenues and tax breaks constitute ways that members of the public support both private and public education and this provides opportunities to create policies encouraging educational institutions to focus on training students for relevant roles in the digital economy.

Ultimately, whether trying to create a more egalitarian marketplace, or helping to train students to find better opportunities when they enter the workforce, the greatest impediment to combating income inequality is greed and disinterest. Greed plays a role whenever corporations decide to increase earnings at the upper levels of their corporate culture, or to shift increased profits into increased revenues for shareholders, rather than reinvesting in the company's workforce. Company leaders are expected to maximize profits for the benefits of ownership and shareholders, and so corporate culture is not designed to benefit workers, but to exploit the workforce by limiting labor expenses in order to maximize profit. Nevertheless, greed plays a role in the individual decisions made by members of corporate boards and management groups in terms of how to distribute the company's profits.

On the broader level, Americans are faced with so many different challenges and issues that even extremely important issues fail to gain widespread focus among the electorate. Voters choosing which candidates to support in municipal, state, or federal elections may choose candidates based on the candidate's position on one of a large number of issues, and this greatly reduces focus on other political issues. Polls indicate that, while most Americans believe that income inequality is a problem and approve of policies to redistribute wealth, most Americans do not make this issue a top voting priority. Until and unless this changes, and income inequality become a more prominent political focus in the United States, it is unlikely that governments will enact policies that would significantly alter the status quo to encourage a more even distribution of wealth and resources.

Works Used

Bennett, Neil, Jonathan Eggleston, Laryssa Mykyta, and Briana Sullivan. "19% of U.S. Households Could Not Afford to Pay for Medical Care Right Away." *Census*. 7 Apr. 2021. https://www.census.gov/library/stories/2021/04/who-had-medical-debt-in-united-states.html.

Ferreira, Francisco, H. G. "Inequality in the Time of COVID-19." *IMF*. 2021. https://www.imf.org/external/pubs/ft/fandd/2021/06/inequality-and-covid-19-ferreira.htm#.

Haynes, Berneta L. "The Racial Health and Wealth Gap: Impact of Medical Debt on Black Families." National Consumer Law Center, Inc., 2022.

Jones, Maurice, and Ed Skyler. "Here's a Solution to Economic Inequity: Invest More in Job Training." *USA Today*. 10 Mar. 2020. https://www.usatoday.com/story/opinion/2020/03/10/invest-more-job-training-reduce-income-inequality-column/4922248002/.

O'Neill, Martin. "Predistribution: An Unsnappy Name for an Inspiring Idea." *The Guardian*. 12 Sept. 2012. https://www.theguardian.com/commentisfree/2012/sep/12/ed-miliband-predistribution.

"The Power of Education to Fight Inequality." *Oxfam*. Oxfam International. 2019. https://www-cdn.oxfam.org/s3fs-public/file_attachments/bp-education-inequality-170919-summ-en.pdf.

Reardon, Sean. "Income Inequality Affects Our Children's Educational Opportunities." *Washington Center for Equitable Growth*. 1 Sept. 2014.

Smith, Jacob. "Walmart Among Top Three Companies with Largest Wage Inequality Between CEO and Employees, Study Finds." *KNWA*. 5 Jan. 2022. https://www.nwahomepage.com/northwest-arkansas-news/walmart-among-top-three-companies-with-largest-wage-inequality-between-ceo-and-employees-study-finds/.

Wiltshire, Justin. "Walmart Is a Monopsonist That Depresses Earnings and Employment Beyond Its Own Walls, but U.S. Policymakers Can Do Something About It." *Washington Center for Equitable Growth*. 29 Mar. 2022. https://equitablegrowth.org/walmart-is-a-monopsonist-that-depresses-earnings-and-employment-beyond-its-own-walls-but-u-s-policymakers-can-do-something-about-it/.

Notes

1. Ferreira, "Inequality in the Time of COVID-19."
2. Haynes, "The Racial Health and Wealth Gap: Impact of Medical Debt on Black Families."
3. Bennett, Eggleston, Mykyta, and Sullivan, "19% of U.S. Households Could Not Afford to Pay for Medical Care Right Away."
4. Smith, "Walmart Among Top Three Companies with Largest Wage Inequality Between CEO and Employees, Study Finds."
5. Wiltshire, "Walmart Is a Monopsonist That Depresses Earnings and Employment Beyond Its Own Walls, but U.S. Policymakers Can Do Something About It."
6. O'Neill, "Predistribution: An Unsnappy Name for an Inspiring Idea."
7. Jones and Skyler, "Here's a Solution to Economic Inequity: Invest More in Job Training."
8. "The Power of Education to Fight Inequality," *Oxfam*.
9. Reardon, "Income Inequality Affects Our Children's Educational Opportunities."

Views on Reducing Economic Inequality

By Juliana Menasce Horowitz, Ruth Igielnik, and Rakesh Kochhar
Pew Research Center, January 9, 2020

Most Americans who say there's too much economic inequality in the country think the federal government and big business should play a role in reducing inequality. Smaller but sizable shares say state governments and wealthy individuals should have a lot of responsibility in this regard.

Most say federal government and large corporations should have a lot of responsibility in reducing inequality

Among those who say there is too much economic inequality, % saying each of the following should have a lot of responsibility in reducing inequality in the country

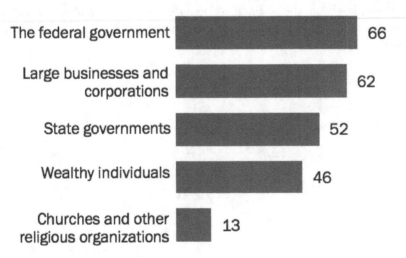

Source: Survey of U.S. adults conducted Sept. 16-29, 2019.
"Most Americans Say There Is Too Much Economic Inequality in the U.S., but Fewer Than Half Call It a Top Priority"

PEW RESEARCH CENTER

Asked how much, if at all, a series of measures would do to reduce economic inequality, those who say there's too much inequality see merit in a variety of approaches. But one stands out in particular: About nine-in-ten say ensuring workers have the skills they need for today's jobs would do at least a fair amount to reduce inequality, with more than half of Democrats and Democratic leaners (65%) and Republicans and Republican leaners (56%) saying this would do *a great deal* to reduce it. Most adults who say there's too much economic inequality (60%) also say increasing taxes on the wealthiest Americans would do a great deal to reduce inequality, but there's less consensus among Democrats and Republicans on this and the other measures asked about in the survey.

About eight-in-ten adults who say there's too much economic inequality say that, in order to reduce inequality, it would be better for the government to invest in education and job training programs for people who are poor. Just 15% say it would be better to give direct assistance to people who are poor in the form of cash payments or tax credits. And while 84% of those who say there's too much economic inequality think the government should raise taxes on the wealthiest Americans in order to reduce inequality, only about one-in-ten—and about a third of those in the top 7% of the sample's adjusted income distribution—say the government should raise taxes on people like them.

The survey also finds that more than half of all U.S. adults think the federal government has a responsibility to provide all Americans with high-quality K-12 education, adequate medical care, health insurance, adequate income in retirement and an adequate standard of living.

Across nearly all questions about reducing economic inequality, the views of Democrats and those who lean Democratic differ widely from those of Republicans and Republican leaners.

About Two-Thirds Who Say There's Too Much Economic Inequality Say the Federal Government Should Have a Lot of Responsibility in Reducing It

Democrats more likely than Republicans to say government, corporations, wealthy individuals should have a lot of responsibility in reducing inequality

Among those who say there is too much economic inequality, % of Republicans and Democrats saying each of the following should have a lot of responsibility in reducing inequality in the country

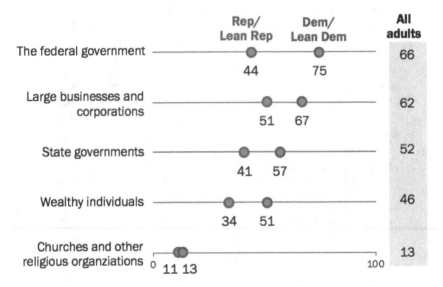

Source: Survey of U.S. adults conducted Sept. 16-29, 2019.
"Most Americans Say There Is Too Much Economic Inequality in the U.S., but Fewer Than Half Call It a Top Priority"

PEW RESEARCH CENTER

Among U.S. adults who think there's too much economic inequality in the country these days, most say the federal government (66%) and large businesses and corporations (62%) should have a lot of responsibility in reducing economic inequality. About half (52%) say state governments should have a lot of responsibility in this area, and 46% say the same about wealthy individuals. Just 13% say churches and other religious organizations should have a lot of responsibility in reducing economic inequality.

Democrats are more likely than Republicans to say the federal government, state governments, large businesses and corporations, and wealthy individuals should have a lot of responsibility in reducing economic inequality. For example, among those who say there is too much inequality, majorities of Democrats say the federal

(75%) and state (57%) governments should have a lot of responsibility in this area. Fewer than half of Republicans who see too much inequality say these groups should have a lot of responsibility for reducing it (44% say the federal government and 41% say state governments should have a lot of responsibility).

Republicans and Democrats Largely Disagree on How Effective Different Measures Would Be at Reducing Economic Inequality

Republicans are less convinced than Democrats that several measures would reduce economic inequality

Among those who say there is too much economic inequality, % of **Republicans** *and* **Democrats** *saying each of the following would do a great deal to reduce economic inequality in the U.S.*

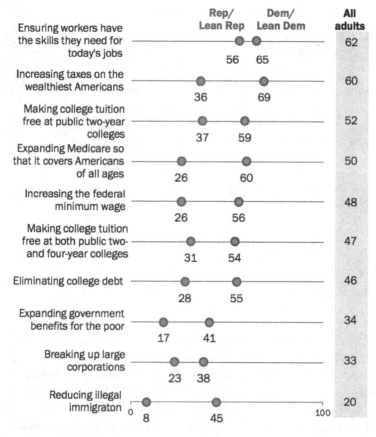

	Rep/ Lean Rep	Dem/ Lean Dem	All adults
Ensuring workers have the skills they need for today's jobs	56	65	62
Increasing taxes on the wealthiest Americans	36	69	60
Making college tuition free at public two-year colleges	37	59	52
Expanding Medicare so that it covers Americans of all ages	26	60	50
Increasing the federal minimum wage	26	56	48
Making college tuition free at both public two- and four-year colleges	31	54	47
Eliminating college debt	28	55	46
Expanding government benefits for the poor	17	41	34
Breaking up large corporations	23	38	33
Reducing illegal immigraton	8	45	20

Source: Survey of U.S. adults conducted Sept. 16-29, 2019.
"Most Americans Say There Is Too Much Economic Inequality in the U.S., but Fewer Than Half Call It a Top Priority"

PEW RESEARCH CENTER

The survey asked U.S. adults how much, if at all, several measures would do to reduce economic inequality in the U.S., regardless of whether they support them. Among those who say there's currently too much economic inequality, 93% say ensuring workers have the skills they need for today's jobs would do at least a fair amount to reduce it,

> **Nine in ten [surveyed] say ensuring workers have the skills they need for today's jobs would do at least a fair amount to reduce inequality.**

with 62% saying this would do a *great deal*. In fact, this is the only measure that majorities of Democrats (65%) and Republicans (56%) who think there's too much economic inequality say would do a great deal to reduce it.

Most adults who say there's too much economic inequality in the country these days (60%) also say increasing taxes on the wealthiest Americans would do a great deal to reduce economic inequality. About half say the same about making college tuition free at public two-year colleges (52%), expanding Medicare so it covers Americans of all ages (50%), and increasing the federal minimum wage (48%).

With the exception of ensuring workers have the skills they need for today's jobs, there is a double-digit gap in the shares of Democrats and Republicans who say each of the measures included in the survey would do a great deal to reduce economic inequality. For example, about seven-in-ten Democrats who say there's too much economic inequality in the U.S. (69%) say increasing taxes on the wealthiest Americans would do a great deal to reduce inequality; 36% of their Republican counterparts say the same. Reducing illegal immigration is the only measure that a larger share of Republicans (45%) than Democrats (8%) see as potentially reducing economic inequality a great deal, among those who say there's too much economic inequality in the country today.

For the most part, lower-income adults who say there's too much economic inequality are more likely than those with middle and upper incomes to say the measures asked about in the survey would do a great deal to reduce economic inequality. There are a few exceptions. When it comes to breaking up large corporations and reducing illegal immigration, lower- and middle-income adults have similar views and are more likely than those with upper incomes to say each would do a great deal to reduce inequality. And on ensuring workers have the skills they need for today's jobs, similar shares across income groups say this would do a great deal to reduce inequality.

About Eight-in-Ten U.S. Adults Who Say There's Too Much Inequality See Investment in Education and Job Training for the Poor as a Better Way to Address It

Education and job training, rather than direct assistance to poor people, seen as better way to address inequality

Among those who say there is too much economic inequality, % saying that, in order to address economic inequality in this country, it would be better for the government to ...

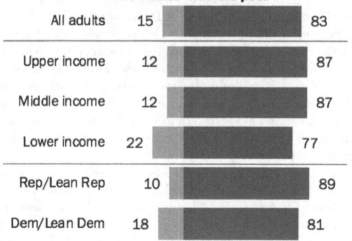

	Give direct assistance to people who are poor in the form of cash payments or tax credits	Invest in education and job training programs for people who are poor
All adults	15	83
Upper income	12	87
Middle income	12	87
Lower income	22	77
Rep/Lean Rep	10	89
Dem/Lean Dem	18	81

Note: Share of respondents who didn't offer an answer not shown. Family incomes are adjusted for differences in purchasing power by geographic region and for household size. Middle income is defined as two-thirds to double the median annual income for the survey sample. Lower income falls below that range, upper income falls above it.
Source: Survey of U.S. adults conducted Sept. 16-29, 2019.
"Most Americans Say There Is Too Much Economic Inequality in the U.S., but Fewer Than Half Call It a Top Priority"

PEW RESEARCH CENTER

When those who say there's too much economic inequality in the U.S. are asked about the best approach for addressing it, most (83%) say it would be better for the government to invest in education and job training programs for people who are poor. Only 15% say a better way to address economic inequality would be for the government to give direct assistance to people who are poor in the form of cash payments or tax credits.

Democrats who say there's too much economic inequality are more likely than their Republican counterparts to say it would be better for the government to give direct assistance to people who are poor, but relatively small shares of both groups say this (18% of Democrats vs. 10% of Republicans). Fully 89% of Republicans and 81% of Democrats who say there's currently too much economic inequality in the country see investments in education and job training programs for people who are poor as a better way to address it.

Among lower-income adults who say there's too much economic inequality, about one-in-five (22%) say giving direct assistance to the poor would be the better way for government to address economic inequality, compared with about one-in-ten of those with middle or upper incomes (12% each).

Most Democrats and Republicans Who Say There's Too Much Economic Inequality Say the Government Should Raise Taxes on the Wealthy to Address It

Most who say there's too much inequality say the government should raise taxes on the wealthiest Americans

Among those who say there is too much economic inequality, % saying that, in order to address economic inequality in this country, the government should ...

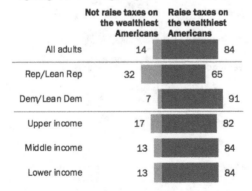

	Not raise taxes on the wealthiest Americans	Raise taxes on the wealthiest Americans
All adults	14	84
Rep/Lean Rep	32	65
Dem/Lean Dem	7	91
Upper income	17	82
Middle income	13	84
Lower income	13	84

Note: Share of respondents who didn't offer an answer not shown. Family incomes are adjusted for differences in purchasing power by geographic region and for household size. Middle income is defined as two-thirds to double the median annual income for the survey sample. Lower income falls below that range, upper income falls above it.
Source: Survey of U.S. adults conducted Sept. 16-29, 2019.
"Most Americans Say There Is Too Much Economic Inequality in the U.S., but Fewer Than Half Call It a Top Priority"

PEW RESEARCH CENTER

More than eight-in-ten U.S. adults who say there's too much economic inequality in the country these days (84%) say the government should raise taxes on the wealthiest Americans in order to address economic inequality. This view is far more widespread among Democrats (91%) than among Republicans (65%), but majorities of both groups share this opinion.

Across income groups, large majorities of those who say there's too much economic inequality in the U.S. these days say that, in order to address the issue, the government should raise taxes on the wealthiest Americans. At least eight-in-ten of those with upper (82%), middle (84%) and lower (84%) incomes say this.

Most Across Income Levels Say the Government Should Not Raise Taxes on People Like Them in Order to Address Economic Inequality

Across income groups, large shares say the government shouldn't raise taxes on people like them to deal with inequality

Among those who say there is too much economic inequality, % saying that, in order to address economic inequality in this country, the government should ...

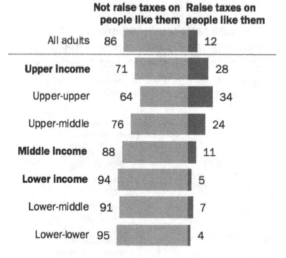

	Not raise taxes on people like them	Raise taxes on people like them
All adults	86	12
Upper income	71	28
Upper-upper	64	34
Upper-middle	76	24
Middle income	88	11
Lower income	94	5
Lower-middle	91	7
Lower-lower	95	4

Note: Share of respondents who didn't offer an answer not shown. Family incomes are adjusted for differences in purchasing power by geographic region and for household size. Middle income is defined as two-thirds to double the median annual income for the survey sample. Lower income falls below that range, upper income falls above it. Lower-lower is less than half, lower-middle is half to two-thirds, upper-middle is two to three, and upper-upper is more than three times the median annual income for the survey sample.
Source: Survey of U.S. adults conducted Sept. 16-29, 2019.
"Most Americans Say There Is Too Much Economic Inequality in the U.S., but Fewer Than Half Call It a Top Priority"

PEW RESEARCH CENTER

The vast majority of Americans who say there's too much economic inequality in the country these days (86%) say the government should *not* raise taxes on people like them in order to address economic inequality; 12% say the government should raise their taxes in order to deal with inequality.

While upper-income adults who say there's too much economic inequality (28%) are more likely than those with middle (11%) and lower (5%) incomes to say the government should raise taxes on people like them in order to address economic inequality, large shares across income groups say the government should not raise their taxes. In fact, among those with the highest incomes – a subset of upper-income adults who are in the top 7% of the sample's adjusted income distribution – about two-thirds (64%) say the government should not raise taxes on people like them, while 34% say the government should do this to deal with economic inequality.

Most U.S. Adults Say the Federal Government Has a Responsibility to Provide Health Insurance and Adequate Medical Care for All Americans

Nearly all Democrats, but only about half of Republicans, say the government has a responsibility to provide adequate medical care for all Americans

*% of **Republicans** and **Democrats** saying the federal government has a responsibility to provide each of the following for all Americans*

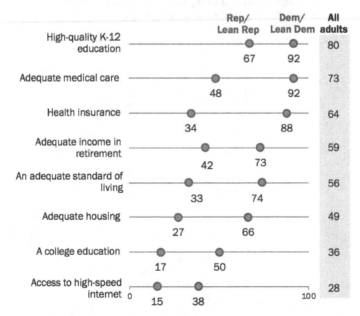

	Rep/ Lean Rep	Dem/ Lean Dem	All adults
High-quality K-12 education	67	92	80
Adequate medical care	48	92	73
Health insurance	34	88	64
Adequate income in retirement	42	73	59
An adequate standard of living	33	74	56
Adequate housing	27	66	49
A college education	17	50	36
Access to high-speed internet	15	38	28

Source: Survey of U.S. adults conducted Sept. 16-29, 2019.
"Most Americans Say There Is Too Much Economic Inequality in the U.S., but Fewer Than Half Call It a Top Priority"

PEW RESEARCH CENTER

Asked more generally about the federal government's role in providing support and services, eight-in-ten U.S. adults say the federal government has a responsibility to provide high-quality K-12 education for all Americans. Majorities also say the federal government has a responsibility to provide adequate medical care (73%), health insurance (64%), adequate income in retirement (59%) and an adequate standard of living (56%). About half or fewer say the federal government has a responsibility to provide adequate housing (49%), a college education (36%) and access to high-speed internet (28%) for all Americans.

Large shares of Democrats see the federal government having a responsibility to provide most of these to all Americans. About two-thirds of Democrats or more say the federal government should provide high-quality K-12 education (92%), adequate medical care (92%), health insurance (88%), adequate retirement income (73%), an adequate standard of living (74%) and adequate housing (66%) for all Americans. In contrast, with the exception of high-quality K-12 education, about half or fewer of Republicans say the federal government has a responsibility to provide each of these to all Americans.

Half of Democrats—vs. just 17% of Republicans—think the federal government has a responsibility to provide a college education to all Americans. And while the share of Democrats (38%) who say the federal government should provide access to high-speed internet is lower than it is for any other of the eight items in the survey, the share of Republicans who hold this view is far lower, at 15%.

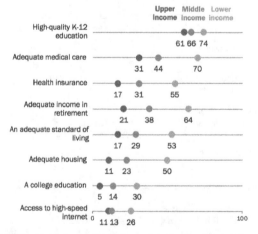

Lower-income Republicans are more likely than those with higher incomes to say the federal government has a responsibility to provide certain things

Among **Republicans and Republican leaners** across income tiers, % saying the federal government has a responsibility to provide each of the following for all Americans

Note: Figures include those who identify with or lean to the Republican Party. Family incomes are adjusted for differences in purchasing power by geographic region and for household size. Middle income is defined as two-thirds to double the median annual income for the survey sample. Lower income falls below that range, upper income falls above it.
Source: Survey of U.S. adults conducted Sept. 16-29, 2019.
"Most Americans Say There Is Too Much Economic Inequality in the U.S., but Fewer Than Half Call It a Top Priority"

PEW RESEARCH CENTER

Overall, lower-income adults are more likely than those with middle or upper incomes to say the government has a responsibility to provide each of the eight items tested in the survey. There are wide income differences among Republicans on all items. Income differences are also present, although less consistent, among Democrats.

By double-digits, larger shares of lower- than middle- or upper-income Republicans say the federal government has a responsibility to provide adequate medical care, health insurance, adequate income in retirement, an adequate standard of living, adequate housing, a college education and access to high-speed internet to all Americans. On each of these items except for access to high-speed internet, middle-income Republicans are more likely than those with upper incomes to see a responsibility for the federal government in providing for all Americans.

Most lower-income Democrats, but fewer than half with middle or upper incomes, say the government has a responsibility to provide a college education to all

*Among **Democrats and Democratic leaners** across income tiers, % saying the federal government has a responsibility to provide each of the following for all Americans*

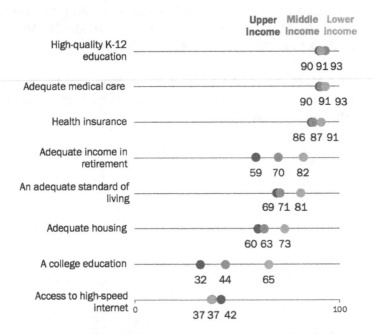

Note: Figures include those who identify with or lean to the Democratic Party. Family incomes are adjusted for differences in purchasing power by geographic region and for household size. Middle income is defined as two-thirds to double the median annual income for the survey sample. Lower income falls below that range, upper income falls above it.
Source: Survey of U.S. adults conducted Sept. 16-29, 2019.
"Most Americans Say There Is Too Much Economic Inequality in the U.S., but Fewer Than Half Call It a Top Priority"

PEW RESEARCH CENTER

Among Democrats, about two-thirds of those with lower incomes (65%) say the federal government has a responsibility to provide a college education to all Americans, compared with 44% of middle-income and 32% of upper-income Democrats. Lower-income Democrats are more likely than those with middle and upper incomes to say the federal government has a responsibility to provide adequate income in retirement, an adequate standard of living and adequate housing. Across income levels, majorities of Democrats (about six-in-ten or more) say the federal government has a responsibility to provide each of these.

Similarly large shares of Democrats across income levels (roughly nine-in-ten) say the federal government has a responsibility to provide high-quality K-12 education, adequate medical care and health insurance. About four-in-ten Democrats with lower, middle and upper incomes say the federal government has a responsibility to provide access to high-speed internet.

Print Citations

CMS: Horowitz, Juliana Menasce, Ruth Igielnik, and Rakesh Kochhar. "Views on Reducing Economic Inequality." In *The Reference Shelf: Income Inequality,* edited by Micah L. Issitt, 157–168. Amenia, NY: Grey House Publishing, 2022.

MLA: Horowitz, Juliana Menasce, Ruth Igielnik, and Rakesh Kochhar. "Views on Reducing Economic Inequality." *The Reference Shelf: Income Inequality,* edited by Micah L. Issitt, Grey House Publishing, 2022, pp. 157–168.

APA: Horowitz, J. M., Igielnik, R., & Kochhar, R. (2020). Views on reducing economic inequality. In Micah L. Issitt (Ed.), *The reference shelf: Income inequality* (pp. 157–168). Amenia, NY: Grey House Publishing.

Tackling the Inequality Pandemic: Is There a Cure?

By Zia Qureshi

The Brookings Institution, November 17, 2020

Inequality was bad and the COVID-19 pandemic is making it worse. The immediate priority is to protect the disadvantaged and the vulnerable from the health and economic impacts of the crisis. But policies must also address the deeper, structural drivers of the rise in inequality.

The Issue

"The COVID-19 recession is the most unequal in modern U.S. history."[1] The pandemic has thrown into stark relief the high and rising economic inequality in the United States and elsewhere. The costs of the pandemic are being borne disproportionately by poorer segments of society. Low-income populations are more exposed to the health risks and more likely to experience job losses and declines in well-being. These effects are even more concentrated in economically disadvantaged minorities. The pandemic is not only exacerbated by the deprivations and vulnerabilities of those left behind by rising inequality but its fallout is pushing inequality higher.[2]

Income and wealth inequality has risen in practically all major advanced economies over the past two to three decades. It has risen particularly sharply in the United States. The increase in inequality has been especially marked at the top end of the income distribution. Those with middle-class incomes have been squeezed and the typical worker has seen largely stagnant real wages over long periods. Intergenerational economic mobility has declined. Income distribution trends are more mixed in emerging economies but many of them have also experienced rising inequality, including some major emerging economies such as China and India.

Rising inequality is a major fault line of our time, with adverse economic, social, and political consequences. It has depressed economic growth by dampening aggregate demand and slowing productivity growth. It has stoked social discontent, political polarization, and populist nationalism. And as the pandemic has revealed, it has increased societal and economic fragility to shocks.

The Ideas

What does research say about why inequality is rising? Many factors affect income distribution but research has increasingly focused on technological change as a key

---

driver of the rise in inequality observed in recent decades.[3] Digital technologies have been transforming markets and how we work and do business, and the latest advances in artificial intelligence are driving the digital revolution further. The benefits of this technological transformation have been shared highly unequally.

> **Rising inequality is a major fault line of our time, with adverse economic, social, and political consequences.**

Inequalities have increased between firms and between workers. Firms at the technological frontier have broken away from the rest, acquiring dominance in increasingly concentrated markets and capturing the lion's share of profits. Increasing automation of low- to middle-skill tasks has shifted labor demand toward higher-level skills, hurting wages and jobs at the lower end of the skill spectrum. With the new technologies favoring capital, winner-take-all business outcomes, and higher-level skills, the distribution of both capital and labor income has become more unequal, and income has shifted from labor to capital.

The COVID-19 pandemic is reinforcing these inequality-increasing dynamics. It is causing the digital transformation of production, commerce, and work to accelerate.[4] While smaller firms struggle, large technologically advanced firms are further increasing market shares, fortifying the shift toward more oligopolistic, less competitive markets.[5] Increased automation and telework are further tilting labor markets against low-skilled, low-wage workers.[6] Industries with business models heavily reliant on human contact and low-skilled workforce are hit especially hard.

Globalization also has contributed to rising inequality within economies—although technological change has been the more dominant factor. But it has been a force for reduced inequality between economies. Expanding global supply chains have been a major spur to economic growth in emerging economies, enabling them to narrow the income gap with advanced economies. The pandemic could disrupt this economic convergence by stoking the backlash against globalization and provoking nationalist trade policy responses, including reshoring of production. This would add to the challenges emerging economies face as increasing automation necessitates search for new growth models less reliant on low skill, low-wage labor as the source of comparative advantage.

A weakening redistributive role of the state also has been a factor pushing inequality higher. As shifts in product and labor markets caused by technological change—and globalization—drove inequality of market incomes within economies higher, the role of the state in alleviating market-income inequality through taxes and transfers diminished. In OECD economies, taxes and transfers typically kept disposable-income inequality one-fifth to one-quarter lower than market-income inequality. In recent years, the role of fiscal redistribution in offsetting the rise in market-income inequality has shrunk because of reduced progressivity of personal income taxes, lower taxes on capital, and tighter spending on social programs.

The Way Forward

Is rising inequality an inevitable consequence of today's technology-driven economic transformations—and globalization? The answer is no. Policies have been slow to respond to the challenges of change. With better, more responsive policies, more inclusive economic outcomes are possible.

The first order of business is to contain the pandemic and address its immediate health and economic consequences that disproportionately hurt the less well-off. Countries have responded in varying degrees by taking preventive measures against the pandemic, shoring up health systems, strengthening safety nets, and implementing policies to cushion the impact on jobs and economic activity. The more successful these actions are in protecting the vulnerable and supporting economic recovery, the less will be the direct impact of the crisis in worsening existing inequalities.

Beyond these immediate actions is a longer-term agenda to address the underlying drivers of the secular rise in inequality. Policies to reduce inequality are often seen narrowly in terms of redistribution—tax and transfer policies. This is of course an important element, especially given the erosion of the state's redistributive role. In particular, systems for taxing income and wealth should be bolstered in light of the new distributional dynamics. But there is a much broader policy agenda of "predistribution" that can make the growth process itself more inclusive.[7]

A core part of this broader agenda is to better harness the potential of technological transformation to foster more inclusive economic growth:

- As technology transforms the world of business, policies and institutions governing markets must keep pace. Competition policies should be revamped for the digital age to ensure that markets provide an open and level playing field for firms, keep competition strong, and check the growth of monopolistic structures. This includes regulatory reform and stronger antitrust enforcement. New issues revolving around data (the lifeblood of the new economy) and market concentration resulting from tech giants that resemble natural or quasi-natural monopolies must be addressed. New thinking is needed on ways to broaden capital ownership and reform corporate governance to reflect wider stakeholder interests.

- In an increasingly knowledge-driven economy, the innovation ecosystem should be improved to promote wider diffusion of technologies embodying new knowledge. Reform of patent regimes and more effective use of public investment and tax policies on research and development can help "democratize" the innovation system so that it serves broader economic and social goals rather than narrow interests of a small group of investors.[8] Biases in the tax system favoring capital relative to labor that create incentives toward "excessive automation"—that destroys jobs without enhancing productivity—should be corrected.[9]

- The foundation of digital infrastructure and digital literacy must be strengthened to expand access to new opportunities. The digital divide remains wide between groups within economies, and is wider still between economies at different levels of development.

- Investment in education and training must be boosted, with stronger programs for worker upskilling, reskilling, and lifelong learning that respond to shifts in the demand for skills. This will require innovation in the content, delivery, and financing of (re)training, including new models of public-private partnerships. Persistent inequalities in access to education and training must be addressed. While gaps in basic capabilities have narrowed, those in higher-level capabilities that will drive success in the 21st century have widened.[10]

- Labor market policies should shift to a more forward-looking focus on improving workers' mobility, helping them to move to new and better jobs rather than seeking to protect existing jobs being rendered obsolete by changing technology. The pandemic has exposed weaknesses in social safety nets. Social protection systems should be strengthened, indeed overhauled. Traditionally based on formal long-term employer-employee relationships, they should be adapted to a job market with more frequent job transitions and more diverse work arrangements. Social contracts need to realign with the changing economy and the nature of work.

At the international level, not only must past gains in establishing a rules-based international trading system be shielded from the rise of protectionist sentiment, new disciplines need to be devised for the next phase of globalization led by digital flows to ensure open access and fair competition. International cooperation on tax matters becomes even more important in view of the new tax challenges of the digital economy.

Inevitably, major economic reform is politically complex. Today's elevated political divisiveness adds to the challenges. One thing reform should not be paralyzed by, however, is continued trite debates about conflicts between growth and equality. Research has increasingly shown this to be a false dichotomy.[11] Crises can shift the political setting for reform. The fault lines exposed by the pandemic can be a catalyst for change.

Notes

1. Heather Long, Andrew Van Dam, Alyssa Fowers and Leslie Shapiro, "The Covid-19 Recession Is the Most Unequal in Modern U.S. History," *The Washington Post,* September 30, 2020, www.washingtonpost.com/graphics/2020/business/coronavirus-recession-equality/.
2. Heather Boushey and Somin Park, "The Coronavirus Recession and Economic Inequality: A Roadmap to Recovery and Long-Term Structural Change," *Center for Equitable Growth,* August 2020; Brown, Caitlin, and Martin Ravallion, "Inequality and the Coronavirus: Socioeconomic Covariates of Behavioral Responses and Viral Outcomes Across U.S. Counties," *NBER Working Paper* 27549, July 2020; and Furceri, Davide, Prakash Loungani, Jonathan Ostry,

and Pietro Pizzuto, "Will COVID-19 Affect Inequality? Evidence from Past Pandemics," *Covid Economics* 12: 138-57, May 2020.

3. Zia Qureshi, "Inequality in the Digital Era," in *Work in the Age of Data,* BBVA, Madrid, February 2020.

4. Alex Chernoff and Casey Warman, "COVID-19 and Implications for Automation," *NBER Working Paper* 27249, July 2020

5. Nancy L. Rose, "Will Competition be Another COVID-19 Casualty?," *The Hamilton Project, Brookings,* July 2020.

6. David Autor, "The Nature of Work after the COVID Crisis: Too Few Low-Wage Jobs," *The Hamilton Project, Brookings,* July 2020.

7. Jacob Hacker, "The Institutional Foundations of Middle Class Democracy," *Policy Network,* May 2011.

8. Dani Rodrik, "Democratizing Innovation," *Project Syndicate,* August 11, 2020.

9. Daron Acemoglu, Andrea Manera, and Pascual Restrepo, "Does the U.S. Tax Code Favor Automation?," *Brookings Papers on Economic Activity,* Spring 2020.

10. United Nations, *Human Development Report 2019: Beyond Income, Beyond Averages, Beyond Today—Inequalities in Human Development in the 21ˢᵗ Century,* New York.

11. Brookings Institution and Chumir Foundation, *Productive Equity: The Twin Challenges of Reviving Productivity and Reducing Inequality,* Report, 2019, Washington, DC; and OECD, *The Productivity-Inclusiveness Nexus,* 2018, Paris.

Print Citations

CMS: Qureshi, Zia. "Tackling the Inequality Pandemic: Is There a Cure?" In *The Reference Shelf: Income Inequality,* edited by Micah L. Issitt, 169–173. Amenia, NY: Grey House Publishing, 2022.

MLA: Qureshi, Zia. "Tackling the Inequality Pandemic: Is There a Cure?" *The Reference Shelf: Income Inequality,* edited by Micah L. Issitt, Grey House Publishing, 2022, pp. 169–173.

APA: Qureshi, Z. (2020). Tackling the inequality pandemic: Is there a cure? In Micah L. Issitt (Ed.), *The reference shelf: Income inequality* (pp. 169–173). Amenia, NY: Grey House Publishing.

Obamacare Is Key to Combating Income Inequality, Study Finds

By Adriana Belmonte
Yahoo! News, January 15, 2021

The Affordable Care Act (ACA), the landmark health care bill known as Obamacare, has been a point of contention since it was implemented back in 2010.

The constitutionality of the ACA is currently being argued in the Supreme Court. If the law were to be overturned, an estimated 21 million Americans would lose their health care coverage.

And a new study from Health Affairs found that repealing ACA would also contribute to income inequality by rescinding key benefits to lower-income Americans.

Poorer Americans (who were able to obtain Medicaid through Obamacare) "are better off because their out-of-pocket health spending is reduced and they do not pay private health insurance premiums," the report found when factoring in government taxes, health care coverage, and tax credits when calculating income.

As a result of Obamacare, the analysis estimated, those in the bottom 10% of income distribution saw their incomes rise by an average of 18.8% of the federal poverty level (FPL). (In 2020, the FPL was $12,670 for an individual, $17,240 for a family of 2, $21,720 for a family of 3, and $26,200 for a family of 4.)

The findings corroborate previous study from the Tax Policy Center found that the ACA has played a major role in keeping low-income Americans from going bankrupt.

"The Medicaid Expansion Makes a Noticeable Difference"

Matt Buettgens, senior fellow at the Urban Institute and one of the authors of the report, said he and his fellow researchers wanted to see what would happen if Obamacare was entirely repealed when factoring in taxes and health care coverage as well.

"It's not exactly the same as going back to 2013 when the ACA was implemented because a lot has changed since then," Buettgens told *Yahoo! Finance*. "We constructed a picture with and without the ACA for 2019."

Those in the bottom 10th percentile in Medicaid expansion states get an estimated 22.4% boost in their income because of the ACA, in comparison to only 11.4% in non-expansion states. Currently, 39 states have adopted the expansion.

"The pattern all the way through is about how the Medicaid expansion makes a noticeable difference just about everywhere," Buettgens said. "There's a lot of research about other benefits of Medicaid expansion, including some papers that show that it actually saves lives. It actually decreases mortality, which is a very strong, strong result. This sort of adds to that."

> **The ACA has played a major role in keeping low-income Americans from going bankrupt.**

If a person's income is below 138% of the FPL and their state has adopted the Medicaid expansion, they qualify for Medicaid. And if someone's income is between 100% and 400% of the federal poverty level, they qualify for premium tax credits that lower their monthly premium.

The premium tax credit is defined by the IRS as "a refundable tax credit designed to help eligible individuals and families with low or moderate income afford health insurance purchased through the health insurance marketplace."

"Those with the Highest Incomes Are Less Well Off Under the ACA"

There are some exceptions to people's incomes benefiting from the landmark health care legislation.

While low-income Americans reap several income perks from the ACA, the study found that middle-income Americans gained no income benefit under it: Americans in the 90th percentile of income distribution see only a 0.9% increase in their income as a result of Obamacare.

Part of this is due to the Supplemental Poverty Measure, a key component of the law for the lowest-income individuals. It deducts insurance premiums from income and "incorporates reductions in out-of-pocket spending, but the premium tax credits are not counted as income," the research stated.

Those in higher-income brackets don't qualify for ACA programs, so the Supplemental Poverty Measure is not applicable to them.

"Those with the highest incomes are less well off under the ACA because their taxes help pay for the ACA's benefits," the study explained, "but their incomes are too high to qualify for those benefits."

A May 2020 study from the Tax Policy Center that found a repeal of the ACA would bring a major tax cut for the richest Americans. The top 0.1% would receive a tax cut of $198,250 per year, while the top 1% of Americans would see a tax cut of $32,370 with a repeal of the ACA.

"We knew that repealing ACA would be a windfall for the wealthy," Seth Hanlon, a senior fellow at CAP, previously told *Yahoo! Finance*. "But the magnitude of the tax cut for the top 0.1%—people making $3.8 million and upwards—is still stunning."

President elect Joe Biden has vowed to raise taxes on wealthy Americans and corporations while also building on Obamacare by expanding Medicaid, lowering drug and insurance prices, and enabling further protections for Americans with pre-existing conditions.

Print Citations

CMS: Belmonte, Adriana. "Obamacare Is Key to Combating Income Inequality, Study Finds." In *The Reference Shelf: Income Inequality*, edited by Micah L. Issitt, 174–176. Amenia, NY: Grey House Publishing, 2022.

MLA: Belmonte, Adriana. "Obamacare Is Key to Combating Income Inequality, Study Finds." *The Reference Shelf: Income Inequality*, edited by Micah L. Issitt, Grey House Publishing, 2022, pp. 174–176.

APA: Belmonte, A. (2021). Obamacare Is key to combating income inequality, study finds. Micah L. Issitt (Ed.), *The reference shelf: Income inequality* (pp. 174–176). Amenia, NY: Grey House Publishing.

Why Socialism Won't Work

By Allison Schrager
Foreign Policy, January 15, 2020

With increasingly ubiquitous iPhones, internet, central air conditioning, flat-screen TVs, and indoor plumbing, few in the developed world would want to go back to life 100, 30, or even 10 years ago. Indeed, around the world, the last two centuries have brought vast improvements in material living standards; billions of people have been lifted from poverty, and life expectancy across income levels has broadly risen. Most of that progress came from capitalist economies.

Yet those economies are not without their problems. In the United States and the United Kingdom, the gap between the rich and poor has become intolerably large as business owners and highly educated workers in urban areas have become richer while workers' wages in rural areas have stagnated. In most rich countries, more trade has brought a bigger, better variety of goods, but it has also displaced many jobs.

With social instability in the form of mass protests, Brexit, the rise of populism, and deep polarization knocking at the capitalist economies' doors, much of the progress of the last several decades is in peril. For some pundits and policymakers, the solution is clear: socialism, which tends to be cited as a method for addressing everything from inequality and injustice to climate change.

Yet the very ills that socialists identify are best addressed through innovation, productivity gains, and better rationing of risk. And capitalism is still far and away the best, if not only, way to generate those outcomes.

Today's socialism is difficult to define. Traditionally, the term meant total state ownership of capital, as in the Soviet Union, North Korea, or Maoist China. Nowadays, most people don't take such an extreme view. In Europe, social democracy means the nationalization of many industries and very generous welfare states. And today's rising socialists are rebranding the idea to mean an economic system that delivers all the best parts of capitalism (growth and rising living standards) without the bad (inequality, economic cycles).

But no perfect economic system exists; there are always trade-offs—in the most extreme form between total state ownership of capital and unfettered markets without any regulation or welfare state. Today, few would opt for either pole; what modern socialists and capitalists really disagree on is the right level of government intervention.

Modern socialists want more, but not complete, state ownership. They'd like to nationalize certain industries. In the United States, that's health care—a plan supported by Democratic presidential candidates Elizabeth Warren (who does not call herself a socialist) and Bernie Sanders (who wears the label proudly). In the United Kingdom, Labour Party leader Jeremy Corbyn, who was trounced at the polls in mid-December, has set his sights on a longer list of industries, including the water, energy, and internet providers.

Other items on the socialist wish list may include allowing the government to be the primary investor in the economy through massive infrastructure projects that aim to replace fossil fuels with renewables, as Green New Deal socialists have proposed. They've also floated plans that would make the government the employer of a majority of Americans by offering guaranteed well-paid jobs that people can't be fired from. And then there are more limited proposals, including installing more workers on the boards of private companies and instituting national rent controls and high minimum wages.

For their part, modern capitalists want some, but less, state intervention. They are skeptical of nationalization and price controls; they argue that today's economic problems are best addressed by harnessing private enterprise. In the United States, they've argued for more regulation and progressive taxation to help ease inequality, incentives to encourage private firms to use less carbon, and a more robust welfare state through tax credits. Over the past 15 years, meanwhile, capitalist Europeans have instituted reforms to improve labor market flexibility by making it easier to hire and fire people, and there have been attempts to reduce the size of pensions.

No economic system is perfect, and the exact right balance between markets and the state may never be found. But there are good reasons to believe that keeping capital in the hands of the private sector, and empowering its owners to make decisions in the pursuit of profit, is the best we've got.

One reason to trust markets is that they are better at setting prices than people. If you set prices too high, many a socialist government has found, citizens will be needlessly deprived of goods. Set them too low, and there will be excessive demand and ensuing shortages. This is true for all goods, including health care and labor. And there is little reason to believe that the next batch of socialists in Washington or London would be any better at setting prices than their predecessors. In fact, government-run health care systems in Canada and European countries are plagued by long wait times. A 2018 Fraser Institute study cites a median wait time of 19.8 weeks to see a specialist physician in Canada. Socialists may argue that is a small price to pay for universal access, but a market-based approach can deliver both coverage and responsive service. A full government takeover isn't the only option, nor is it the best one.

Beyond that, markets are also good at rationing risk. Fundamentally, socialists would like to reduce risk—protect workers from any personal or economywide shock. That is a noble goal, and some reduction through better functioning safety nets is desirable. But getting rid of all uncertainty—as state ownership of most industries would imply—is a bad idea. Risk is what fuels growth. People who take more chances tend to reap bigger rewards; that's why the top nine names on the *Forbes* 400 list of the richest Americans are not heirs to family dynasties but are self-made entrepreneurs who took a leap to build new products and created many jobs in the process.

Some leftist economists like Mariana Mazzucato argue that governments might be able to step in and become laboratories for innovation. But that would be a historical anomaly; socialist-leaning governments have typically been less innovative than others. After all, bureaucrats and worker-corporate boards have little incentive to upset the status quo or compete to build a better widget. And even when government programs have spurred innovation—as in the case of the internet—it took the private sector to recognize the value and create a market.

> **Risk is what fuels growth. People who take more chances tend to reap bigger rewards.**

And that brings us to a third reason to believe in markets: productivity. Some economists, such as Robert Gordon, have looked to today's economic problems and suggested that productivity growth—the engine that fueled so much of the progress of the last several decades—is over. In this telling, the resources, products, and systems that underpin the world's economy are all optimized, and little further progress is possible.

But that is hard to square with reality. Innovation helps economies do more with fewer resources—increasingly critical to addressing climate change, for example—which is a form of productivity growth. And likewise, many of the products and technologies people rely on every day did not exist a few years ago. These goods make inaccessible services more available and are changing the nature of work, often for the better. Such gains are made possible by capitalist systems that encourage invention and growing the pie, not by socialist systems that are more concerned with how the existing pie is cut. It is far too soon, in other words, to write off productivity.

Here, it is worth considering the lessons of a previous productivity boom: the Industrial Revolution. As the economist Joel Mokyr has shown, it took new innovations like the steam engine more than 100 years to appear in productivity estimates. The same could be happening today with smartphones and the internet. Meanwhile, even as that upheaval transformed the human experience, creating a more comfortable existence for most everyone, it was also messy and disruptive. The early part of that innovative cycle—like others since—displaced existing workers while the gains flowed to the owners of capital first, causing social instability.

This time around, the effects may end up being less wrenching: The divisions between owners of capital and workers are not as clear as they used to be. More Americans than ever own stock through their workplace retirement accounts. Stock ownership is on the rise in many non-U.S. capitalist economies, too. And several other countries, such as Australia and the United Kingdom, also offer retirement accounts, making their citizens shareholders as well. Unlike 200 years ago, workers' interests are already more aligned with those of management.

Stock ownership in retirement accounts hints at the kinds of market-friendly policies that can share wealth while preserving innovation and risk-taking. In the United States, there is room to make taxes more progressive, especially when it comes to estate taxes, and to close tax loopholes that make it easier for companies to exploit the system. The social safety net could be expanded to include jobs retraining, an enhanced earned income tax credit, and grants to innovate or work remotely in smaller cities or more rural areas. And the health care industry is indeed in need of reform.

More generally, capitalism can be made more inclusive, and government programs can help smooth its rough edges. But none of these changes require governments to take over entire industries. Depending on the market, the reform could be a less intrusive government option, subsidy, or sometimes just better accountability.

Most fundamentally, inequality is tolerable if the poor have a shot at becoming rich, too. That shot has never been so great as the American dream in particular promised, but there is little evidence that economic mobility has actually gotten worse in recent years. Still, to avoid greater instability—and to ensure the greatest possible buy-in for the capitalist system—today's business and political leaders can do more to make sure everyone at least has a chance to roll the dice. Here, education reform and development of rural areas are necessary to close the gap.

And that's not socialism—it's building off capitalism and making better use of today's and tomorrow's workers.

Print Citations

CMS: Schrager, Allison. "Why Socialism Won't Work." In *The Reference Shelf: Income Inequality,* edited by Micah L. Issitt, 177–180. Amenia, NY: Grey House Publishing, 2022.

MLA: Schrager, Allison. "Why Socialism Won't Work." *The Reference Shelf: Income Inequality,* edited by Micah L. Issitt, Grey House Publishing, 2022, pp. 177–180.

APA: Schrager, A. (2020). Why socialism won't work. In Micah L. Issitt (Ed.), *The reference shelf: Income inequality* (pp. 177–180). Amenia, NY: Grey House Publishing.

How a Default Union Membership Could Help Reduce Income Inequality

By Mark Harcourt, Gregor Gall, Margaret Wilson,
and Nisha Novell
The Conversation, January 21, 2019

A more equal society with less income disparity is good for well-being.

In their latest book, epidemiologists Richard Wilkinson and Kate Pickett argue people living in more equal societies empathise more and worry less about income, possessions and social status.

But income inequalities have been increasing, notably in New Zealand, and research suggests this growing economic gap is associated with a range of social ills and political instability.

In our research, we argue that making union membership the default option would help reduce inequality while protecting workers' rights to opt out.

Unions and Inequality

Unions have traditionally played a key role in reducing income disparities. They negotiate higher pay for virtually all workers, but especially the low waged.

In the United States, evidence suggests the union pay premium has been a consistent 10% to 20% since the 1930s, and is as high as 30% to 40% for the lowest paid. Countries that have higher union membership levels and collective bargaining coverage usually have lower income inequality. Those that have declining membership and coverage usually have worsening inequality.

In the US, research suggests the decline in union membership since the 1960s explains up to a third of the growth in male wage inequality since that time.

Preferences for Union Membership

Despite widespread de-unionisation, surveys show roughly half of all workers across richer Anglophone countries, such as Australia and New Zealand, want to be union members but a majority cannot exercise their preference because they belong to a non-union workplace.

Recruitment of members was less of an issue in the past. Unions, once established, could negotiate closed-shop clauses in their collective agreement. Such a clause means an employer agrees to employ only workers who are already members of a particular union or agree to join once employed.

But more recently, governments in Australia, New Zealand, the UK and the US have increasingly adopted a policy of voluntary unionism, banning the closed-shop clause or declaring it unenforceable. In the European Union, the European Court of Human Rights, in the Sorensen and Rasmussen v. Denmark case, declared the closed shop was a breach of the freedom not to associate.

> **Default employees to union membership in workplaces where unions already have some members or a collective agreement.**

How, then, can employees retain the freedom to choose while reaping the benefits of union membership in reducing inequality? In our research we propose an innovative solution, drawing on insights from behavioural economics, which involves defaulting employees to union membership in workplaces where unions already have some members or a collective agreement. Once employed, employees would be automatically enrolled in the on-site union, but retain the freedom to opt out at least after some time.

Union Default and Increased Membership

Our work indicates a union default would likely increase union membership in four main ways. It would lower the costs of joining, membership would become the norm, inertia would keep workers in the union and they would not want to lose the benefits of unions.

The cost of union membership would be significantly lower because, for the union, it would be solely associated with establishing an initial presence and collective agreement. The cost of recruiting additional members would be effectively zero. For members, enrolment would be automatic.

Once enrolled, employees would be more likely to remain members through inertia. Making decisions can be difficult, especially when the choices are complex. This is certainly true of unions, given the broad range of their services and the difficulties in forecasting whether these services will be needed (for example, in the case of a dismissal). If membership is the default, inertia means workers would stay with the status quo.

A union default would also help to normalise union membership. It would send a clear signal to employees that the state approves of union membership as the right thing to do and that it's commonplace. Beyond that, a union default would set a reference point for employees' assessments of gains and losses, with losses typically given more importance in any decision to leave a union.

It's difficult to predict how much union membership would rise with a union default, but the extensive empirical research on default effects in various contexts would suggest a lot.

Print Citations

CMS: Harcourt, Mark, Gregor Gall, Margaret Wilson, and Nisha Novell. "How a Default Union Membership Could Help Reduce Income Inequality." In *The Reference Shelf: Income Inequality,* edited by Micah L. Issitt, 181–183. Amenia, NY: Grey House Publishing, 2022.

MLA: Harcourt, Mark, Gregor Gall, Margaret Wilson, and Nisha Novell. "How a Default Union Membership Could Help Reduce Income Inequality." *The Reference Shelf: Income Inequality,* edited by Micah L. Issitt, Grey House Publishing, 2022, pp. 181–183.

APA: Harcourt, M., Gall, G., Wilson, M., & Novell, N. (2019). How a default union membership could help reduce income inequality. In Micah L. Issitt (Ed.), *The reference shelf: Income inequality* (pp. 181–183). Amenia, NY: Grey House Publishing.

Can Rights Combat Economic Inequality

By Mila Versteeg
Harvard Law Review, April 10, 2020

Introduction

Few recent academic-press books have spurred as much public and scholarly debate as Professor Samuel Moyn's *Not Enough: Human Rights in an Unequal World*.[1] This is unsurprising given its topical and important subject: the growing gap between rich and poor in many countries around the world.[2] Rising inequality, which Moyn and others attribute largely to neoliberal policies of free trade and free markets, is often blamed for the rise of populist movements and the resulting threats to liberal democracy (pp. 216–18). Moyn explores this phenomenon from the perspective of human rights: What, if anything, have human rights done to address the economic inequality at the heart of these disturbing trends?

"Not enough," answers Moyn. The book is therefore a critique of the modern human rights movement, which, Moyn believes, has barely attempted to address economic inequality. As Moyn puts it, human rights have been "unambitious in theory and ineffectual in practice in the face of market fundamentalism's success" (p. 216). While human rights "have occupied the global imagination," they have "contributed little of note, merely nipping at the heels of the neoliberal giant" (p. 216). Even worse, the human rights movement has been tainted by association with unconstrained capitalism because the movement gained prominence while laissez-faire policies were gaining favor globally (p. 217). Moyn believes that "[t]he coexistence of the human rights phenomenon with the death of socialism . . . is a historical fact that needs to be named" (p. 217) because past decades show that "even perfectly realized human rights . . . are compatible with . . . radical inequality" (p. 213).

Moyn acknowledges that some advocacy efforts have addressed social rights, such as the rights to healthcare, to social security, and to education (pp. xi, 68–69, 143). But these efforts are not enough either, as they have focused only on *sufficiency*: a minimum of resources for the poorest of the poor, rather than comparable resources for all (p. 3). For Moyn, there exists a crucial distinction between the former, that is, "sufficiency," and the latter, what he calls "material equality" (p. 3) (also "distributive equality" (p. 3), "economic justice" (p. 3), or just "equality" (p. 218)). Sufficiency captures "how far an individual is from having nothing and how well she is doing in relation to some minimum of provision of the good things in life" (p. 3).[3] In contrast, material equality "concerns how far individuals are from one another in the portion of those good things they get" (p. 3).[4] A commitment to material equality therefore effectively requires limiting inequality in any given country and a "commitment to a universal middle class" (p. 4). Moyn believes that promoting sufficiency is not enough to achieve equality: even if we realize higher levels of sufficiency for more people, the rich can still become richer (pp. 4–5).[5]

Not Enough is a strong indictment of the human rights movement. Yet in the end, Moyn concludes that human rights law is actually the wrong vehicle for promoting material equality.[6] One reason is that human rights law—with its individualistic premise of constraining the state from committing human rights abuses against discrete persons—is simply a bad fit for the task of effecting material equality (p. 218). "[W]henever inequality has been limited," he says, "it was never on the sort of individualistic and often antistatist basis that human rights share with their market fundamentalist *Doppelgänger*" (p. 218). Another, related reason is that human rights law's toolkit—litigation and "naming and shaming" violators—is ill-equipped to promote economic justice (pp. 10, 218). According to Moyn, "When it comes to mobilizing support for economic fairness, the chief tool[] of the human rights movement—playing informational politics to stigmatize the repressions of states . . .—[is] simply not fit for use" (p. 218). In addition, the movement's hopes for litigation have never materialized: Moyn concludes that litigation opportunities at the international level are ineffectual or nonexistent, while at the domestic level, courts have been unwilling and unable to do much of note (pp. 199–201). In fact, Moyn even questions whether human rights have any role to play in combating inequality: "[A] critical reason that human rights have been a powerless companion of market fundamentalism is that they simply have nothing to say about material inequality" (p. 216).

What, then, is Moyn's solution? Moyn's primary objective is to force redistribution and cap inequality (p. 218). To accomplish that, he argues, we need not only to provide a basic minimum of subsistence but also to set an income ceiling, lift up the middle classes, prevent the dismantling of existing social welfare states, and build new ones (pp. 214, 218–21). His own plan therefore entails a more radical shift than a mere change in human rights advocacy strategies. He appears to envision economic transformation realized through global economic interventionism, massive tax reforms, and new antitrust rules (p. 214). The end goal is a strong social welfare state, preferably extended to the global level. "The truth is that local and global economic justice requires redesigning markets or at least redistributing from the rich to the rest, something that naming and shaming are never likely to achieve . . . ." (p. 218).

Moyn's critique and proposal leave the reader wondering: If human rights law by its nature is not the right vehicle for achieving his redistributive vision, why indict the movement for not addressing it adequately? Political economists and policymakers have been increasingly concerned with rising economic inequality.[7] Moyn masterfully forces his readers to grapple with the connection between human rights and this growing inequality. He places their relationship in historical perspective, taking us back to times when political leaders imagined a world with relative economic equality. *Not Enough* introduces us to the thinkers of the French Revolution, the architects of the mid-twentieth-century European social welfare states, and the drafters of the Universal Declaration of Human Rights, all of whom sought to close the gap between rich and poor. These leaders built societies genuinely concerned with material equality, with the post–World War II European social welfare state as Moyn's primary example. They were also the first to put social rights into writing, although they viewed these rights as "regulatory guidelines" rather than as human rights in the modern sense (p. 55). By the end of the book, though, it remains unclear why the human rights movement is the object of Moyn's scorn.

This Book Review addresses the question that *Not Enough* prompts but does not ultimately answer: Can human rights *law*, including litigation and other forms of legal mobilization, be used to promote material equality? To do so, this Review takes an angle mostly absent from *Not Enough*: the phenomenon of courts around the world interpreting their domestic constitutions to promote economic equality. Courts in Colombia, Mexico, Argentina, Peru, Hungary, Portugal, Russia, Romania, Lithuania, and Latvia have all, on occasion, rendered decisions that tackled economic inequality.[8] Some of these courts have provided access to social rights–related goods and services to the poor and the middle classes alike. Others have protected middle-class entitlements in the face of harsh austerity measures or have prevented tax cuts for the rich or new tax burdens on the poor. In essence, these courts have used constitutional rights to do exactly what Moyn says human rights law has failed to do: attempt to advance economic equality.

One takeaway from these foreign examples is that rights *do* have a potential role to play in promoting economic equality. Many courts have deployed their constitutions to promote economic justice and, in doing so, have illuminated numerous possible connections between rights and material equality.[9] Even though these decisions may fall short of Moyn's transformative vision, they do ensure equality gains if faithfully implemented.

Another takeaway is that the political economy of these judicial interventions is very different from Moyn's description of the international human rights movement. Notably, many of these interventions were not primarily concerned with sufficiency for the poor, but with protecting the middle classes.[10] Indeed, some of the courts that have addressed economic equality beyond a minimum subsistence for the poor have been heavily criticized for pursuing a majoritarian agenda and engaging in "judicial populism," that is, catering justice to the middle class.[11] Commentators have argued that, in doing so, courts have strayed from the core objective of justiciable social rights: protecting society's most vulnerable.[12]

This Review argues that if rights are to play a role in promoting material equality, some judicial populism is probably helpful. When large segments of the population benefit from judicial interventions, equality gains are likely larger than when interventions focus on the poor alone. Such interventions are not necessarily inconsistent with the judicial role: protecting the rights of the groups that lack political power, even if those groups comprise numerical majorities, is arguably a proper function of constitutional courts. What is more, such interventions can be particularly impactful. A large body of empirical social science literature on rights effectiveness has shown that, although rights enforcement is often difficult, rights are most impactful when mobilized groups of citizens push for their enforcement.[13] Such mobilization is more likely to occur for rights that benefit majorities than for rights that protect vulnerable minorities alone.[14] It follows that a human rights agenda focused on economic justice that also benefits the middle classes can be particularly powerful.

> **We need not only to provide a basic minimum of subsistence but also to set an income ceiling.**

Ultimately, however, whether rights can promote economic equality is an empirical question, and neither Moyn nor I have done the work required to answer it with certainty. But I imagine that the readers of this Review will feel more optimistic about such an endeavor than those who only read *Not Enough*. At a minimum, my analysis suggests that it may be premature to abandon human rights law as a tool for fighting economic inequality.

My conclusions differ from Moyn's chiefly because I introduce three perspectives that are mostly absent from *Not Enough*. First, my account draws heavily on the comparative constitutional law literature. *Not Enough* is an intellectual history focused on political thought in Western Europe and Northern America. Yet the comparative literature has shown that most of the action on social rights has occurred in the Global South, and particularly in Latin America.[15] Second, my account takes seriously the many different doctrinal connections between rights and material equality. *Not Enough* uses the term "human rights" broadly, to encompass both the political project of building a social welfare state and the legal project of the modern human rights movement. This approach may explain why *Not Enough* largely abstracts from doctrine. Taking doctrine seriously, however, reveals that judicial decisions that promote equality are rooted not only in social rights but also in property and equality rights. Thus, focusing on social rights alone does not reveal the full potential of human rights law to address economic inequality. Third, this Review engages the social science literature on human rights effectiveness. Sorting out the causal effect of human rights law is notoriously difficult.[16] Nonetheless, *Not Enough* makes a strong causal claim: human rights have been ineffective in reigning in the soaring income inequality around the globe (p. 201). In developing its claim, *Not Enough* does not engage the voluminous empirical social science literature that has attempted to sort out the causal impact of human rights law.[17] Granted, this literature has addressed social rights in only a limited way, and, to date, few studies have directly explored the impact of rights on material equality.[18] What is more, this literature has shown that rights protections are no panacea: it is only under a limited set of circumstances that they make a difference in practice.[19] Nonetheless, some of the literature's findings do offer cause for optimism on the impact of social rights.

The remainder of this Review is organized as follows. Part I explores the relationship between rights and material equality by introducing the well-known concepts of the Lorenz curve and the Gini coefficient and providing some stylized examples of how rights can improve equality *in theory*. This Part reveals that there are a number of different ways that law can promote economic equality other than by capping the wealth of the rich, including successful efforts to promote sufficiency and the protection of middle-class entitlements. Part II gives examples of how courts around the world have used rights to promote economic equality. It focuses especially on judicial interventions in austerity measures and regressive tax reform, as these most directly seek to mitigate the neoliberal agenda. It observes that not all these cases were decided based on social rights provisions, and that some courts used the rights to property and equality to promote economic equality. Part III concludes by exploring the lessons we can draw from these foreign examples.

1. The book has spurred many reviews and debates. See, e.g., Gráinne de Búrca, Samuel Moyn. *Not Enough: Human Rights in an Unequal World*, 16 *INT'L J. CONST. L.* 1347 (2018) (book review); Ioannis Kampourakis, Samuel Moyn, *Not Enough: Human Rights in an Unequal World*, 83 *MODERN L. REV.* 229 (2020) (book review); Jennifer Pitts, *Not Enough: Human Rights in an Unequal World*, by Samuel Moyn, 47 *POL. THEORY* 267 (2019) (book review); Mitchell Cohen, *Did the Crusade for Human Rights Lead to More Inequality?*, *N.Y. TIMES* (May 18, 2018), https://nyti.ms/2k4HuqO [https://perma.cc/ZLS2-3G2N] (book review); Katharine Young, *Inequality and Human Rights*, *INFERENCE* (Dec. 12, 2019), https://inference-review.com/article/inequality-and-human-rights [https://perma.cc/T9JD-Z4VF] (book review). The blog *Law and Political Economy* featured some seven response pieces. See *Category Archives: Not Enough Symposium*, *LAW & POL. ECON.*, https://lpeblog.org/category/not-enough-symposium [https://perma.cc/2GAS-N8F6].

2. See Richard Partington, *Inequality: Is It Rising, and Can We Reverse It?*, *THE GUARDIAN* (Sept. 9, 2019, 1:00 AM), https://www.theguardian.com/news/2019/sep/09/inequality-is-it-rising-and-can-we-reverse-it [https://perma.cc/ENY4-KWEF].

3. Emphasis has been omitted.

4. Emphasis has been omitted.

5. Moyn conjectures that promotion of sufficiency alone could lead to a world in which "the poor will come closer to sufficient provision as the rich reap ever greater gains for themselves" (p. 5).

6. There is some ambiguity here, as Moyn also claims that the human rights movement could do more: "If human rights movements today focused even more than they do on social rights, for example, especially in the promotion of labor rights that functioned as mechanisms of collective empowerment, it might make a significant difference to material outcomes" (p. 217).

7. See, e.g., Christopher Ingraham, *U.N. Warns that Runaway Inequality Is Destabilizing the World's Democracies*, *WASH. POST* (Feb. 11, 2020, 8:03 AM),

https://www.washingtonpost.com/business/2020/02/11/income-inequality-un-destabilizing [https://perma.cc/3Y8T-LVLE].

8. See infra Part II, pp. 2029–52.

9. See infra Part II, pp. 2029–52.

10. See infra pp. 2033–37, 2044, 2048–49.

11. See infra pp. 2053–54.

12. See infra p. 2054.

13. See infra notes 265–272 and accompanying text.

14. See infra notes 265–272 and accompanying text.

15. David Bilchitz, *Constitutionalism, the Global South, and Economic Justice*, in *CONSTITUTIONALISM OF THE GLOBAL SOUTH: THE ACTIV-IST TRIBUNALS OF INDIA, SOUTH AFRICA, AND COLOMBIA* 41, 47 (Daniel Bonilla Maldonado ed., 2013) (noting that for many constitutions in the Global South, "matters of economic distributive justice . . . are central"). Latin American courts are especially known for their social rights activism. See, e.g., César Rodríguez-Garavito, *Beyond the Courtroom: The Impact of Judicial Activism on Socioeconomic Rights in Latin America*, 89 TEX. L. REV. 1669, 1672–73 (2011). They were the first to enforce social rights and have been most aggressive in deploying them toward material equality. See Benedikt Goderis & Mila Versteeg, *The Diffusion of Constitutional Rights*, 39 INT'L REV. L. & ECON. 1, 5–10 (2014). What is more, Latin American countries were the first to constitutionalize many social rights. See id. The right to public education was first constitutionalized in Haiti in 1801. Mila Versteeg & Emily Zackin, *American Constitutional Exceptionalism Revisited*, 81 U. CHI. L. REV. 1641, 1688 (2014); see *CONSTITUTION DE 1801*, art. 68 (Haiti). The right to asylum was first constitutionalized in Colombia in 1811. Lucas Kowalczyk & Mila Versteeg, *The Political Economy of the Constitutional Right to Asylum*, 102 CORNELL L. REV. 1219, 1261 (2017); see *ACTA DE FEDERACIÓN DE LAS PROVINCIAS UNIDAS DE LA NUEVA GRANADA [CONSTITUTION]* (1811) art. 39 (Colom.). Children's rights were first constitutionalized in Haiti in 1816. See Revised 1806 *CONSTITUTION D'HAÏTI* (June 2, 1816) art. 35; id. art. 53. Rights for the disabled were also first constitutionalized in Haiti in 1816. Id. art. 35. The right to work was first constitutionalized in Mexico in 1857. *CONSTITUCIÓN POLÍTICA DE LA REPÚBLICA MEXICANA* (1857) art. 4. And the right to food was first enshrined in the constitution of Argentina in 1949. See *CONSTITUCIÓN DE LA NACIÓN ARGENTINA* (1949) art. 37, § I.6. Notably, *Not Enough* does not cover the stories of the Latin American drafters who first imagined and constitutionalized these rights; its focus is on the 1791 French Constitution (which mentioned poor relief and public education) and other European constitutions (pp. 20–25). Indeed, Moyn mentions only the Mexican Constitution of 1917 and then moves on to the drafters of the 1919

Weimar Constitution and the 1921 Yugoslav Constitution, leaving untold the stories of the Latin American drafters who constitutionalized these rights (p. 35).

16. ADAM S. CHILTON & MILA VERSTEEG, *HOW CONSTITUTIONAL RIGHTS MATTER* (forthcoming 2020) (manuscript at 100–03) (on file with the Harvard Law School Library); see Adam S. Chilton, *Essay, Experimentally Testing the Effectiveness of Human Rights Treaties*, 18 CHI. J. INT'L L. 164, 166–68 (2017); see also Ryan Goodman & Derek Jinks, *Measuring the Effects of Human Rights Treaties*, 14 EUR. J. INT'L L. 171, 171–78 (2003); Eric A. Posner, *Some Skeptical Comments on Beth Simmons's Mobilizing for Human Rights*, 44 N.Y.U. J. INT'L L. & POL. 819, 823–30 (2012).

17. For Moyn's view on the debate, see Samuel Moyn, *Beyond the Human Rights Measurement Controversy*, 81 LAW & CONTEMP. PROBS., no. 4, 2018, at 121, 121–22. He argues that the controversy in the empirical literature over whether human rights treaties matter "[s]ettles [n]othing," id. at 122, because "both sides have put similar or even identical intellectual and political options on the table" and that the debate "ought to end," id. at 121.

18. See infra notes 265–266 and accompanying text.

19. See infra notes 285–287 and accompanying text.

Print Citations

CMS: Versteeg, Mila. "Can Rights Combat Economic Inequality?" In *The Reference Shelf: Income Inequality,* edited by Micah L. Issitt, 184–190. Amenia, NY: Grey House Publishing, 2022.

MLA: Versteeg, Mila. "Can Rights Combat Economic Inequality?" *The Reference Shelf: Income Inequality,* edited by Micah L. Issitt, Grey House Publishing, 2022, pp. 184–190.

APA: Versteeg, M. (2020). Can rights combat economic inequality? In Micah L. Issitt (Ed.), *The reference shelf: Income inequality* (pp. 184–190). Amenia, NY: Grey House Publishing.

Bibliography

Allec, Logan. "What Are Taxes?" *The Balance*. 15 Dec. 2021. https://www.thebalance.com/what-are-taxes-5213316.

Atkinson, Robert D., and Michael Lind. "Debunking the Myth of Small Business Job Creation." *MIT Press*. 30 May 2019. https://thereader.mitpress.mit.edu/small-business-job-creation-myth/.

Baker, Dean. "CORRECTION: The Productivity Adjusted Minimum Wage Would Be $21.50 in 2020 and $23 in 2021." *CEPR*. 16 Mar. 2022. https://cepr.net/correction-the-productivity-adjusted-minimum-wage-would-be-21-50-in-2020-and-23-in-2021/.

Beamer, Glenn. *Creative Politics: Taxes and Public Goods in a Federal System*. U of Michigan P, 1999.

Belsie, Laurent. "Taxes and the Rich: America's History of Favoritism and Crackdowns." *The Christian Science Monitor*. 21 June 2021. https://www.csmonitor.com/USA/Politics/2021/0621/Taxes-and-the-rich-America-s-history-of-favoritism-and-crackdowns.

Bennett, Neil, Jonathan Eggleston, Laryssa Mykyta, and Briana Sullivan. "19% of U.S. Households Could Not Afford to Pay for Medical Care Right Away." *Census*. 7 Apr. 2021. https://www.census.gov/library/stories/2021/04/who-had-medical-debt-in-united-states.html.

Bloomenthal, Andrew, Somer Anderson, and Peter Rathburn. "Can a Family Survive on the US Minimum Wage?" *Investopedia*. 18 Mar. 2022. https://www.investopedia.com/articles/personal-finance/022615/can-family-survive-us-minimum-wage.asp.

Carey, Kevin. "Do Not Be Alarmed by Wild Predictions of Robots Taking Everyone's Jobs." *Slate*. 31 Mar. 2021. https://slate.com/technology/2021/03/job-loss-automation-robots-predictions.html.

DeSimone, Bailey. "From the Serial Set: The History of the Minimum Wage." *LOC*. Library of Congress. 3 Sept. 2020. https://blogs.loc.gov/law/2020/09/from-the-serial-set-the-history-of-the-minimum-wage/#:~:text=Serial%20Set%20Vol.-,No.,and%20Arbitration%20Act%20of%201894.

Dunn, Amina. "Most Americans Support a $15 Federal Minimum Wage." *Pew Research Center*. 22 Apr. 2021. https://www.pewresearch.org/fact-tank/2021/04/22/most-americans-support-a-15-federal-minimum-wage/.

Ferreira, Francisco, H. G. "Inequality in the Time of COVID-19." *IMF*. 2021. https://www.imf.org/external/pubs/ft/fandd/2021/06/inequality-and-covid-19-ferreira.htm#.

Flemming, Sean. "A Short History of Jobs and Automation." *We Forum*. World Economic Forum. 3 Sept. 2020. https://www.weforum.org/agenda/2020/09/short-history-jobs-automation/.

Geiger, A. W. "How Americans See Automation and the Workplace in 7 Charts." *Pew Research Center*. 9 Apr. 2019. https://www.pewresearch.org/fact-tank/2019/04/08/how-americans-see-automation-and-the-workplace-in-7-charts/.

"Gini Coefficient by Country 2022." *World Population Review*. https://worldpopulationreview.com/country-rankings/gini-coefficient-by-country.

"Gini Index." *World Bank*. World Bank Group. 2022. https://data.worldbank.org/indicator/SI.POV.GINI?name_desc=false.

Graafland, Johan. *Ethics and Economics: An Introduction to Free Markets, Equality and Happiness*. Routledge, 2022.

Greenhouse, Steven. *Beaten Down, Worked Up*. Anchor Books, 2019.

Grizzard, Frank E., and D. Boyd Smith. *Jamestown Colony: A Political, Social, and Cultural History*. ABC-CLIO, 2007.

Hanauer, Amy. "Faulty Fact Check on Tax Breaks for the Rich and Corporations." *ITEP*. 5 Feb. 2021. https://itep.org/faulty-fact-check-on-tax-breaks-for-the-rich-and-corporations/.

Hanlon, Seth. "The Forbes 400 Pay Lower Tax Rates Than Many Ordinary Americans." *American Progress*. Center for American Progress. 7 Oct. 2021. https://www.americanprogress.org/article/forbes-400-pay-lower-tax-rates-many-ordinary-americans/#:~:text=According%20to%20the%20Tax%20Policy,0.5%20percent%20in%20excise%20taxes.

Haynes, Berneta L. "The Racial Health and Wealth Gap: Impact of Medical Debt on Black Families." National Consumer Law Center, Inc., 2022.

Hiltzik, Michael. *The New Deal: A Modern History*. Free Press, 2011.

"History of Federal Minimum Wage Rates Under the Fair Labor Standards Act, 1938–2009." *U.S. Department of Labor*. https://www.dol.gov/agencies/whd/minimum-wage/history/chart.

Horowitz, Juliana Menasce, Ruth Igielnik, and Kochhar Rakesh. "Views of Economic Inequality." *Pew Research Center*. 9 Jan. 2020. https://www.pewresearch.org/social-trends/2020/01/09/views-of-economic-inequality/.

Jones, Maurice, and Ed Skyler. "Here's a Solution to Economic Inequity: Invest More in Job Training." *USA Today*. 10 Mar. 2020. https://www.usatoday.com/story/opinion/2020/03/10/invest-more-job-training-reduce-income-inequality-column/4922248002/.

Lindert, Peter, and Jeffrey Williamson. "Unequal Gains: American Growth and Inequality Since 1700." *Vox EU*. CEPR. 16 June 2016. https://voxeu.org/article/american-growth-and-inequality-1700#:~:text=Colonial%20America%20was%20the%20most,than%2020%25%20of%20total%20income.

"Living Wage Calculator." *Massachusetts Institute of Technology*. https://livingwage.mit.edu/.

Marquart, Sarah. "Reports Reveal Millions of Jobs Are Threatened by Automation: Does This Spell Doom?" *Futurism*. 25 Feb. 2016. https://futurism.com/85-jobs-threatened-automation-spell-doom.

Mekouar, Dora. "Today's Democracy Isn't Exactly What Wealthy US Founding Fathers Envisioned." *VOA*. 24 Jan. 2021. https://www.voanews.com/a/usa_all-about-america_todays-democracy-isnt-exactly-what-wealthy-us-founding-fathers-envisioned/6201097.html.

Miller, Andrea. "How Companies Like Amazon, Nike and FedEx Avoid Paying Federal Taxes." *CNBC*. 14 Apr. 2022. https://www.cnbc.com/2022/04/14/how-companies-like-amazon-nike-and-fedex-avoid-paying-federal-taxes-.html.

"A Minimum Wage." *New Zealand Herald*. 5 July 1894. *National Library of New Zealand*. https://paperspast.natlib.govt.nz/newspapers/NZH18940705.2.19.

Moran, William. *The Belles of New England: The Women of the Textile Mills and the Families Whose Wealth They Wove*. Macmillan, 2002.

"National Poverty in American Awareness Month: January 2022." *Census*. Census Bureau. Jan. 2022. https://www.census.gov/newsroom/stories/poverty-awareness-month.html.

Newport, Frank. "U.S. Public Opinion and Increased Taxes on the Rich." *Gallup*. 4 June 2021. https://news.gallup.com/opinion/polling-matters/350555/public-opinion-increased-taxes-rich.aspx.

O'Neill, Martin. "Predistribution: An Unsnappy Name for an Inspiring Idea." *The Guardian*. 12 Sept. 2012. https://www.theguardian.com/commentisfree/2012/sep/12/ed-miliband-predistribution.

"On This Day: 'No Taxation without Representation!'" *Constitution Center*. 7 Oct. 2021. https://constitutioncenter.org/blog/no-taxation-without-representation.

Peck, Emily. "These Companies Paid Little to No Taxes Last Year." *Axios*. 26 Apr. 2022. https://www.axios.com/2022/04/26/these-companies-paid-little-to-no-taxes-last-year.

"The Power of Education to Fight Inequality." *Oxfam*. Oxfam International. 2019. https://www-cdn.oxfam.org/s3fs-public/file_attachments/bp-education-inequality-170919-summ-en.pdf.

Reardon, Sean. "Income Inequality Affects Our Children's Educational Opportunities." *Washington Center for Equitable Growth*. 1 Sept. 2014.

Schaeffer, Katherine. "6 Facts About Economic Inequality in the U.S." *Pew Research*. Pew Research Center. 7 Feb. 2020. https://www.pewresearch.org/fact-tank/2020/02/07/6-facts-about-economic-inequality-in-the-u-s/#:~:text=The%20share%20of%20American%20adults,from%2025%25%20to%2029%25.

Shapiro, Thomas M. *Toxic Inequality: How America's Wealth Gap Destroys Mobility, Deepens the Racial Divide, & Threatens our Future*. Basic Books, 2017.

Semuels, Alana. "The Founding Fathers Weren't Concerned with Inequality." *The Atlantic*. 25 Apr. 2016. https://www.theatlantic.com/business/archive/2016/04/does-income-inequality-really-violate-us-principles/479577/.

Shierholz, Heidi. "Working People Have Been Thwarted in Their Efforts to Bargain for Better Wages by Attacks on Unions." *Economic Policy Institute*, Aug. 2019. Retrieved from https://www.epi.org/publication/labor-day-2019-collective-bar-gaining/.

Smith, Jacob. "Walmart Among Top Three Companies with Largest Wage Inequal-ity Between CEO and Employees, Study Finds." *KNWA*. 5 Jan. 2022. https://www.nwahomepage.com/northwest-arkansas-news/walmart-among-top-three-companies-with-largest-wage-inequality-between-ceo-and-employees-study-finds/.

Smith, Stephen. *Taxation: A Very Short Introduction*. Oxford UP, 2015

Upmeyer, Linda. "Minimum Wage Levels—Let the States and Free Markets De-cide." *Alec*. 7 June 2018. https://alec.org/article/minimum-wage-levels-let-the-states-and-free-markets-decide/.

Watson, Bruce. *Bread and Roses: Mills, Migrants, and the Struggle for the American Dream*. Penguin Books, 2005.

White, Richard. *And the Republic for Which It Stands*. Oxford UP, 2017.

Williams, Claire "The Tax Man Cometh for the Wealthy and Corporations in House Democrats' Plan: And Voters Are OK with It." *Morning Consult*. 22 Sept. 2021. https://morningconsult.com/2021/09/22/house-democrats-tax-plan-raising-tax-es-wealthy-corporations-poll/.

Wiltshire, Justin. "Walmart Is a Monopsonist That Depresses Earnings and Em-ployment Beyond Its Own Walls, but U.S. Policymakers Can Do Something About It." *Washington Center for Equitable Growth*. 29 Mar. 2022. https://eq-uitablegrowth.org/walmart-is-a-monopsonist-that-depresses-earnings-and-em-ployment-beyond-its-own-walls-but-u-s-policymakers-can-do-something-about-it/.

Websites

Center on Budget and Policy Priorities (CBPP)
www.cbpp.org

The Center on Budget and Policy Priorities (CBPP) is a progressive nonprofit that supports, funds, and collects data on governmental budget and policy and lobbies for policies aimed at helping low-income families and individuals. The CBPP has published dozens of research reports on issues including income and wealth inequality, taxation, poverty, unemployment, and the social welfare system.

Economic Policy Institute (EPI)
www.epi.org

The Economic Policy Institute (EPI) is a nonprofit think tank that supports and funds research and studies of economic policies and issues in America. Founded in the 1980s, the EPI is closely linked to the American Federation of Labor and Congress of Industrial Organizations (AFL-CIO) and other organizations representing the labor movement and has produced a variety of research on workers' rights and welfare issues. The EPI provides links to a variety of no-cost articles for journalists, students, educators, and citizens interested in the nation's economic history and current issues in fiscal policy.

Fight for $15
Fightfor15.org

The Fight for 15 is a national, union led activist organization campaigning to raise the minimum wage to $15 across the United States. The Fight for 15 organization has the support of some of America's largest and most powerful unions and has drawn widespread media attention. In addition to their direct campaign for a $15 minimum wage, the Fight for $15 organization has been involved in a number of other workers' rights and welfare campaigns, including the Starbuck's unionization controversy.

The Heritage Foundation
www.heritage.org

The Heritage Foundation is a conservative research and lobbyist organization founded in the 1970s and active in promoting a number of traditional conservative, neoconservative, and libertarian policy initiatives on issues including government spending, debt, corporate regulation, and taxation. The Heritage Foundation provides access to archived reports and opinion articles on a wide variety of topics and also provides articles to local and national news outlets with regard to current economic debates.

International Monetary Fund (IMF)

www.imf.org

The International Monetary Fund (IMF) is an international organization, established in 1945, and focused on trade, economic issues, and international economic cooperation. IMF studies and data on inequality have global relevance as the interconnected economies of the world evolve and develop in concert over time. The IMF provides a wealth of data about income equality and inequality in societies around the world, as well as comparative economic studies that can help students to better understand US inequality in relation to global economic dynamics.

RAND Corporation

www.rand.org

The RAND Corporation is a nonprofit think tank that began in 1948 as a research wing for the United States military. The RAND Corporation is still financed by governmental revenues and RAND researchers provide original research and analysis for politicians seeking guidance on policy, or a better understanding of a key issue. RAND provides educational programs for students seeking to pursue research in technology and many other fields and the organization funds and publishes research reports on a number of issues, including budget, governmental spending, and policy proposals. RAND corporation researchers have published a variety of research on economic issues, including long-term studies of income and governmental policy.

World Bank (WB)

www.worldbank.org

The World Bank (WB) is an international economic organization allied with the United Nations (UN) and created in 1948 to facilitate economic cooperation between UN member nations. The WB funds and publishes research on a wide variety of economic topics including international trade, the oil and petroleum industry, and military spending. World Bank data is available for journalists, researchers, and students of different levels and provides international information on economic topics like gross domestic product (GDP) growth, international treaties and economic partnerships, trade, employment, and comparative economic influence/stability between the world's nations.

Index